W9-BKF-201

This Day in
Presidential History

Also by Paul Brandus:

Under This Roof: The White House and the Presidency—21 Presidents, 21 Rooms, 21 Inside Stories

This Day in Presidential History

Paul Brandus

WEST WING
REPORTS

Bernan Press
Lanham • Boulder • New York • London

Published by Bernan Press
An imprint of The Rowman & Littlefield Publishing Group, Inc.
4501 Forbes Boulevard, Suite 200, Lanham, Maryland 20706
www.bernan.com
800-462-6420; info@bernan.com

Library of Congress Cataloging-in-Publication Data Available

ISBN: 978-1-59888-943-7 (cloth : alk. paper)
ISBN: 978-1-59888-944-4 (electronic)

To Julia, the light of my life.

The first known photograph of the White House. Believed to have been taken by John Plumbe in 1846 in the middle of the Polk presidency, it shows the south side of the mansion. The Truman Balcony would be added a century later. Library of Congress.

Table of Contents

Preface and Acknowledgments

Journalism is a grand profession, and it's a great honor for me to be able to practice my chosen craft in a place where news is made each day: the White House. It never fails to amaze me—each time I walk through the Northwest Gate on my way to the briefing room—that I'm surrounded by such incredible history. War and peace, triumph and tragedy, sex and scandal, all this and more have happened here.

A few years ago, these doings of the presidents, their families, and the great mansion on Pennsylvania Avenue became a daily feature on my Twitter account (@WestWingReport). Now, for the first time, it's a book. From George Washington to Donald Trump, from New Year's Day to New Year's Eve, the highlights (and a few lowlights) are all here.

At the end of this book, you'll see a list of how the presidents rank in terms of greatness. The rankings come from C-SPAN's third "Historians Survey of Presidential Leadership," in which it surveyed a cross-section of ninety-one presidential historians who ranked the forty-three former occupants of the White House on ten attributes of leadership. Donald Trump, new to the job, is not ranked. Thank you to C-SPAN for their terrific work.

I'd especially like to thank my fellow history buff, Holly McGuire of Bernan Press for her enthusiasm and guidance. Her suggestions have been invaluable and I'm very appreciative. Thank you, Holly!

In putting this book together, I had a simple goal: for students, researchers, fellow journalists, and anyone interested in the White House and presidency to enjoy it and perhaps learn a thing or two. The responsibility for any errors or oversights is mine alone, and if you find something wrong, please let me know.

Paul Brandus
Washington, D.C.

January

January 1

1801: The White House celebrated its first New Year's Day with a reception hosted by President John Adams and his wife Abigail (the term "First Lady" would not be used until decades later). Dinner was served and guests were entertained by the U.S. Marine Band. It was the White House debut of the band—"the President's Own"—which consisted of eight to ten musicians.

Adams, the second U.S. president and the first to live in the White House, had only been a resident there for two months—but was already a lame duck, having been beaten by Thomas Jefferson in the nasty election of 1800. And the White House itself, still unfinished, wasn't even called the White House: in those days it was referred to as the "President's Palace," "Presidential Mansion," or "President's House." Built—largely by slaves—between 1792 and 1800 at a cost of $232,000 (about $75 million today), the imposing mansion at 1600 Pennsylvania Avenue would be the largest residence in the United States until after the Civil War.

1802: Thomas Jefferson's "Danbury Letter." In one of the most important letters ever written by a president, Thomas Jefferson wrote that the First Amendment to the Constitution created a "wall of separation between church and state."

A group of Baptists in Danbury, Connecticut, had written him to complain that because their state had an official religion—the colony of Connecticut had been founded by Calvinist Protestants—it was an infringement upon their own religious liberty. "What religious privileges we enjoy," they told Jefferson, "we enjoy as favors granted, and not as inalienable rights."

Jefferson sympathized with the Connecticut Baptists, writing that "religion is a matter which lies solely between Man & his God, that he owes account to none other for his faith or his worship." By noting the First Amendment, Jefferson was saying that the federal government had no right to legislate, or get involved in, anyone's religious views. But it did not prevent states from having official churches. Connecticut eventually did away with its official religion in 1818.

1863: President Abraham Lincoln's Emancipation Proclamation went into effect, liberating slaves held in the "rebellious states." The proclamation also allowed black men to fight for the Union—as war casualties mounted, every man was needed. On April 13, 1865, the Thirteenth Amendment to the Constitution was passed, formally abolishing slavery. "Neither slavery nor involuntary servitude, except as a punishment for crime whereof the party shall have been duly convicted, shall exist within the United States, or any place subject to their jurisdiction," it stated. It was ratified by the states on December 6, 1865.

1942: Franklin D. Roosevelt signed the Declaration of the United Nations. The president and leaders from twenty-five other countries fighting the Axis Powers of Germany, Italy, and Japan pledged that America and the Allied nations allies would use their "full resources" to defeat "Hitlerism," which was identified as a threat to life and human rights. The term "United Nations" would be extended after the war to 1946 world organization.

★ QUOTE OF THE DAY

I never, in my life, felt more certain that I was doing right than I do in signing this paper.

Abraham Lincoln, on signing the Emancipation Proclamation

The White House has been home to a head of state—the president of the United States—longer than kings and queens have resided in London's Buckingham Palace. John Adams moved into the White House on November 1, 1800—thirty-seven years before Buckingham Palace became the official residence of the British monarch.

January 2

1974: Richard M. Nixon lowered the speed limit to save gas. As the United States reeled under a crippling Arab oil embargo—which caused shortages of gasoline nationwide—the president signed a bill lowering the U.S. speed limit to 55 mph. In late 1973, as the embargo began to hurt the U.S. economy, he asked Americans to drive less and for gas stations to close for twenty-seven hours on weekends. Nixon also called for limits on commercial air travel, and during the holidays urged citizens not to hang Christmas lights.

1980: Jimmy Carter told the Soviet Union "Nyet." Outraged over the Soviet invasion of Afghanistan, the president asked the Senate to postpone deliberation of SALT II—a nuclear arms control treaty—with the Kremlin. He also ordered the American ambassador at Moscow, Thomas J. Watson, Jr., home. Carter's actions sent a signal to the Soviets that "détente"—the era of friendlier political and economic relations that had begun during the Nixon administration was over.

The Soviets ignored Carter's demand to withdraw from Afghanistan. Carter then cut off exports of food and high technology to the U.S.S.R., and, in a more controversial move, ordered an American boycott of the Summer Olympics, which were scheduled to be held that year in Moscow. The United States quietly began sending military aid to anti-Soviet fighters in Afghanistan.

★ QUOTE OF THE DAY

Our independence will depend on maintaining and achieving self-sufficiency in energy.

Richard M. Nixon

January 3

1903: Theodore Roosevelt shut down the post office in Indianola, Mississippi, because the city refused to accept a black woman as its postmaster. This bigotry reared its ugly head despite the fact that Minnie Cox had been serving as postmaster since 1891. She was known for her professionalism and dedication, working long hours and helping her customers by paying their late rent on post office boxes. Cox even personally paid for a post office telephone so that citizens could call to see if they had any mail to pick up.

But as post–Civil War Reconstruction—which had helped African-Americans find work in the deep South—faded away in the early twentieth century, white citizens in Indianola argued that important (and well-paying) jobs such as postmaster should be held by whites. A petition called for Cox to resign.

Word reached the White House. President Roosevelt, outraged at the treatment toward Cox, refused to accept her resignation and ordered mail service eliminated until citizens relented and allowed her back on the job. But intimidated and fearing for her safety, Minnie Cox moved away. Roosevelt ordered his attorney general to prosecute those who had threatened her.

1938: With war clouds gathering in Europe, Franklin D. Roosevelt began emphasizing national security. In his State of the Union Address, the president, while focusing on the nation's continuing economic and social problems, also cited the necessity to be "adequately strong in self-defense." He asked Congress for a big military buildup, particularly in the navy.

1938: Franklin Delano Roosevelt started the March of Dimes. The president, who'd been stricken by polio in 1921, founded the National Foundation for Infantile Paralysis, later renamed the March of Dimes Foundation. Polio—which damages the central nervous system—killed or paralyzed thousands of Americans each year, and Roosevelt, who had lost the use of his legs, decided to fight it. The foundation raised millions of dollars over the years, and in 1949 named Dr. Jonas Salk to lead a research team to develop a polio vaccine. Salk tested the first successful polio vaccine in 1955.

1961: Dwight Eisenhower cut off diplomatic ties with Cuba. Unhappy about having a communist neighbor—Cuba—in America's backyard, the president closed the U.S. embassy in Havana and severed diplomatic relations. He blamed Cuban leader Fidel Castro for the move, claiming that Castro wanted to reduce the number of American diplomats in Havana.

That Cuba not only had turned to communism but had established close ties with the Soviet Union deeply worried Eisenhower. His administration—which would end in just seventeen days—had been quietly laying the groundwork for a secret invasion of Cuba. A decision on whether to proceed with the invasion would be handed off to Eisenhower's successor, John F. Kennedy.

★ QUOTE OF THE DAY

The only limit to our realization of tomorrow will be our doubts of today.

Franklin D. Roosevelt

January 4

1965: Lyndon B. Johnson unveiled his "Great Society." In his State of the Union address, Lyndon B. Johnson unveiled a sweeping list of domestic priorities: civil rights, health care, education, and the environment. He said it would all help build what he called a "Great Society." Johnson, who became president after John F. Kennedy, was assassinated in 1963, was elected in his own right by a massive landslide in November 1964. He believed he had a mandate to act big—and act big he did. A former congressman, senator, and senate majority leader, Johnson knew how the machinery of Congress worked, and lawmakers soon passed the Voting Rights Act, the Civil Rights Act, and created Medicare and Medicaid. Johnson also launched a war on poverty, fought to improve childhood education and helped create the National Endowment for the Arts and the National Endowment for the Humanities. As all this legislation was going on, he also reached for the stars: pouring money into the space program, helping America—as John F. Kennedy urged—to land a man on the moon and return him safely to the earth before the decade was out.

1974: Richard M. Nixon refused to hand over Watergate tapes. As congressional investigators and journalists kept up their probe of the 1972 burglary of Democratic National Committee offices in Washington's Watergate Office Building, the president said he would not relinquish hundreds of tape recordings and documents that had been subpoenaed by the Senate Watergate Committee. Nixon's refusal added to the growing public perception that he was stonewalling and had something to hide. The president would resign seven months later.

★ QUOTE OF THE DAY

We do not intend to live in the midst of abundance, isolated from neighbors and nature, confined by blighted cities and bleak suburbs, stunted by a poverty of learning and an emptiness of leisure.

Lyndon B. Johnson

January 5

1933: Calvin Coolidge died at his home, The Beeches, in Northampton, Massachusetts. He was the thirtieth president, serving from 1923 to 1929. Coolidge assumed the nation's highest office when Warren Harding died in 1923.

Coolidge was responsible for the most significant addition to the White House in a century, when he had an entire third floor built on top of

This Day in Presidential History

the mansion. It included a sleeping porch where the president often took naps. Unfortunately, the weight of this third floor nearly led to the White House's collapse two decades later. (See July 4 for more about Coolidge.)

1949: Harry Truman's "Fair Deal." During his State of the Union address, Harry Truman said that every American deserved a "Fair Deal" from the government. World War II had concluded almost four years ago, and many Americans—tired of wartime sacrifices—wanted change.

In a sweeping proposal reminiscent of his predecessor, Franklin D. Roosevelt, Truman—fresh off his surprise win in the election of 1948—proposed a national health insurance plan, more public housing, more education spending, and civil rights legislation. He also asked for a higher minimum wage and an expansion of Social Security.

Conservatives in Congress, tired of what they viewed as nearly two decades of liberal leadership, balked, complaining that Truman's plans reeked of socialism. Even so, the president got much of what he wanted: a near doubling of the minimum wage (from 40 cents to 75 cents), 800,000 new homes for the poor, and more Social Security. But Truman's dream of national health insurance would be left for another president, Barack Obama, to achieve six decades later.

1957: The Eisenhower Doctrine. Worried about communism gaining a foothold in the Middle East, Dwight Eisenhower proposed to step up economic and military cooperation with friendly nations in the region. Eisenhower, a former five-star Army general, also proposed sending U.S. troops to the region as needed "to secure and protect the territorial integrity and political independence of such nations."

Eisenhower was particularly worried about the biggest country in the Arab world, Egypt, which was making friendly overtures to the Soviet Union. The Eisenhower Doctrine had its first real test in 1958, when civil unrest threatened the government of Lebanon. Lebanon's president, Camille Chamoun, asked Eisenhower for help, and the United States sent nearly 15,000 troops to help maintain order. He would not be the last president to send Americans into harm's way in the Middle East.

1972: Richard M. Nixon and the space shuttle. The Apollo program, which put the first man on the moon, had been a spectacular success—but it had also been spectacularly expensive. Now that it was winding down, what would replace it? The answer: a reusable vehicle that could be launched into space more than once. Thus, Richard M. Nixon signed a bill authorizing $5.5 million in funding to develop the space shuttle. The first shuttle, named *Columbia*, would be launched nine years later.

★ QUOTE OF THE DAY

The chief business of the American people is business. … It is only those who do not understand our people who believe that our national life is entirely absorbed by material motives…. . I cannot repeat too often that America is a nation of idealists.

Calvin Coolidge, January 17, 1925, to the Society of American Newspaper Editors

January 6

1919: Theodore Roosevelt, sixty years old, died in his sleep at his home, Sagamore Hill, in Oyster Bay, New York. His last words were, "Please put out that light."

Roosevelt was the twenty-sixth president, serving from 1901 to1909. Assuming office upon the assassination of William McKinley, he was, at forty-two, the youngest person to become president (though the youngest elected was forty-three-year-old John F. Kennedy). TR, as he was known, had previously been, among other things, New York City police commissioner, assistant Navy secretary, and governor of New York.

Roosevelt's presidency was one of consequence. He oversaw the construction of the Panama Canal and won the Nobel Peace Prize for his efforts to end the 1905 war between Japan and Russia. He was the first conservationist president, protecting 130 million acres of forests and creating 5 national parks and 51 wildlife refuges. He spoke out against racism, saying whites should adjust their attitudes toward minorities. If whites were the leading race in the United States, he argued, they had a responsibility to preserve American civilization by improving the status of minorities (see February 13).

Roosevelt also sought to make industry more competitive. In a 20,000-word speech in 1901, he asked Congress to curb the power of monopolistic corporations (trusts); he became known as the "trust-buster." His administration sued dozens of monopolies, including John D. Rockefeller's Standard Oil and J.P. Morgan's Northern Securities Co.

Roosevelt also changed the name of the "Executive Mansion" to its current name: the White House.

1941: Franklin Roosevelt's "Four Freedoms." With war raging in Europe and Japan on the march in the Pacific, Roosevelt, in his State of the Union, address, outlined four freedoms that all Americans were entitled to:

- Freedom of speech
- Freedom of religion
- Freedom from want
- Freedom from fear

In 1943, FDR's "Four Freedoms" were portrayed by the artist Norman Rockwell in a beautiful series of covers for the *Saturday Evening Post*.

★ QUOTE OF THE DAY

Far better is it to dare mighty things, to win glorious triumphs, even though checkered by failure... than to rank with those poor spirits who neither enjoy nor suffer much, because they live in a gray twilight that knows not victory nor defeat.

Theodore Roosevelt

Wedding Bells

Two future presidents were married on this day: George Washington married Martha Dandridge Custis in 1759, and George H.W. Bush married Barbara Pierce in 1945. The Bush marriage is the longest in presidential history—with the 1946 union of Jimmy Carter and Eleanor Rosalynn Smith close behind.

January 7

1800: Millard Fillmore was born in Moravia, New York. He was the thirteenth president, serving from 1850 to 1853. Fillmore, America's sixth president in just nine years, is regarded as one of America's most ineffectual presidents because of his failure to address the deepening divide between North and South over the issue of slavery. He opposed the proposal to keep slavery out of the territories annexed during the Mexican-American War in order to appease the South, and thus backed the Compromise of 1850, including the Fugitive Slave Act ("Bloodhound

This Day in Presidential History

Millard Fillmore. Library of Congress.

Law") which was part of the compromise. After his presidency, Fillmore opposed President Abraham Lincoln during the Civil War.

1969: Congress doubled the presidential salary to $200,000. As of 2017, it is $400,000.

1999: Bill Clinton's Senate trial began. After being impeached by the House of Representatives for perjury and obstruction of justice (see December 19), the Senate—controlled by President Clinton's fellow Democrats—weighed the charges against him. He would easily be acquitted. The only other president to be impeached was Andrew Johnson—who also won Senate acquittal.

★ QUOTE OF THE DAY

May God save the country, for it is evident that the people will not.

Millard Fillmore

January 8

1790: The first State of the Union address. Speaking to Congress in New York—then the site of the federal government—George Washington became the first president to deliver the annual address, which is required by the Constitution. Washington noted that "the welfare of our country is the great object to which our cares and efforts ought to be directed. And I shall derive great satisfaction from a cooperation with you, in the pleasing though arduous task of ensuring to our fellow citizens the blessings which they have a right to expect."

Beginning in 1801, Thomas Jefferson put his State of the Union in writing, a practice that continued until 1913, when Woodrow Wilson delivered it in person to lawmakers, beginning a tradition that continues to this day.

1918: As World War I raged, Woodrow Wilson unveiled his "14 Points" plan aimed at bringing peace to a devastated Europe. Among other items, Wilson called for the soon-to-be victorious United States and its allies to offer a magnanimous peace deal to Germany and Austria-Hungary and the establishment of a postwar world body—the League of Nations—to resolve future disputes. Wilson's plan helped bring the war to an end that November. The president would win the Nobel Peace Prize in 1920.

1964: Lyndon B. Johnson's "War on Poverty." In his first State of the Union address—it had been just seven weeks since John F. Kennedy's assassination—President Johnson said it was unacceptable that one in five Americans lived in poverty. "Very often a lack of jobs and money is not the cause of poverty, but the symptom," Johnson declared. "The cause may lie deeper in our failure to give our fellow citizens a fair chance to develop their own capacities, in a lack of education and training, in a lack of medical care and housing, in a lack of decent communities in which to live and bring up their children."

Of his war on poverty, LBJ said, "The richest nation on earth can afford to win it. We cannot afford to lose it."

2002: George W. Bush signed the No Child Left Behind Act into law. It supported measurable goals for students in reading and math, and required states to give assessment tests to students in certain grades if they wanted to receive federal school funding.

With its emphasis on testing, report cards, and teacher qualifications, "NCLB" furthered the federal government's role in public education; in 2015, it was replaced by the "Every Student Succeeds Act," which returned education authority to the states.

2002: Seven nations were targeted for nuclear attack in a secret Bush administration report to Congress. The "Nuclear Posture Review" stated that the Pentagon needed to be prepared to use nuclear weapons against

China, Russia, Iraq, North Korea, Syria, Iran, and Libya if needed. A furor erupted when the report was leaked to the press.

⭐ QUOTE OF THE DAY

Unfortunately, many Americans live on the outskirts of hope—some because of their poverty, and some because of their color, and all too many because of both. Our task is to help replace their despair with opportunity.

Lyndon B. Johnson

January 9

1913: Richard M. Nixon was born in Yorba Linda, California. The thirty-seventh president, serving from 1969 to 1974, was a World War II veteran, congressman, senator, and Dwight Eisenhower's vice president. He won the Republican nomination for president in 1960, but lost that year to John F Kennedy, and, after a humiliating run for California governor in 1962, seemed finished in politics.

But promising to "bring us together" as a nation, Nixon came roaring back to win the White House in 1968. Yet the Watergate scandal—the most notorious in American history—helped tear it apart; in 1974, he resigned the presidency, the only person to do so.

Although Nixon will forever be remembered for Watergate, his presidency had notable successes. On the foreign policy front, he reached out to China, forged "détente" with the Soviet Union, and ended the Vietnam War.

At home, Nixon championed the environment, forming the Environmental Protection Agency, and oversaw tough new regulations to safeguard air and water. In fact, he probably imposed more regulations on the economy than any president since Franklin D. Roosevelt. He also raised taxes on the rich while cutting them for the poor—and exempting nine million low-income citizens from paying taxes. He oversaw a sharp boost in Social Security benefits.

All of this, in the end, was overshadowed by Watergate. It began with a burglary of Democratic National Committee headquarters in the Watergate

This Day in Presidential History

Richard M. Nixon. Library of Congress.

office complex. Eventually, journalists, primarily Robert Woodward and Carl Bernstein of the *Washington Post,* tied the break-in—and attempts to cover it up—to the White House. It became a grave constitutional scandal and cost Nixon support even among fellow Republicans, who eventually persuaded the president to step aside. He did so on August 9, 1974.

★ QUOTE OF THE DAY

I reject the cynical view that politics is a dirty business.

Richard M. Nixon

January 10

1789: The first American presidential election concluded. Voting—white male property owners only—had begun three weeks earlier, on December 15, 1788, and resulted in a resounding win for George Washington. As it does today, the election was determined by the Electoral College system. Established by the Constitution, today it gives all American citizens over the age of eighteen the right to vote for electors, who in turn vote for the president. The president and vice president are the only elected federal officials chosen by the Electoral College instead of by direct popular vote.

1941: With Britain fighting alone against Nazi Germany in World War II, President Franklin Roosevelt unveiled the lend-lease program—allowing arms shipments to any nation whose defense was considered vital to U.S. security. Lend-lease program ended the pretense of American neutrality in the war; the amount equivalent of $760 billion in 2016 was sent to allies such as Britain and the Soviet Union. In return for sending military aid to Britain, the United States took Britain's gold reserves and various other assets.

1967: Lyndon B. Johnson's war tax. With some 485,000 American troops in Vietnam—a number that would peak a year later at 536,000—Lyndon B. Johnson asked Congress to raise taxes to help pay for the war. Congress responded by approving a 6% surcharge on personal and corporate incomes.

2007: George W. Bush's Iraq surge: the president announced a "surge" of 21,000 additional U.S. troops to Iraq. In a nationwide television address, the president said the bulk of the troops were needed to help secure the Iraqi capital of Baghdad, but that some 4,000 troops would go to Anbar province west of the capital to work with regional forces and pursue the terrorist group al Qaeda.

★ QUOTE OF THE DAY

To impose taxes when the public exigencies require them is an obligation of the most sacred character, especially with a free people.

James Monroe

January 11

1908: Theodore Roosevelt designated the Grand Canyon as a national monument. Roosevelt was the first truly conservationist president. He protected 130 million acres of forests and created 5 national parks (the Grand Canyon was upgraded to one in 1919) and 51 wildlife refuges. It is for these efforts to safeguard America's natural beauty that President Roosevelt was chosen as one of the four busts to be chiseled into Mount Rushmore.

1943: Franklin D. Roosevelt became the first sitting president to fly in an airplane, when he traveled to Casablanca, Morocco, for war talks with

British prime minister Winston Churchill (Soviet premier Josef Stalin, also invited, was unable to attend because the Red Army was engaged in a major offensive against German forces at the time). In great secrecy, FDR boarded a Boeing-made Pan American aircraft—the Dixie Clipper—in Miami, startling the crew, who had no idea that the president of the United States would be their passenger.

1989: Bidding farewell to Americans after eight years in the White House, President Reagan declared that the United States had been revitalized as a nation, "respected again in the world and looked to for leadership." Reagan claimed that under his leadership, America had returned to "common sense" that "told us that to preserve the peace, we'd have to become strong again after years of weakness." Polls showed that most Americans agreed—his final Gallup approval rating was 63%—though critics noted that during Reagan's time in office the federal debt had soared, and that his claims for helping to wind down the Cold War should be shared with Soviet leader Mikhail Gorbachev, British prime minister Margaret Thatcher, and Pope John Paul II.

★ QUOTE OF THE DAY

Let this great wonder of nature remain as it now is. You cannot improve on it. But what you can do is keep it for your children, your children's children, and all who come after you, as the one great sight which every American should see.

Theodore Roosevelt

January 12

1942: Franklin Roosevelt created the National War Labor Board (NWLB). Its aim was to prevent work stoppages that might harm the war effort. One thing that FDR particularly wanted to prevent was labor strikes, which he feared would slow production at weapons factories. Roosevelt's NWLB was comprised of political, business, and labor leaders, and had the authority to impose its own settlements in any dispute between labor and management that might erupt. The Truman administration shuttered the NWLB in 1946.

1966: Lyndon B. Johnson: America would remain in Vietnam. The president insisted that U.S. forces would keep fighting in South Vietnam until Communist aggression ended. Johnson, a believer in the domino theory—which said that if one country fell to communism, others, like in a cascading line of dominoes, would soon follow—considered the growing war in that southeast Asian country a matter of U.S. national security. Johnson backed up his words by sharply escalating the U.S. war effort: when he became president in November 1963, there were 16,000 American troops in Vietnam; by the end of 1965, there were approximately 200,000; and at war's peak in 1968–1969, there would be 538,000.

1991: Congress approved George H.W. Bush's request to use force against Iraq. The House and Senate approved Bush's request to use military force to push Iraq out of Kuwait. The House's 250-183 and Senate's 52-47 vote was the first time since the Vietnam War that Congress approved the use of force by a president. Operation Desert Storm began four days later.

★ QUOTE OF THE DAY

I'm not going to rush to send somebody else's kids into a war.

George H.W. Bush

January 13

1833: Andrew Jackson wrote Vice President Martin Van Buren to express his opposition to South Carolina's defiance of federal authority. The Palmetto state had nullified an earlier federal tariff that it said favored Northern manufacturing over Southern agriculture. Complicating matters was John C. Calhoun—a South Carolina native and Jackson's vice president when that original tariff was passed—who opposed Jackson, saying states could reject federal laws. South Carolina citizens vowed to use force to resist collection of any federal tariffs. In his letter to Van Buren, Jackson wrote, "Nothing must be permitted to weaken our government at home or abroad."

1942: Franklin D. Roosevelt established the U.S. War Production Board, designed to help coordinate the transition of American business and industry from a civilian to a wartime focus.

1966: The first black cabinet member in American history was named when Lyndon B. Johnson nominated Robert Weaver to head the Department of Housing and Urban Development (HUD). HUD is responsible for developing and implementing national housing policy and enforcing fair housing laws. The nomination of Weaver—who earned his doctorate in economics from Harvard and worked in both the administrations of Franklin D. Roosevelt and John F. Kennedy—reflected Johnson's desire to improve race relations and eliminate urban decay.

1972: Richard M. Nixon announced more troop withdrawals from Vietnam. Nixon, accelerating his efforts to get the United States out of Vietnam, said some 70,000 Americans would come home by May, reducing troop strength to about 69,000. When Nixon became president in January 1969, there were 540,000 Americans in Vietnam; he would wind down the war by spring 1973.

★ QUOTE OF THE DAY

There are no problems we cannot solve together, and very few that we can solve by ourselves.

Lyndon B. Johnson

January 14

1942: Franklin Roosevelt ordered aliens from Japan, Germany, and Italy to register with the U.S. government. After Pearl Harbor was attacked, thrusting the United States into World War II, it was feared that citizens of German, Italian, or Japanese descent could sabotage the war effort. Roosevelt was particularly worried about the West Coast, which he feared could be attacked by Japan.

1943: Franklin Roosevelt and British prime minister Winston Churchill met to discuss World War II strategy. At their conference in Casablanca, Morocco, the leaders decided to demand that the Axis powers (Germany, Italy, and Japan) surrender unconditionally.

1964: Jacqueline Kennedy thanked the nation. Making her first public appearance since her husband's assassination twelve weeks before, Mrs. Kennedy said she was touched by the hundreds of thousands of condolence letters and telegrams—nearly 800,000—she had received.

"The knowledge of the affection in which my husband was held by all of you has sustained me and the warmth of these tributes is something I shall never forget," she said. "Whenever I can bear to, I read them. All his bright light's gone from the world. All of you who have written to me know how much we all loved him and that he returned that love in full measure."

Mrs. Kennedy said the letters—there would be 1.5 million by 1965—would be archived at the yet-to-be built John F. Kennedy Presidential Library in Boston.

1979: Jimmy Carter proposed to make Martin Luther King Jr.'s birthday a federal holiday. Months after King—the iconic civil rights leader—was murdered on April 4, 1968, legislation to make his birthday (January 15) a holiday was introduced, but it went nowhere until Carter said he would support it. It took another four years to make it official, however—leaving a new president, Ronald Reagan, to sign the bill.

★ QUOTE OF THE DAY

Dr. King spoke of two kinds of peace, of negative peace, which meant the absence of fear and tension, and he spoke of a positive peace, which meant the presence of justice.

It's a positive peace that we now seek-peace that keeps alive his audacious dream that all people can have food and health care for their bodies, education and culture for their minds, and dignity, equality, and freedom for their spirits.

Jimmy Carter

January 15

1953: After one of the most consequential presidencies in U.S. history, Harry Truman bid farewell to the American people. Truman's speech reflected the modesty and humility that was characteristic of him:

When Franklin Roosevelt died, I felt there must be a million men better qualified than I to take up the presidential task. But the work was mine to do, and I had to do it. And I have tried to give it everything that was in me.

1962: John F. Kennedy fudged on Vietnam. Asked a blunt question at a news conference—"Are American troops now in combat in Vietnam?" John F. Kennedy gave a one word answer: "No." The president neglected to mention, however, that U.S. troops were serving as combat advisers with the South Vietnamese army, and U.S. pilots were flying missions with the South Vietnamese Air Force. During these operations some Americans were wounded.

The Vietnam War is primarily associated with the two presidents who followed Kennedy—Lyndon B. Johnson and Richard M. Nixon. Yet Kennedy, during his short presidency, was beginning to be drawn in: there were about 3,000 American troops in Vietnam when his presidency began in 1961—and some 16,000 at the time of his assassination in November 1963.

1973: Richard M. Nixon ordered an end to the bombing of North Vietnam as peace talks between the United States and Hanoi gathered momentum. A peace treaty would be announced two weeks later, bringing the war—at the time the longest in American history—to an end. In terms of duration, the war in Vietnam would be exceeded by two wars that the United States fought simultaneously: in Afghanistan and Iraq.

★ QUOTE OF THE DAY

War: An act of violence whose object is to constrain the enemy, to accomplish our will.

George Washington

January 16

1833: In a foreshadowing of the tensions leading to the Civil War, Andrew Jackson waded into a battle over state's rights, ordering that force be used to collect tariffs in South Carolina. South Carolina said the tariffs were too high. Southern states bristled over federal tariffs, which, along with slavery (of course), widened the rift between North and South.

1883: Chester Arthur signed the Pendleton Act, creating the basis for the U.S. Civil Service system. It said that jobs in the federal government would be given on the basis of merit instead of political affiliation. It also made it illegal to fire or demote government officials for political reasons and prohibited soliciting campaign donations on federal property.

1991: The Persian Gulf War began, when George H.W. Bush announced the start of Operation Desert Storm, a U.S.-led military coalition formed to push Iraq out of Kuwait. Iraqi leader Saddam Hussein had invaded Kuwait the previous August. Bush quickly said, "This will not stand." After a five-week bombing campaign and a 100-hour ground war, the president ordered an end to hostilities. One hundred and twenty-five American soldiers were killed in the Persian Gulf War, with another twenty-one declared missing in action. The United States did not occupy Iraq itself in 1991; Defense Secretary Dick Cheney said it wasn't worth the casualties or "getting bogged down."

2001: Bill Clinton awarded former president Theodore Roosevelt a posthumous Medal of Honor for his service in the Spanish-American War.

★ QUOTE OF THE DAY

This is an historic moment. We have in this past year made great progress in ending the long era of conflict and cold war. We have before us the opportunity to forge for ourselves and for future generations a new world order—a world where the rule of law, not the law of the jungle, governs the conduct of nations. When we are successful—and we will be—we have a real chance at this new world order, an order in which a credible United Nations can use its peacekeeping role to fulfill the promise and vision of the U.N.'s founders.

George H.W. Bush

January 17

1893: Rutherford B. Hayes died in his home, Spiegel Grove, in Fremont, Ohio. The nineteenth president, he served from 1877 to 1881. Hayes came to office after what was arguably the most controversial presidential election in U.S. history—so controversial and contentious that for security reasons he had to be sworn in secretly in the Red Room of the White House (see March 3). A true high-tech president, Hayes sought friendship with the great inventors of the day like Thomas Edison and Alexander Graham Bell, inviting them to the White House to display their creations. He did so knowing that the corresponding attention would speed the integration of these new products into the U.S. economy and spur economic growth. Hayes, in fact, would have the White House's first telephone installed; its number was "1."

1929: Calvin Coolidge signed the Kellogg-Briand Pact, with the lofty goal of outlawing war. A byproduct of World War I, the pact banned aggression, but not self-defense.

1961: Dwight D. Eisenhower warned of the "military-industrial complex." In his farewell address to the nation, the president, a five-star general who led the Allied invasion of Nazi-occupied France on D-Day, told Americans that the U.S. defense establishment was too big, too costly, and, perversely, presented a threat to the institutions and liberty it was designed to protect. He said the U.S. defense industry was profiting off Americans' national security paranoia, and warned of the danger of "misplaced power."

Eisenhower knew that threats America faced in the second half of the twentieth century—notably from the Soviet Union and Red China—meant that America could no longer be unprepared for war, as it was before World War II. But he was also a fiscal conservative who believed that the American people needed to guard against the "danger that public policy could itself become the captive of a scientific-technological elite."

Other than George Washington's, Eisenhower's farewell address is regarded as the most important in American history—and well worth a read.

1994: A sexual harassment suit against a sitting president: Bill Clinton. Paula Jones, a former Arkansas state clerk, claimed that Clinton—while governor of Arkansas—sexually harassed her and then tried to undermine her after she went public with her accusations. She asked for $700,000 in damages. Citing presidential immunity, Clinton's lawyers sought to dismiss Jones's suit. A federal judge ruled that the investigation into Jones' allegations could proceed, but that Clinton could not stand trial until leaving office. Jones was eventually awarded $850,000.

⭐ QUOTE OF THE DAY

Beware of "the impulse to live only for today, plundering, for ease and convenience, the precious resources of tomorrow."

Dwight D. Eisenhower

First Lady Michelle Obama (2009–2017) was born Michelle Robinson on this day in 1964 in Chicago, Illinois. As first lady, Obama took on the issue of childhood obesity and encouraged healthful eating. She oversaw a vegetable garden at the White House.

January 18

1803: Thomas Jefferson asked Congress to fund the Lewis and Clark expedition. The United States hadn't even purchased the Louisiana Territory from Napoleon yet, but Jefferson, always planning for the future, asked for $2,500 from lawmakers (the expedition's true cost was later tabulated at around $50,000). In fact, Jefferson's request for funds came even before Napoleon offered to sell France's territorial holdings in North America to the United States. But in the spring of 1803 he did. The deal—negotiated by future president James Monroe and ambassador to France Robert Livingston—was swiftly concluded, and the Jefferson, beaming, announced it to the American people on July 4.

1919: Woodrow Wilson, in Paris, joined post-World War I talks. The president, along with the victorious leaders of Britain, France, and Italy, spent the next six months discussing the future of Europe and the formation of an international peacekeeping organization—and Wilson's pet project—called the League of Nations.

Britain and France, who had suffered tremendous losses in the war, sought to punish Germany severely and keep it weak; Wilson was determined to show magnanimity. But Wilson, eager to garner support for the League, compromised on the treatment of Germany. The Germans were forced to relinquish territory and pay steep reparations; it left a lingering and angry resentment among many Germans—helping to plant the seeds for the even more devastating war that would begin two decades later.

1862: John Tyler died at his Virginia plantation, Sherwood Forest. The tenth president, who served from 1841 to 1845, was in office when Texas was annexed in 1844—it would become the twenty-eighth state in the Union the following year. His principal contribution to the nation, however, may have been in the wake of President William Henry Harrison's

Two grandsons of President John Tyler—who was born in 1790—are still alive!

death in April 1841. Tyler, the vice president, insisted that upon the death of a sitting president, the vice president should officially become president. Harrison's cabinet said that Tyler was merely the "acting president." Tyler's view prevailed. The reason for the dispute in the first place was the fact that the Constitution was not explicit about what would happen if a president died in office. It was later rectified. Tyler was also elected to office in the Confederate government during the Civil War. He died before actually assuming that office—and was buried in a coffin bearing the Confederate flag.

1962: The Kennedy administration began "Operation Ranch Hand"—a massive U.S. Air Force effort to defoliate forests of Vietnam, Cambodia, and Laos with a herbicide that came to be known as Agent Orange. The United States believed the defoliation would expose transportation routes and staging areas used by Communist forces. It is estimated that over 6,000 spraying missions, eighteen and twenty million gallons of the herbicide were dropped. The operation—which continued until 1971—was originally called "Operation Hades," before being changed.

☆ QUOTE OF THE DAY

I know that the acquisition of Louisiana has been disapproved by some ... that the enlargement of our territory would endanger its union.... The larger our association the less will it be shaken by local passions; and in any view is it not better that the opposite bank of the Mississippi should be settled by our own brethren and children than by strangers of another family?

Thomas Jefferson

January 19

1886: Grover Cleveland signed the Presidential Succession Act, changing the order of who would succeed a chief executive who died in office. The vice president remained at the top of the list, but now, the secretary of state was second. The old law, established in 1792 (see February 21), said that after the vice president, the president pro tempore of the Senate was next. The order of succession would be changed again in 1947 (see July 18), putting the Speaker of the House of Representatives second in line.

1955: Dwight Eisenhower held the first (taped) televised presidential news conference. "Well, I see we are trying a new experiment this morning," he told the assembled White House press corps. "I hope it doesn't prove to be a disturbing influence." Eisenhower's spokesman, James Hagerty, feared that the president might get asked about a very big rumor: that he was weighing the possible use of nuclear weapons against China. "Don't worry, Jim," the president said. "If that question comes up I'll just confuse them."

1977: Gerald R. Ford pardoned Tokyo Rose. During World War II, several Japanese women broadcast propaganda over the radio to Allied troops. One was a Japanese-American woman named Iva Toguri. Born in Los Angeles, California, she was in Japan taking care of a sick relative in 1941; but when she tried to return to the United States, she was not allowed to leave. After Japan attacked Pearl Harbor later that year, Toguri was forced to make broadcasts designed to undermine the Allied war effort. Arrested in 1945, she spent a decade in prison in the United States and then was deported back to Japan. Over the next twenty years she fought to clear her name—and after a sympathetic story about her on the CBS television news program *60 Minutes*, President Ford, on his last full day in office, pardoned her.

★ QUOTE OF THE DAY

It has been my experience that folks who have no vices have very few virtues.

Abraham Lincoln

Who Takes Over if the President Dies?
1. Vice President
2. Speaker of the House
3. President pro tempore of the Senate
4. Secretary of State
5. Secretary of the Treasury

January 20

1801: John Adams nominated John Marshall to the Supreme Court as chief justice of the United States. The Senate confirmed him seven days later. Marshall served in that role for thirty-four years.

1937: Franklin Roosevelt became the first president to be inaugurated on January 20. Prior to 1937, Inauguration Day had been March 4. In his inaugural address, he said the fight against the Great Depression was far from over: "I see one-third of a nation ill-housed, ill-clad, ill-nourished."

1949: Harry Truman was sworn in for his own term as president. He had been the thirty-third president since Franklin Roosevelt's death on April 12, 1945.

1953: The first live, coast-to-coast TV broadcast of a presidential inauguration occurred, as Dwight D. Eisenhower became the thirty-fourth president.

1961: John F. Kennedy was sworn in as the thirty-fifth president. At forty-three, he was the youngest person ever elected president. The youngest president ever, however, was Theodore Roosevelt, who was sworn in at age forty-two, after President William McKinley's murder (see September 14).

1965: Lyndon B. Johnson was sworn in for his own term as president; LBJ had ascended to the presidency after the assassination of John F. Kennedy fourteen months before (see November 22).

1969: Richard M. Nixon was sworn in as the thirty-seventh president. After his 1960 loss to John F. Kennedy and a humiliating attempt to become governor of California in 1962, Nixon's comeback was regarded as one of the most remarkable in American history.

1977: Jimmy Carter was sworn in as the thirty-ninth president—and last to be inaugurated on the east front of the Capitol. Starting in 1981, presidents were sworn in on the west front, overlooking the Mall.

1981: Ronald Reagan was sworn in as the fortieth president—and, at age sixty-nine, the second oldest ever elected. Minutes after he assumed office—taking over from Jimmy Carter—Iran released fifty-two Americans who had been held hostage for 444 days.

1989: George H. W. Bush was sworn in as the forty-first president. He was the first sitting vice president to be elected president in 151 years.

1993: Bill Clinton was sworn in as the forty-second president—at age forty-six, the second-youngest ever elected.

2001: George W. Bush was sworn in as the forty-third president—and the second son of a president to become president himself (John Adams and his son John Quincy Adams were the other pair).

2009: Barack Obama was sworn in as the forty-fourth president, using the Bible that Abraham Lincoln had used for his inaugural in 1861. He was the first African American ever elected president. (Due to a few verbal mix-ups during the oath, Chief Justice John Roberts readministered the oath to Obama privately that evening in the White House.)

2017: Donald Trump was sworn in as the forty-fifth president—at the age of seventy-one, he is the oldest person ever elected to a first term as chief executive.

☆ QUOTE OF THE DAY

Ask not what your country can do for you. Ask what you can do for your country.

John F. Kennedy

Only four sitting vice presidents have been elected president: John Adams, Thomas Jefferson, Martin Van Buren, and George H.W. Bush.

January 21

When January 20 fell on a Sunday, several presidents were inaugurated on the following day, January 21:

1957: Dwight Eisenhower was sworn in for his second term as the thirty-fourth president of the United States.

1977: Jimmy Carter pardoned Vietnam draft dodgers. Hoping to put the Vietnam War in America's rear-view mirror, the president, on his first full day in office, granted an unconditional pardon to Americans who evaded the draft during the Vietnam War. Some 90% of those who had evaded the draft had moved to Canada, where they were—after some initial controversy—welcomed as immigrants. Still others hid inside the United States. Carter's decision was harshly criticized by veterans' groups.

1985: Ronald Reagan was sworn in for his second term as the fortieth president of the United States. The coldest inauguration temperature on record (7 °F at noon) forced the ceremony indoors to the Capitol Rotunda.

2013: Barack Obama was sworn in for his second term as the forty-fourth president of the United States. He used Bibles previously owned by Abraham Lincoln and Martin Luther King, Jr.

★ QUOTE OF THE DAY

Officeholders are the agents of the people, not their masters.

Grover Cleveland

January 22

1807: Thomas Jefferson told Congress of the "Burr Conspiracy," the treason charges leveled against his former vice president Aaron Burr. Jefferson informed Congress that Burr tried to split several western states and the new Louisiana territory from the Union and make himself ruler. Burr was arrested and tried—but acquitted.

1932: Herbert Hoover established the Reconstruction Finance Corporation, a government agency that lent money to banks, insurance companies, and other institutions in an effort to jump start the economy in the Great Depression.

1944: Franklin Roosevelt established the War Refugee Board, tasked with the "immediate rescue and relief of the Jews of Europe and other victims of enemy persecution." After World War II, the WRB's first director, John Pehle, described it as "little and late." But it has been credited with saving as many as 200,000 lives during the Holocaust.

1973: Lyndon B. Johnson died. The thirty-sixth president, aged sixty-four, passed away at his ranch in Stonewall, Texas—the second former president to die in a month (Harry Truman passed away on December 26, 1972). Johnson, who became president after John F. Kennedy was assassinated in 1963, was elected in his own right the next year. His presidency was known for sweeping domestic achievements: his "Great Society" included the Voting Rights Act, the Civil Rights Act, and improvements in housing. Johnson was also a staunch supporter of the space program, which landed a man in the moon six months after he left office. But the Johnson era was also defined by the Vietnam War, which tore the country apart and proved to be the president's undoing.

1982: Ronald Reagan dangled nuclear arms cuts before Moscow—on one condition. The president said he'd consider nuclear talks with the Soviet Union if they stopped oppressing Poland, which was a key member of the Warsaw Pact, the Soviet-controlled military alliance. The Americans and Soviets had been squabbling over the status of intermediate-range nuclear forces (INF) in Europe and each had accused the other of acting in bad faith.

Reagan's offer came after the Moscow-backed Polish government imposed martial law, seeking to control growing unrest in that country. The Reagan administration claimed that arms reduction talks could not be "insulated from other events" and that "the continuing repression of the Polish people—in which Soviet responsibility is clear—obviously constitutes a major setback to the prospects for constructive East-West relations."

★ QUOTE OF THE DAY

The presidency has made every man who occupied it, no matter how small, bigger than he was; and no matter how big, not big enough for its demands.

Lyndon B. Johnson

January 23

1845: Congress set the future date for presidential elections. Lawmakers determined that "the Tuesday after the first Monday in November" would be the date when all states must appoint electors for president and vice president. Since 1848, every presidential election has been held on this date.

1968: A U.S. Navy intelligence ship was seized by North Korea, sparking a yearlong crisis for Lyndon B. Johnson. The U.S.S. *Pueblo*—which the United States said was in international waters—was fired upon, wounding the commander and two crewmen, before being captured and taken to a North Korean port. The eighty-three-man crew was bound and blindfolded, charged with espionage, and held captive for eleven months. During their time in captivity, they were regularly beaten and tortured; one American died during the ordeal.

This Day in Presidential History

1973: Nixon announced an end to the Vietnam War. The president said the agreement with North Vietnam would bring "peace with honor" to what was then the longest war in U.S. history, in which 58,209 Americans died.

2017: Donald Trump signed an executive order pulling the United States out of the Trans-Pacific Partnership (TPP), a twelve-nation free trade deal. The president called TPP—which had been negotiated during the presidency of Barack Obama but never ratified by the Senate—"a rape of our country."

★ QUOTE OF THE DAY

It is common sense to take a method and try it. If it fails, admit it frankly and try another. But above all, try something.

Franklin D. Roosevelt

January 24

2003: The Department of Homeland Security (DHS) began operation. Created by George W. Bush and approved by Congress in the wake of the September 11, 2001, terrorist attacks on New York and Washington, D.C., DHS today encompasses a variety of U.S. government security agencies, such as the Secret Service, Immigration and Customs Enforcement, the Federal Emergency Management Agency, Transportation Security Administration, and more.

★ QUOTE OF THE DAY

I believe the most solemn duty of the American president is to protect the American people.

George W. Bush

January 25

1961: John F. Kennedy held the first presidential news conference carried live on radio and TV. In contrast to today's presidents, who hold their televised news conferences in the White House, Kennedy held his in an auditorium at the State Department, which had more room. Topics that day included everything from relations with Cuba to food aid for America's poor.

Kennedy is rightly called the first president of the television era. It began with his first TV debate with Richard M. Nixon during the 1960 campaign. Kennedy knew that his charisma, intelligence, and good looks played well on the small screen, and helped with his ability to influence public opinion.

1972: Richard M. Nixon revealed secret details of Vietnamese peace talks. The president, criticized for not doing enough to end the Vietnam War, disclosed that his National Security advisor Henry Kissinger held twelve secret negotiating sessions with Vietnamese officials in Paris between August 4, 1969, and August 16, 1971. Nixon also disclosed details of an eight-point plan given to the North Vietnamese that outlined his proposal to end the war. A peace agreement would be signed a year later.

★ QUOTE OF THE DAY

This has been the longest, the most difficult war in American history. Honest and patriotic Americans have disagreed as to whether we should have become involved at all nine years ago; and there has been disagreement on the conduct of the war. The proposal I have made tonight is one on which we all can agree. Let us unite now, unite in our search for peace—a peace that is fair to both sides—a peace that can last.

Richard M. Nixon

January 26

1871: A decade after Abraham Lincoln's income tax went into effect, it was repealed. The first federal income tax (a 3% surcharge on income) was levied by Congress in 1861 at Lincoln's request; he recognized that Americans needed to pay for their wars.

1961: Two years before her son assassinated John F. Kennedy, the mother of Lee Harvey Oswald visited the White House—to ask for help finding her son. Oswald, a former Marine Corps marksman, had defected to the Soviet Union more than a year before, but Marguerite Oswald had no information on him. The U.S. government also wanted more information on the defector. Oswald would return to the United States in 1962 with help, ironically, from Navy Secretary John Connally—who would be shot by Oswald during the November 22, 1963, murder of President Kennedy.

1973: Richard M. Nixon announced the signing of the Paris Peace Accords, officially ending the Vietnam War. The conflict killed 58,209 Americans. Once the longest war in U.S. history, it has since been exceeded by Afghanistan (#1) and Iraq (#2).

1998: "I did not have sexual relations with that woman," an angry president Clinton insisted, in response to allegations of an affair with former intern Monica Lewinsky. The Lewinsky scandal eventually led to the president's impeachment by the House of Representatives; he was acquitted in a Senate trial.

2005: George W. Bush's pick for secretary of state, Condoleezza Rice, won Senate confirmation; she was the first black woman to serve in that position. The first black woman to serve in a cabinet was Patricia Roberts Harris, who served as President Carter's secretary of housing and urban development, and United States secretary of health, education, and welfare (now health and human services).

★ QUOTE OF THE DAY

A long and trying ordeal for America has ended. Our nation has achieved its goal of peace with honor in Vietnam.

Richard M. Nixon

January 27

1838: An early speech by Abraham Lincoln hinted of greatness. The future president's "Lyceum Address," given at the age of twenty-eight, described problems that modern-day Americans would certainly recognize:

I hope I am over wary; but if I am not, there is, even now, something of ill-omen, amongst us. I mean the increasing disregard for law which pervades the country; the growing disposition to substitute the wild and furious passions, in lieu of the sober judgment of Courts; and the worse than savage mobs, for the executive ministers of justice.

This disposition is awfully fearful in any community; and that it now exists in ours, though grating to our feelings to admit, it would be a violation of truth, and an insult to our intelligence, to deny.

1862: Abraham Lincoln ordered Union forces to take the offensive against the Confederate Army. The president's General War Order No. 1 was a reflection of Lincoln's frustration that his army and navy commanders weren't acting boldly enough in taking the battle to the enemy.

1967: Three astronauts—Virgil Grissom, Edward White, and Roger Chaffee—died in a fire during an *Apollo* 1 launch test; their deaths occurring hours after President Johnson signed a space treaty with fifty-nine nations governing the exploration of space. Johnson was informed of the *Apollo* 1 tragedy during a White House party. He read this memo to his stunned guests:

Three valiant young men have given their lives in the Nation's service. We mourn this great loss. Our hearts go out to their families.

1973: By proclamation of Richard M. Nixon, the United States observed a day of prayer and Thanksgiving to commemorate the end of the Vietnam War. "I urge all men and women of goodwill to join the prayerful hope that this moment marks not only the end of the war in Vietnam, but the beginning of a new era of world peace and understanding for all mankind," the president said.

2017: In one of his first major actions as president, Donald Trump signed an executive order banning entry, for ninety days, of citizens from seven Muslim-majority nations, and indefinitely halting the flow of refugees from another, Syria. The order, driven by security concerns, sparked nationwide protests and was soon blocked by a federal judge. A revised executive order would be issued in March, but was blocked by court order before it took effect.

January 28

1915: Woodrow Wilson vetoed an immigration bill that would have required literacy tests for new arrivals to the United States. Supporters of tighter immigration laws argued that the United States was allowing people in who were illiterate and thus not able to contribute.

This Day in Presidential History

1916: Appointed by Woodrow Wilson, Louis D. Brandeis became the first Jewish justice on the Supreme Court. After being nominated, Brandeis faced—and faced down—anti-Semitic opposition; during his twenty-three years on the high court, his decisions affirmed his strong belief in individual liberty and privacy, and his opposition to unchecked governmental power.

1938: With war clouds gathering over Europe and Asia, Franklin Roosevelt called for the construction of a two-ocean navy. "We cannot assume that our defense would be limited to one ocean and one coast and that the other ocean and the other coast would with certainty be safe," Roosevelt said. In 1940, the Two-Ocean Navy Act would be approved by Congress, providing funds for a massive expansion of the fleet.

1986: A stunned Ronald Reagan postponed his State of the Union address after the space shuttle *Challenger* exploded, killing all seven crew members aboard. Reagan instead gave one of the finest speeches of his presidency—arguably one of the most eloquent given by any president—a paean to American courage, openness, and resilience. The *Challenger* disaster came a day after the anniversary of a 1967 fire that had killed three Apollo astronauts. A third space disaster, the 2003 explosion of the shuttle *Columbia*, would occur on February 1, 2003.

★ QUOTE OF THE DAY

The future doesn't belong to the fainthearted; it belongs to the brave.

Ronald D. Reagan

January 29

1834: Andrew Jackson became the first president to use federal troops to put down labor unrest. Indentured laborers digging the Chesapeake & Ohio Canal were angry over working conditions and low pay.

1843: William McKinley was born in Niles, Ohio. He was the twenty-fifth president, serving from 1897 to 1901. A Civil War hero, he was elected to Congress in 1877 and rose through the House ranks rapidly. He served seven terms and was then elected Governor of Ohio. In 1896, McKinley was elected president.

The defining event of his presidency was the war with Spain. It was America's first two-front war—fought in both the Pacific and the Caribbean—and vaulted America onto the world stage as a true global power. Americans saw this as the culmination of the "Manifest Destiny" philosophy that had first emerged half a century before during the Polk years—the last time Americans vanquished a foreign enemy. McKinley was reelected in 1900, but assassinated in September 1901—the third U.S. president to be murdered in just thirty-six years. His death put Vice President Theodore Roosevelt in the White House at age forty-two—the youngest president in American history.

1923: Scandal rocked Warren Harding's Veterans' Bureau. The head of the bureau, Charles Forbes, resigned as a Senate investigation began to uncover rampant fraud, bribery, and conspiracy. Forbes would be convicted, adding to the growing perception that the president's administration was rife with corruption (see April 7, May 31).

2002: George W. Bush's "Axis of Evil" speech. Four-and-a-half months after terrorists attacked New York and Washington, President Bush, in his State of the Union speech, said three countries—North Korea, Iran, and Iraq—were rogue states that harbored, financed, or aided terrorists. He vowed that none of these countries would be allowed to obtain weapons of mass destruction—but in 2006 Bush was unable to prevent North Korea from testing its first nuclear weapon.

William McKinley. Library of Congress.

This Day in Presidential History

☆ QUOTE OF THE DAY

Everywhere that freedom stirs, let tyrants fear.

George W. Bush

January 30

1835: An assassination attempt against Andrew Jackson. His attacker, an unemployed British housepainter, had two guns. Both of them misfired. The 67-year-old Jackson—known as "Old Hickory" for his toughness—fought with his assailant, beating him with his cane. The president had just left a funeral service in the House chamber of the U.S. Capitol. Jackson was convinced that political opponents had hired his attacker, Richard Lawrence. It was more likely, however, that Lawrence was mentally unstable—he was confined for the rest of his life in a mental institution.

1882: Franklin D. Roosevelt was born in Hyde Park, New York. He was the thirty-second president, serving from 1933 to 1945. Roosevelt, regarded by historians as perhaps the second or third greatest president, guided the

The first assassination attempt against a president failed when, miraculously, both of Richard Lawrence's guns failed to fire. Andrew Jackson, then 67, beat his would-be-killer with his cane. Library of Congress.

United States through two of its most challenging and dangerous crises: the Great Depression and World War II. FDR was elected four times; no other president has been elected more than twice. After his death, the constitution was amended, saying a president could serve just two consecutive terms.

1968: Confidence in Lyndon B. Johnson's management of the Vietnam was shattered by Tet—a surprise North Vietnamese offensive against South Vietnam. Historians say Tet wound up as a U.S. military victory, but at home it damaged the government's insistence that the Vietnam War was under control.

1974: In his State of the Union address, Richard M. Nixon refused to resign over the growing Watergate scandal. Declaring that two years of Watergate was enough, he demanded an end to the investigation. Lawmakers and the American people disagreed. Nixon would resign the presidency less than seven months later.

★ QUOTE OF THE DAY

The only limit to our realization of tomorrow will be our doubts of today. Let us move forward with strong and active faith.

Franklin D. Roosevelt

Herbert Hoover (left) and Franklin Delano Roosevelt en route to Roosevelt's inauguration, March 4, 1933. Library of Congress.

This Day in Presidential History

January 31

1865: Slavery came one step closer to being abolished when the House of Representatives passed the Thirteenth Amendment to the Constitution. The Senate had previously passed the amendment, which said "neither slavery nor involuntary servitude … shall exist within the United States, or any place subject to their jurisdiction." It would soon be ratified by the required three-quarters of states—becoming the law of the land in December 1865. Sadly, Abraham Lincoln—assassinated in April of 1865—did not live to see it.

1950: Harry Truman vowed to build the hydrogen bomb. The president's decision came five months after the American monopoly on nuclear weapons ended with the Soviet Union's first test of its own atomic bomb. On November 1, 1952, America's first hydrogen bomb—"Ivy Mike"—was tested on Elugelab in the Enewetak Atoll. It was vastly more powerful than the nuclear devices dropped on Japan during World War II.

1995: Bill Clinton bailed out Mexico. After Congress rejected a $50 billion bailout of Mexico, the president, using his executive powers, okayed a $20 billion loan to that country. Mexico's economy was crumbling and its currency, the peso, plunged in value. Clinton, fearing unrest south of the border, said U.S security was at stake and authorized the bailout.

★ QUOTE OF THE DAY

Whenever I hear any one arguing for slavery I feel a strong impulse to see it tried on him personally.

Abraham D. Lincoln

February

February 1

1790: Representing the third branch of the federal government—the judiciary—the Supreme Court held its first session. Chief Justice John Jay—who had been both nominated and confirmed that very day by President George Washington—presided. The Supreme Court was established by Article Three of the Constitution, which took effect in March 1789. Six months later, the Judiciary Act was passed, allowing for six justices who would serve on the court for life.

1861: President-elect Lincoln's problems grew, when Texas seceded from the Union. It was the seventh state to do so and came over the objections of Texas Governor Sam Houston. Houston was replaced as governor after he refused to take an oath of allegiance to the Confederacy. Texas joined the Confederacy on March 12, 1861.

1865: Abraham Lincoln signed a joint congressional resolution proposing that a Thirteenth Amendment—abolishing slavery—be added to the Constitution.

1905: Theodore Roosevelt established the National Forest Service.

2003: George W. Bush addressed the nation after the space shuttle *Columbia* exploded during reentry into the earth's atmosphere, killing all seven crew members. The disaster came just four days after the anniversary of the first shuttle explosion—*Challenger*—in 1986, and five days after the anniversary of a fire on board *Apollo* 1, which killed three astronauts during a training exercise.

★ QUOTE OF THE DAY

The crew of the shuttle *Columbia* did not return safely to Earth but we can pray they are safely home.

George W. Bush

February 2

1848: A victory for America—and James K. Polk: the Treaty of Guadalupe Hidalgo was signed, ending the Mexican-American War. The war added 525,000 square miles to the United States, including the area that would become the states of California, Nevada, Utah, New Mexico, and Arizona, as well as parts of Colorado and Wyoming. It also recognized the annexation of Texas. The United States was now a continental power, with the American flag flying from the Atlantic to the Pacific. "The results of the war with Mexico," Polk told Congress, "have given to the United States a national character abroad which our country never before enjoyed."

Although Polk's war was successful, he lost public support after two bloody years of fighting during which the United States lost 1,773 men and spent $100 million—a huge sum in those days.

1934: By executive order, Franklin D. Roosevelt established the Export-Import Bank to encourage trade between the United States and foreign nations, particularly Latin America.

1948: Harry Truman moved to desegregate the U.S. military. The president told Congress that he had ordered the secretary of defense to take steps "to have the remaining instances of discrimination in the armed services eliminated as rapidly as possible" (see July 26).

☆ QUOTE OF THE DAY

There is more selfishness and less principle among members of Congress than I had any conception of, before I became President of the U.S.

James Polk

There shall be firm and universal peace between the United States of America and the Mexican Republic.
Article I, Treaty of Guadalupe Hidalgo, signed February 2, 1848.

February 3

1917: Woodrow Wilson cut off diplomatic ties with Germany, as the United States edged closer to war. Wilson—angry that Germany had announced a policy of unrestricted submarine warfare in the Atlantic Ocean—would soon ask for a declaration of war. The United States would enter World War I—"the war to end all wars"—that spring.

1924: Woodrow Wilson died at Washington, D.C. He was the twenty-eighth president—and eighth from Virginia—serving from 1913 to 1921. A scholar who was president of Princeton University, he was elected governor of New Jersey and served from 1911 to 1913. A Democrat, he was elected president in 1912 and served two terms.

As president, Wilson oversaw an expansion of the federal government, with the creation of the Federal Reserve and Federal Trade Commission. Thanks to the Sixteenth Amendment to the Constitution ("The Congress shall have power to lay and collect taxes on incomes, from whatever source derived"), the Revenue Act of 1913 revived the income tax (which had first been introduced during the Civil War). Wilson's presidency also saw the ratification of the Nineteenth Amendment, which granted American women the right to vote.

The World War I was also fought on Wilson's watch. He tried to keep America neutral, but eventually asked for a declaration of war on Germany in 1917. When the war ended in November 1918, Wilson unveiled a fourteen-point plan aimed at preventing future conflict. One key proposal was for the creation of the League of Nations, an international peacekeeping body similar to today's United Nations. The Senate dealt Wilson a blow by rejecting the Versailles Treaty and U.S. membership in the League of Nations. Yet for his efforts, Wilson received the Nobel Peace Prize.

1994: Bill Clinton ended a trade embargo against Vietnam. The president agreed to lift the embargo, which had been in place since 1975—when South Vietnam fell to communist North Vietnam—because of its cooperation in helping the United States locate the 2,238 Americans still listed as missing from the Vietnam War.

2005: Alberto Gonzales—nominated by George W. Bush—became the nation's first Hispanic attorney general. The 60-36 Senate vote reflected squabbling between Republicans and Democrats over whether the administration's counterterrorism policies had led to torture.

★ QUOTE OF THE DAY

The ear of the leader must ring with the voices of the people.

Woodrow Wilson

This Day in Presidential History

February 4

1789: Electors unanimously chose George Washington to be the first president of the United States. Washington won sixty-nine electoral votes, more than enough to be elected; John Adams received thirty-six and John Jay received seven. The only drama in the election was who would become vice president. In that first election, each elector cast two votes; if a person received a vote from a majority of the electors, that person became president, and the runner-up became vice president. Since John Adams was the runner-up, he became the vice president. The Twelfth Amendment, ratified in 1804, would change this procedure, requiring each elector to cast distinct votes for president and vice president.

For the first thirteen years of its existence—from 1776 to 1789—the United States had no president, of course. The federal government was run by the Confederation Congress, which had a ceremonial presiding officer and several executive departments, but no independent executive branch.

1861: A month before Abraham Lincoln was inaugurated, southern states met to form the Confederate States of America. Representatives from South Carolina, Mississippi, Florida, Alabama, Georgia, and Louisiana elected Jefferson Davis as president. Within two months, Texas, Virginia, Arkansas, North Carolina, and Tennessee would also join—and the Civil War was on.

1945: Franklin D. Roosevelt, British prime minister Winston Churchill, and Soviet leader Josef Stalin—the "big three"—attended the Yalta talks, which shaped post–World War II Europe. The talks—held in Soviet Crimea—are today seen as controversial since it helped cement communist control by the Soviet Union over Eastern Europe. Some historians say the Cold War—a half-century struggle between the United States and Soviet Union—began at Yalta. (See February 11.)

★ QUOTE OF THE DAY

To be prepared for war is one of the most effectual means of preserving peace.

George Washington

Eight presidents were born in Virginia—more than in any other state:
George Washington
Thomas Jefferson
James Madison
James Monroe
William Henry Harrison
John Tyler
Zachary Taylor
Woodrow Wilson

February 5

1917: Congress overrode Woodrow Wilson's veto of a bill severely limiting Asian immigration. Anti-immigrant feelings had been rising in prior years, and with the United States edging closer to participation in World War I, xenophobia—fear of foreigners—rose still higher. In late 1916, Congress passed its immigration bill, which required a literacy test for newcomers to the United States. Wilson vetoed it.

1937: To howls of protest, Franklin D. Roosevelt announced his "court packing" plan to add up to five new Supreme Court justices. Roosevelt's plan, the Judicial Procedures Reform Bill, was in reaction to the Supreme Court's repeated striking down of his New Deal programs. FDR's idea provoked national outrage; some accused him of trying to rig the judiciary system.

1987: Congress overrode Ronald Reagan's veto of the Clean Water Act. Reagan had vetoed the bill three months earlier, saying its $20 billion cost was too much. Reagan said he was "committed to the act's objectives" but wanted states and municipalities to absorb more of the financial burden.

★ QUOTE OF THE DAY

I ask you to judge me by the enemies I have made.

Franklin D. Roosevelt

February 6

1911: Ronald Reagan was born in Tampico, Illinois. He was the fortieth president, serving from 1981 to 1989—and winning both of his elections in landslides. Known as the "Great Communicator," Reagan did not see himself as one, but said, "I communicated great things." Reagan was known for his optimism and enduring faith in America's future; his vision was that of a "shining city on a hill." Many historians credit him for helping to win the Cold War against the Soviet Union, a goal he predicted in a famous 1982 speech in which he said that "the march of freedom and democracy" would leave Marxism-Leninism on the "ash heap of history."

A Democrat until switching to the Republican Party at age fifty-one, Reagan served two terms as Governor of California (1966-1974), a tenure that gave him more executive experience than any of the fifteen prior presidents who had also been governors. It can be argued that Reagan arrived in the White House as seasoned an executive—if not more so—than most of his predecessors.

At home, Reagan presided over a robust economic rebound from the deep recession of 1980–82. Some 5.3 million and 10.7 million jobs were created, respectively, during his two terms in office. He also helped preserve Social Security by taxing benefits and raising the retirement age.

Ronald Reagan. Library of Congress.

This Day in Presidential History

The 1986 Tax Reform Act closed loopholes and raised taxes on businesses, yet despite this increased revenue, the national debt increased (in absolute terms) some 256% during his time in office.

Reagan, who came within seconds of dying after a 1981 assassination attempt, supported measures to reduce gun violence. In 1986, he signed the Firearm Owners Protection Act, which was hailed by gun rights activists for its numerous protections for gun owners. But it also banned ownership of any fully automatic rifles that weren't already registered on the day the law was signed. He also supported an assault weapons ban and the Brady Bill on background checks for prospective gun buyers.

During President Reagan's second term, the White House became snared in what became a constitutional crisis: the Iran-Contra scandal, in which Reagan admitted that money from Iranian arms sales had been used to buy weapons for U.S.-backed rebels in Nicaragua. Many Americans were angry that Reagan appeared to be doing business with Iranian officials—while publicly labeling them terrorists. There was talk of impeachment. Eleven White House officials were convicted (all of those convictions were vacated or pardoned).

A *Vanity Fair* poll in 2010 solicited choices for a fifth face on Mount Rushmore. Reagan was the choice of Republicans, while Democrats opted for John F. Kennedy.

★ QUOTE OF THE DAY

I know in my heart that man is good, that what is right will always eventually triumph, and there is purpose and worth to each and every life.

Ronald Reagan

February 7

1963: John F. Kennedy banned travel, financial, and commercial transactions with Communist Cuba. It was the latest in a series of ever-tightening restrictions on the island nation. The previous fall, in the wake of the dangerous Cuban Missile Crisis, Kennedy imposed travel restrictions, and in the summer of 1963 began the Cuban Assets Control Regulations program, in which Cuban assets in the United States were frozen and existing restrictions were consolidated.

This Day in Presidential History

2002: George W. Bush unveiled a plan to federally fund faith-based initiatives. He said that faith-based organizations could assume a greater role in helping the needy without violating America's traditional separation of church and state. Under the president's plan, religious groups could receive federal funding for programs that were usually carried out by secular nonprofit organizations, and that anyone donating to those religious groups should get tax breaks. But Bush's plan to use federal funds for faith-based programs was attacked by many secularists, who challenged both its constitutionality and effectiveness.

★ QUOTE OF THE DAY

This legislation will not only provide a way for Government to encourage faith-based programs to exist without breaching the separation of church and state; it will also encourage charitable giving, as well. And we have an opportunity to capture the compassion of the country, focus it in the right direction.

George W. Bush

The Perks of Power

Before the ban on commercial transactions with Cuba went into effect, John F. Kennedy, who loved Cuban cigars, ordered press secretary Pierre Salinger to purchase 1,200 of them for future use. Salinger succeeded, returning in the morning with 1,201 Petit H. Upmann cigars, Kennedy's favorite cigar size and brand.

February 8

1809: James Madison was declared the victor of the 1808 presidential election. Madison, who was Thomas Jefferson's secretary of state, won 122 electoral votes to Federalist opponent Charles C. Pinckney's 47.

1887: Grover Cleveland signed the Dawes Act. Inspired by an 1881 book *A Century of Dishonor*, which detailed the federal government's mistreatment of Native Americans, the Dawes Act divided tribal lands of Native Americans into individual allotments and encouraged Indian assimilation into American society. But it had the effect of reducing land owned by Native Americans from 138 million acres in 1887 to 78 million in 1900. In addition, the law created new schools in which children were punished for speaking their native language or performing native rituals. Scholars regard the Dawes Act as a failed policy that only deepened the distrust and resentment that Native Americans had of the federal government.

1922: Warren Harding had the White House's first radio installed. Radio was a hot new medium in the 1920s—and politicians saw it as a way to reach voters. Harding would be the first president to have his voice broadcast on the radio, but it was two of his three immediate successors—Calvin Coolidge and Franklin D. Roosevelt—who truly used the power of radio to change not just the presidency, but America itself.

★ QUOTE OF THE DAY

What is the use of being elected or re-elected, unless you stand for something?

Grover Cleveland

February 9

1773: William Henry Harrison was born at his family's Berkeley Plantation in the Colony of Virginia. The ninth president, he served the shortest time in office—just one month—in 1841. At sixty-eight, the oldest president prior to Ronald Reagan and Donald Trump, Harrison gave a two-hour long inaugural address in cold, wet weather. He died a month later—of pneumonia, according to his doctor, but probably of typhoid fever. His grandson Benjamin was also elected president and served from 1889 to 1893—the only presidential grandfather-grandson in American history.

1825: John Quincy Adams was declared the winner of the 1824 election—even though he lost *both* the popular *and* electoral college vote to Andrew Jackson. How could Adams lose both the popular vote *and* electoral college—and yet win the presidency? Because the 1824 election was a four-man race. Jackson won the most electoral votes, 99, Adams had 84, William Crawford had 41, and Henry Clay 37. Thus, Jackson had a *plurality* but not a *majority* as required by the Constitution. In such a scenario, the Twelfth Amendment to the Constitution lets Congress decide, and it gave the election to Adams. Ironically, Adams hated the presidency, calling it the "four most miserable years of my life." Jackson got his revenge, winning their election rematch in 1828.

This Day in Presidential History

William Henry Harrison. Library of Congress.

To this day, the election of 1824 remains one of the most controversial in American history. The 1800 election was also decided by the House (see February 17). A third bitterly contested election, in 1876, was decided by an electoral commission consisting of five senators, five members of the House, and five Supreme Court justices (see March 2). And, of course, there was the election of 2000, which was decided when the Supreme Court stopped the recount of damaged ballots in Florida—giving the presidency to George W. Bush (see December 12).

1886: Grover Cleveland declared martial law in Seattle, Washington, as anti-Chinese rioting broke out. The job market was tough in 1886 and some citizens in the Pacific Northwest blamed what they said was cheap competition from Chinese immigrants. Protests broke out and quickly turned violent; the president declared martial law and ordered Army troops from Fort Vancouver to restore law and order.

1965: Lyndon B. Johnson ordered North Vietnam to be bombed, following an attack on a U.S. barrack that killed nine American soldiers.

☆ QUOTE OF THE DAY

To believe all men honest would be folly. To believe none so is something worse.

John Quincy Adams

This Day in Presidential History

February 10

1807: Worried about British aggression, Thomas Jefferson asked Congress to boost defense spending. The president wanted to buy more gun boats to better protect the long U.S. coastline. Jefferson was concerned about growing tension with Great Britain, fueled in part by the British belief that the young United States was rapidly becoming a threat to British maritime supremacy. A battle that summer between an American and British warship off the coast of Virginia was exactly the sort of thing that Jefferson worried about; the United States was also angry that Britain was interfering with American trade with France (which was at war with Britain). Growing tensions between the United States and Britain would lead to the War of 1812—often called America's "second war for independence."

1954: Dwight Eisenhower warned against United States' involvement in Vietnam. In 1954, there was heavy fighting between communist forces—led by Ho Chi Minh—and France, which had long enjoyed colonial rule over Vietnam. The French asked Eisenhower for help, but the president refused to send American troops. In a news conference he said: "I cannot conceive of a greater tragedy for America than to get heavily involved now in an all-out war." Yet after the French were defeated—and Vietnam divided in two by the Geneva Accords—Eisenhower did begin sending military aid to South Vietnam, laying the foundation for direct American involvement in the 1960s.

1967: A major flaw in the Constitution was fixed, with the ratification of the Twenty-fifth Amendment. After John F. Kennedy was assassinated in 1963, Vice President Lyndon B. Johnson became president—but no one replaced Johnson as vice president. Thus, for fourteen months, the United States had no vice president. It was finally filled in January 1965, when Johnson—winner of the 1964 presidential election—and his new vice president Hubert Humphrey were sworn in.

The Twenty-fifth amendment fixed this situation, saying, "Whenever there is a vacancy in the office of the Vice President, the President shall nominate a Vice President who shall take office upon confirmation by a majority vote of both Houses of Congress." The amendment would quickly come in handy. After Vice President Spiro Agnew resigned in disgrace in 1973, President Richard M. Nixon selected Representative Gerald Ford (R-Michigan) to replace him. In 1974, after Nixon himself resigned, thrusting Ford into the presidency, Ford selected former New York governor Nelson Rockefeller to be vice president.

This Day in Presidential History

★ QUOTE OF THE DAY

Of all the enemies of public liberty, war is perhaps the most to be dreaded, because it comprises and develops the germ of every other.

James Madison

Prior to the Twenty-fifth amendment being ratified in 1967, there were plenty of times when America had no vice president. After the deaths of eight presidents—four of whom were assassinated—the vice president took over, and the vice presidential job was left vacant. And seven vice presidents who died in office were never replaced.

February 11

1811: Angered that Britain—which was at war with France—would not honor American neutrality, James Madison ordered a trade ban with Britain. Madison was also concerned that the British were aiding some Native Americans to fight the United States. Relations between the United States and Britain would continue to deteriorate—Madison would ask for a declaration of war in 1812.

1945: Franklin Roosevelt signed the Yalta agreement. The agreement, also signed by British prime minister Winston Churchill and Soviet leader Josef Stalin, finalized the post–World War II future of Europe. Germany, soon to surrender, would be divided into four portions, with the United States, Britain, France, and the Soviet Union each controlling one. The Soviets also agreed to declare war on Japan ninety days after Germany's surrender.

1953: Dwight Eisenhower denied clemency for Julius and Ethel Rosenberg, who were convicted of passing atomic secrets to the Soviet Union. They were executed four months later.

★ QUOTE OF THE DAY

It is our duty still to endeavor to avoid war; but if it shall actually take place, no matter by whom brought on, we must defend ourselves.

Thomas Jefferson

February 12

1809: Abraham Lincoln was born on a farm near Hodgenville, Kentucky. He was the sixteenth president, serving from 1861 to 1865. Lincoln— widely regarded as America's greatest president—preserved the Union during the Civil War and helped end slavery in the United States. For this effort, he was known as the "Great Emancipator," though he waffled on the issue of slavery in the early stages of his presidency.

Lincoln had soaring oratorical skills. His speeches—including the Gettysburg Address (see November 19) and his second Inaugural Address (see March 4) are considered among the finest ever given by an American president. One week after the South surrendered, ending the Civil War (see April 9), Lincoln was assassinated—the first of four presidents to be murdered (see April 14).

1999: Bill Clinton—facing removal from office—was acquitted by the Senate. Clinton had earlier been impeached by the House of Representatives on charges of perjury obstruction of justice, relating to an affair he had with a White House intern, Monica Lewinsky. Only one other president has ever been impeached: Andrew Johnson (see March 13).

Abraham Lincoln. Library of Congress.

This Day in Presidential History

★ QUOTE OF THE DAY

The struggle of today is not altogether for today—it is for a vast future also.

Abraham Lincoln

February 13

1793: Four more years for George Washington; the first president won an easy reelection victory. His vice president, again, was John Adams.

1861: Making his way toward Washington, D.C., by train, Abraham Lincoln, in Columbus, Ohio, received word that he had won the presidency. At 5:00 p.m. he was informed that the electoral votes had been counted and that he was officially president-elect. Despite looming war clouds, the president-elect minimized the nation's difficulties when he addressed well-wishers: "There is nothing going wrong."

1905: In a speech focusing on America's wide racial divide, Theodore Roosevelt said whites should adjust their attitudes toward minorities. Speaking at the New York City Republican Club, the president said whites were the leading race in the United States and therefore had a responsibility to preserve American civilization by working to improve the status of all minorities. He added that the well-being of both blacks and whites were linked, saying if "morality and thrift among the colored men can be raised," then those same virtues among whites, which most Americans assumed to be more advanced, would "rise to an even higher degree." At the same time, he warned that "the debasement of the blacks will, in the end, carry with it [the] debasement of the whites."

1965: Lyndon B. Johnson approved "Operation Rolling Thunder," a plan for sustained bombing of North Vietnam. The goal was to hit North Vietnamese transportation routes that were being used to introduce personnel and supplies into South Vietnam. It was the beginning of a steady and massive escalation of the war.

★ QUOTE OF THE DAY

Every immigrant who comes here should be required within five years to learn English or leave the country.

Theodore Roosevelt

February 14

1849: The first surviving photo of a sitting president—James K. Polk—was taken. This daguerreotype, taken by Matthew Brady (whose fame would be sealed by his later photographs of Abraham Lincoln), shows Polk in the final weeks of his presidency. He would retire on March 4, and die three months later. It's believed that the first photo of a sitting president ever was taken of William Henry Harrison on March 4, 1841.

1945: Franklin Roosevelt became the first president to meet with the King of Saudi Arabia.

During the World War II, the United States had courted Saudi support, and declared the Kingdom's defense to be of vital interest to the United States. The president also made the Saudis eligible for military assistance through the lend-lease program, as he did earlier, and more famously, with Great Britain, the Soviet Union and others. FDR' smiting with King Abdel Aziz—aboard a U.S. Navy warship in the Suez Canal—was the beginning of what today continues to be a tacit oil-for-security relationship between the two nations.

1971: The installation of Richard M. Nixon's secret tape-recording system was finished, allowing the president to record conversations in the Oval Office, Cabinet Room, Old Executive Office Building, and Camp David. Some 3,700 hours of recordings, including telephone calls, were made between February 16, 1971, and July 18, 1973. In his memoirs, Nixon wrote that he wanted the recordings made for historical purposes; he said his administration would be "the best chronicled in history." Unfortunately for him, those recordings also captured his involvement in the Watergate scandal—which forced him to resign the presidency in August 1974.

★ QUOTE OF THE DAY

There will be no whitewash in the White House.

Richard M. Nixon

February 15

1879: Female attorneys could argue cases before the U.S. Supreme Court, thanks to a bill signed by Rutherford Hayes.

This Day in Presidential History

1903: With Theodore Roosevelt's permission, a toy store began selling the first "Teddy bears." The inspiration for the Teddy bear was one of Roosevelt's hunting trips. TR, an avowed conservationist, was also a big game hunter. President Roosevelt described himself as a conservationist; yet on one trip to Africa alone, he and his party killed some 6,000 animals.

1933: President-elect Franklin D. Roosevelt escaped an assassination attempt. It happened in Miami, Florida, when a gunman, Giuseppe Zangara, fired five shots at Roosevelt's car. The bullets missed the president-elect, but hit five people, including Chicago Mayor Anton Cermak, who had gone to FDR to seek federal aid for his city. After the shooting, FDR's car sped to the hospital. At the hospital Cermak told Roosevelt, "I am glad it was me instead of you." Cermak died on March 6, though his doctor later said the cause of death was ulcerative colitis, and not the bullet wound. Another shooting victim, Mabel Gill, did die of her injuries. There was quick justice: Zangara was convicted and executed five weeks later on March 20.

★ QUOTE OF THE DAY

We've got to teach history based not on what's in fashion but what's important.

Ronald Reagan

February 16

1913: With just three weeks left in his presidency, William Howard Taft said that the United States would not intervene in Mexico's internal affairs, despite political turbulence that threatened not only Americans in Mexico but lucrative U.S. business interests in that country. But the American ambassador to Mexico—Henry Lane Wilson—engineered a coup against the Mexican government anyway. President-elect Woodrow Wilson, who wasn't consulted, was livid; after he took office on March 4, he refused to recognize the new Mexican government.

★ QUOTE OF THE DAY

Those who trust to chance must abide by the results of chance.

Calvin Coolidge

This Day in Presidential History

February 17

1801: After a tie in the 1800 election, the House of Representatives declared Thomas Jefferson the winner of the presidency over his running mate Aaron Burr.

Jefferson's election was the first peaceful transfer of power between two U.S. political parties. The Federalist Party began to fade away, and the Democratic-Republican Party began a generation of dominance. The 1800 election was also one of the nastiest in American history, setting precedents for smear campaigns and personal attacks.

The deadlocked 1800 presidential election was one of two that were decided by the House of Representatives. The other: 1824 (see February 9).

1974: Security scare: An Army private unhappy about failing flight school stole a helicopter and landed on the White House lawn at 2:00 in the morning. Robert K. Preston stole the chopper, a UH-1 Iroquois from nearby Fort Meade, Maryland, flew to Washington D.C., and hovered for six minutes over the White House before landing—just 100 yards from the Oval Office. President Richard M. Nixon was out of town and no attempt was made to shoot the helicopter down. Preston then took off, and after a chase by Maryland State Police helicopters, tried to land on the South Lawn again. This time the Secret Service opened fire with shotguns and submachine guns. Preston, injured slightly, landed the helicopter. He later pled guilty to "wrongful appropriation and breach of the peace," and was sentenced to a year in prison and fined $2,400. There would be another aviation scare just five days later (see February 22).

2009: Barack Obama signed a $787 billion stimulus plan, designed to boost the U.S. economy. It was a mix of federal spending programs and tax cuts; most single wage earners got a tax cut of $400, while couples got $800. The stimulus was needed, the president claimed, to help turn around an economy that had seen in autumn 2008—before he became president—a collapse of the housing market, the stock market, and bailouts of the mortgage industry (see September 7), banks (see October 3), and automakers (see December 19).

★ QUOTE OF THE DAY

Where the press is free and every man able to read, all is safe.

Thomas Jefferson

February 18

1930: To combat the deepening economic downturn, Herbert Hoover urged Congress to speed up passage of a bill to raise trade tariffs. Referring the Smoot-Hawley bill, the president said, "The matter is one of pressing character because, as you know, the business situation of the country is more sensitive now than it normally would be to legislative reactions, and the delays in legislation have a tendency to slowdown recovery a little."

Smoot-Hawley had been passed by the House in May 1929, before the economic crash began; it was passed by the Senate in March 1930, and Hoover signed it. It cut both American imports and exports in half. "Economists still agree that Smoot-Hawley and the ensuing tariff wars were highly counterproductive and contributed to the depth and length of the global Depression," the then Federal Reserve chairman Ben Bernanke argued in 2013. Other economists say its effects were not as severe as is commonly believed.

1939: As war clouds gathered in Europe, Franklin D. Roosevelt spoke of his "Good Neighbor Policy." The president said it was more important than ever that the United States and its neighbors in North America, as well as nations in Central and South America, maintain good relations, which would set an example for the rest of the world. "Nothing is more true than that we here in the New World carry the hopes of millions of human beings in other less fortunate lands," he said. "By setting an example of international solidarity, cooperation, mutual trust, and joint helpfulness, we may keep faith alive in the heart of anxious and troubled humanity, and at the same time, lift democracy high above the ugly truculence of autocracy."

1968: With the Vietnam War at its peak, Lyndon B. Johnson remained firm. Addressing the crew of the aircraft carrier U.S.S. *Constellation*, he said, "In Vietnam today, the foes of freedom are making ready to test America's will. Quite obviously, the enemy believes—he thinks—that our will is vulnerable. Quite clearly, the enemy hopes that he can break that will. And quite certainly, we know that the enemy is going to fail—so we have taken our stand."

But with forty-six Americans dying every day in the war, pressure was growing on Johnson. One rival in his own Democratic party—Senator Eugene McCarthy—was already challenging him for the Democratic nomination on an antiwar platform. Another senator, Robert Kennedy, would enter the race in early March. By the end of March, Johnson stunned the nation by announcing that he would not seek reelection.

☆ QUOTE OF THE DAY

Laws made by common consent must not be trampled on by individuals.

George Washington

February 19

1807: Aaron Burr, the former vice president to Thomas Jefferson, was arrested in Alabama on charges of treason. Burr was accused of plotting to create a new country from the recently purchased Louisiana Territory—with himself as its leader. Burr was eventually acquitted.

1903: Theodore Roosevelt: Trust-Buster. The president ordered the Justice Department to prosecute the Northern Securities Company (a subsidiary of J.P. Morgan) for violating the Sherman Antitrust Act. It was a key domestic objective of TR's presidency: making sure that no company got so big as to become a monopoly. In March 1904, the Supreme Court gave Roosevelt a big win, by ordering that Northern Securities Co. be broken up.

1942: Fearing sabotage during World War II, Franklin D. Roosevelt ordered the forcible removal of Japanese-Americans from parts of the West Coast. The president's executive order 9066 was quickly followed by the relocation of approximately 110,000 Japanese-Americans and Japanese from the Pacific coast to internment camps. In the aftermath of Japan's attack on Pearl Harbor, there was fear that the West Coast would be attacked. Oregon was actually balloon-bombed in September 1942.

But Roosevelt's order was not applied equally. While all who lived on the West Coast were interned, only about 1% of the 150,000-plus Japanese-Americans in Hawaii (which was attacked, of course) were. Those 150,000 comprised about one-third of Hawaii's population, and of the small number that was interned, most were American citizens. In 1944, the Supreme Court upheld the constitutionality of the executive orders. How did the government identify Japanese-Americans? With the help of the Census Bureau, which provided confidential information.

In 1980, President Jimmy Carter oversaw an investigation meant to determine whether the internment order was justified. The Commission on Wartime Relocation and Internment of Civilians found little evidence of Japanese disloyalty and recommended the government pay reparations to the survivors. They formed a payment of $20,000 to each individual internment camp survivor. These were the reparations passed by President Ronald Reagan.

1976: Gerald Ford signed an executive order banning political assassinations. The president's executive order 11905 came in the wake of revelations that the Central Intelligence Agency (CIA) tried to assassinate Cuban leader Fidel Castro in the 1960s.

1987: Ronald Reagan lifted economic sanctions against communist Poland. The president said it was a reward for its release of political prisoners and other moves toward reconciliation with the banned Solidarity movement and the Roman Catholic Church. Communism control in Poland and the rest of Eastern Europe would collapse two years later.

☆ QUOTE OF THE DAY

The successful prosecution of the war requires every possible protection against espionage and against sabotage to national-defense material, national-defense premises, and national-defense utilities.

Franklin D. Roosevelt

February 20

1792: George Washington created the U.S. Postal Service (USPS). One of the few government agencies explicitly authorized by the Constitution, it is, today, an independent government agency responsible for providing postal service in the United States. The USPS traces its roots to 1775, when Benjamin Franklin was appointed the first postmaster general. The USPS has not directly received taxpayer dollars since the early 1980s with the minor exception of subsidies for costs associated with the disabled and overseas voters.

1862: William (Willie) Lincoln, the third son of Abraham and Mary Lincoln, died of typhoid fever in the White House at age eleven. He was the second son the Lincolns lost. "My poor boy, he was too good for this earth. God has called him home," Lincoln said, as he gazed lovingly into the face of his dead son. "I know that he is much better off in heaven, but then we loved him so. It is hard, hard to have him die!" The president then burst into tears.

1907: Theodore Roosevelt signed the Immigration Act of 1907, which targeted Japanese immigration. The president had said in his 1905 State of the Union address that many immigrants, "including most of the undesirable class," did not come to the United States on their own initiative, but were "cajoled" into coming, "often against their best interest" by transportation companies. In 1908, the Japanese government agreed to stop issuing visas for Japanese workers to emigrate to the United States.

1962: A nervous John F. Kennedy watched as John Glenn became the first American to orbit the earth. Glenn's successful mission on *Friendship 7* thrilled Kennedy and the nation, which was involved in an intense competition with the Soviet Union to dominate space.

★ QUOTE OF THE DAY

We have a long way to go in the space race. We started late. But this is the new ocean, and I believe the United States must sail on it and be in a position second to none.

John F. Kennedy

February 21

1792: Congress passed the Presidential Succession Act, which said that after the vice president, the president pro tempore of the Senate was next in line of the presidency. It would be changed again in 1886 (see January 19) and for the final time in 1947 (see July 18).

1972: Arguably the most dramatic trip ever taken by a president of the United States: Richard M. Nixon arrived in China for an eight-day visit. In the summer of 1971, the announcement that Nixon, a lifelong hardline anticommunist, would visit China stunned the world. The United States and China had been bitter foes for a quarter-century, but Nixon recognized the need for better ties—which would also help the United

States in its Cold War standoff with the Soviet Union. During the visit, Nixon met with Chairman Mao and Zhou En-Lai; it is seen today as the beginning of China's drive to modernize and enter the modern world. China's economy is now the world's second largest, trailing only that of the United States itself. Nixon called it "the week that changed the world," and the phrase "Nixon going to China" has since become a metaphor for an unexpected or uncharacteristic action by a politician.

1975: Richard M. Nixon's former attorney general was sentenced for his role in Watergate. John Mitchell received 2½ to 8 years in prison. Former Nixon White House chief of staff H.R. Haldeman and presidential counsel John Ehrlichman were also sentenced to 2½ to 8 years.

★ QUOTE OF THE DAY

I never took a dollar. I had somebody else do it.

> Richard M. Nixon (as recalled by Alexander Haig)

February 22

1732: George Washington was born on the family plantation at Bridges Creek, Colony of Virginia. He was the first president of the United States, serving from 1789 to 1797. Washington was also the commander of the Continental Army during the Revolutionary War from 1775 to 1783. Because of his significant role in the American Revolution and in the formation of the United States, Washington is often referred to as "Father of His Country." Historians today generally regard Washington as the second or third greatest president.

1974: A man attempted to hijack a plane flying out of Baltimore-Washington Airport and crash into the White House. The attempted hijacking left a police officer and the pilot dead. The suspect, Samuel Byck, said he wanted to kill President Nixon. Byck, who called his plot "Operation Pandora's Box," committed suicide. The attempted hijacking—the second aviation scare involving the White House in less than a week (see February 17)—prompted the Secret Service to upgrade White House air defense systems.

George Washington. Library of Congress.

☆ QUOTE OF THE DAY

Associate with men of good quality if you esteem your own reputation; for it is better to be alone than in bad company.

George Washington

George Washington never had wooden teeth: he wore a series of dentures made from metal and cow or hippopotamus bone.

February 23

1848: John Quincy Adams died in Washington, D.C. He was the sixth president, serving from 1825 to 1829, and the first president whose father (John Adams) was also president. Adams was serving as U.S. representative for Massachusetts when he collapsed on the floor of the House on February 21. He died two days later in the Capitol Building.

1861: Dodging an assassination plot, president-elect Abraham Lincoln arrived in Washington in secrecy. As Lincoln prepared to take office, seven states had already left the Union, and civil war was imminent. Allen Pinkerton, a private detective, had uncovered a plot to murder Lincoln as his train passed through Baltimore. Lincoln did not want to appear cowardly, but felt the threats were serious, and agreed to the secret arrival.

This Day in Presidential History

With Pinkerton and Ward Hill Lamon, Lincoln's former law partner, the president-elect sneaked out of a hotel in Harrisburg, Pennsylvania, on the evening of February 22, wearing a soft felt hat instead of his famous stovepipe hat. He also stooped slightly to disguise his height. The group boarded a sleeper car and arrived in Baltimore in the middle of the night. They slipped undetected from the Calvert Street Station to Camden Station across town, where they boarded another train and arrived in Washington at dawn. On the platform, the party was surprised when a voice boomed, "Abe, you can't play that on me." It was Congressman Elihu B. Washburne, a friend of Lincoln's from Illinois. Washburne escorted Lincoln to the Willard Hotel near the White House.

1915: Asked to speak out against the lynching of black women in the Deep South, Woodrow Wilson was silent. The Civil War may have ended slavery in the United States, but not racial hatred; lynching—of men, women, even children—was commonplace. Yet the Woodrow Wilson Presidential Library and Museum acknowledges that the president—born in Virginia to a father who defended slavery—"took no action against such practices." It would not be until 1918, after additional lynchings, that the president—under growing pressure—would speak out (see July 26).

1927: Calvin Coolidge signed a bill requiring radio broadcasters to provide politicians equal time to keep elections fair. The "Radio Act of 1927," which created the Federal Radio Commission (which became the Federal Communications Commission in 1934), gave the government power to fine stations or revoke their broadcast licenses for violating the act. From that point the "equal-time rule" would play an integral role in both national and local elections.

⭐ QUOTE OF THE DAY

Patience and perseverance have a magical effect before which difficulties disappear and obstacles vanish.

John Quincy Adams

February 24

1803: A hallmark of American democracy—the principle of checks and balances—was affirmed by the Supreme Court. Led by Chief Justice John

Marshall, the landmark *Marbury vs. Madison* case determined that the Supreme Court had the authority to limit congressional power by declaring legislation unconstitutional. In writing the decision, Marshall argued that acts of Congress that conflict with the Constitution are not law and therefore nonbinding to the courts. The judiciary's first responsibility, he said, is to uphold the Constitution; if two laws conflict, the court must decide which law applies in any given case.

1868: Andrew Johnson was impeached. The House of Representatives voted eleven articles of impeachment against the president, saying his efforts to fire Secretary of War Edwin M. Stanton were illegal and a violation of the Tenure of Office Act. The actions, lawmakers declared in a 126-47 vote, constituted "high crimes and misdemeanors," the Constitutional threshold for impeachment. But to actually be removed from office, an impeached president must be convicted by a two-thirds vote in the Senate. In his dramatic Senate trial, Johnson was acquitted by a single vote. Only one other president has been impeached: Bill Clinton, who was also acquitted by the Senate.

★ QUOTE OF THE DAY

I never considered a difference of opinion in politics, in religion, in philosophy, as cause for withdrawing from a friend.

Thomas Jefferson

February 25

1791: George Washington signed a bill creating the Bank of the United States. The idea for the bank first originated with Alexander Hamilton, the president's secretary of the treasury.

1793: George Washington held the first cabinet meeting. Four advisors attended: Secretary of State Thomas Jefferson, Secretary of the Treasury Alexander Hamilton, Secretary of War Henry Knox, and Attorney General Edmund Randolph. All four, of course, were friends of the president—but that didn't stop them from disagreeing among themselves. Hamilton and Jefferson in particular clashed "like two fighting cocks," as Jefferson put it. It was such differences that laid the foundation for the eventual creation of our political parties.

Where did the term "cabinet" come from? It came from meetings that Washington often had with advisors in his kitchen. Cabinet secretaries are appointed by the president and must be confirmed by the Senate. The only qualification is that a Cabinet secretary cannot be a member of Congress or hold any other elected office.

1862: Congress passed—and Abraham Lincoln would sign—the Legal Tender Act, allowing for the printing of money. It was the first time the federal government printed money (called "greenbacks") that wasn't backed by gold or silver. Civil War spending was draining the government's gold and silver reserves; the law created a new way for it to meet its obligations. The act legitimized paper currency in "payment of all taxes, internal duties, excises, debts, and demands of every kind due to the United States, except duties on imports, and of all claims and demands … and [it] shall also be lawful money and legal tender in payment of all debts, public and private, within the United States."

1863: Abraham Lincoln signed the National Currency Act, which established the governing framework for the U.S. banking system. It helped organize and administer a system of nationally chartered banks and a uniform national currency.

★ QUOTE OF THE DAY

We should not look back unless it is to derive useful lessons from past errors, and for the purpose of profiting by dearly bought experience.

George Washington

February 26

1917: A livid Woodrow Wilson learned of the Zimmermann telegram, an attempt by Germany to form a Mexican-German alliance against the United States in World War I. Since the war began in 1914, the United States had been neutral. But German submarine attacks on American ships wore the president's patience down, and the Zimmermann telegram was the final straw. The president would soon ask for a declaration of war.

1929: Calvin Coolidge dedicated land for what became Grand Teton National Park. It was one of Coolidge's final acts as president. The park would be expanded in 1943 and again in 1950, and now is more than 300,000 acres in size.

1987: The Tower Commission rebuked President Ronald Reagan for failing to control his staff in the wake of the Iran-Contra affair. Iran-Contra was a complicated scheme in which Reagan administration officials, seeking to free U.S. hostages in Lebanon, sold weapons to Iran—and then used the revenue to fund anticommunist rebels in Nicaragua. Although Reagan took responsibility for the scandal and called it a "mistake," no conclusive evidence has been found showing he authorized the Iran-Contra deal. There was talk of impeaching the president, and eleven administration officials were convicted, though many were eventually overturned. President George H.W. Bush also pardoned some of those who had been convicted of wrongdoing.

☆ QUOTE OF THE DAY

I not only use all the brains that I have, but all that I can borrow.

Woodrow Wilson

February 27

1860: Abraham Lincoln's Cooper Union address outlined the platform of the Republican Party—notably its no-compromise stance on slavery. The speech vaulted Lincoln into the frontrunner's position for the Republican presidential nomination.

1951: The Twenty-second Amendment to the Constitution was ratified, limiting presidents to two terms in office. It was passed after the death of Franklin D. Roosevelt—who was elected to the presidency four times.

1972: The Shanghai Communiqué was issued by Richard M. Nixon and Chinese Premier Chou En-Lab. The Shanghai Communiqué came at the end of the president's historic trip to China, arguably the most dramatic journey ever made by an American president. The communiqué pledged that both countries would work to normalize relations, expand "people-to-people contacts" and trade opportunities. It also referred not so subtly to the Soviet Union—a rival of both the United States and China—by declaring that neither nation "should seek hegemony in the Asia-Pacific region and each is opposed to efforts by any other country or group of countries to establish such hegemony." Nixon's trip to China opened the People's Republic to the rest of the world—an event of monumental consequence.

1991: George H.W. Bush declared victory over Iraq in the Persian Gulf War. In announcing an end to Operation Desert Storm, Bush said his principal strategic goal—pushing Iraq out of Kuwait, which it had invaded the prior August—had been achieved.

1993: Reacting to the bombing of the World Trade Center, Bill Clinton vowed to keep Americans safe. Islamic terrorists detonated a truck bomb in the basement parking garage of the North Tower, thinking that the tower would topple over onto the South Tower, bringing both down and killing tens of thousands. The blast killed six people and wounded an estimated 1,042 others.

★ QUOTE OF THE DAY

This is not a time of euphoria, certainly not a time to gloat. But it is a time of pride: pride in our troops; pride in the friends who stood with us in the crisis; pride in our nation and the people whose strength and resolve made victory quick, decisive, and just. And soon we will open wide our arms to welcome back home to America our magnificent fighting forces.

George H.W. Bush

No person shall be elected to the office of the President more than twice, and no person who has held the office of President, or acted as President, for more than two years of a term to which some other person was elected President shall be elected to the office of the President more than once.

Twenty-second Amendment

February 28

1844: A close call for John Tyler. As the president hosted a pleasure cruise along the Potomac River on the U.S.S. *Princeton*, a cannon exploded during a demonstration, killing eight people, including two members of Tyler's Cabinet: Secretary of State Abel P. Upshur and Secretary of the Navy Thomas Gilmer. The daughter of one victim—a prominent New York businessman named David Gardiner—later became Tyler's wife. Julia Gardiner was thirty-four years younger than the fifty-four-year-old president. Tyler's first wife, Letitia, had died in 1842.

1854: The Republican Party was formally organized. Citizens meeting in Ripon, Wisconsin, were angry at the looming passage in Congress of the Kansas-Nebraska Act, which stated that settlers could decide for themselves whether to permit slavery in those new territories. The legislation repealed the Missouri Compromise of 1820, which had banned slavery in that region. A week earlier, a similar meeting had taken place in Jackson, Michigan. Both the Ripon and Jackson groups called themselves "Republicans," a tribute to the "Democratic-Republican" philosophy of Thomas Jefferson and James Madison.

★ QUOTE OF THE DAY

Wealth can only be accumulated by the earnings of industry and the savings of frugality.

John Tyler

February 29

1864: Abraham Lincoln nominated a future president—Ulysses S. Grant—for promotion to lieutenant general of the U.S. Army. As a major general, Grant had deeply impressed his commander-in-chief and lawmakers with smashing victories over Confederate forces at Vicksburg and Chattanooga. A congressional bill was proposed elevating Grant, who had distinguished himself with his "courage, skill, and ability." Only two men, George Washington and Winfield Scott, had held the rank of lieutenant general before Grant, and Scott's was a brevet (honorary) appointment.

1904: Theodore Roosevelt appointed the Panama Canal Commission to oversee construction of the massive project.

1956: Despite heart problems, Dwight Eisenhower announced that he would run for reelection. Eisenhower, then the fourth-oldest person ever elected president, had suffered a serious heart attack five months earlier, raising concerns about his ability to serve. He was reelected by a landslide and completed his second term successfully.

1968: Lyndon B. Johnson's commission on civil unrest said racism was the primary cause. The Kerner Commission, as it was popularly known, was formed after rioting in several big cities. The president wanted to know three things: "What happened? Why did it happen? And what can be done to prevent it from happening again and again?" The commission— led by Illinois Governor Otto Kerner—blamed "white racism" for causing the violence—not a conspiracy by militant African-American political groups, as some critics had charged.

The report said that America was "moving toward two societies, one black, one white—separate and unequal" and blamed "white society" for allegedly isolating and neglecting African-Americans. It urged, among other things, greater efforts to promote racial integration, federally subsidized job training programs, and decent, affordable housing.

☆ QUOTE OF THE DAY

Nearly all men can stand adversity, but if you want to test a man's character, give him power.

Abraham Lincoln

March

March 1

1809: Thomas Jefferson signed the Non-Intercourse Act. It allowed the United States to trade with countries other than Britain or France; trade with them continued to be banned until Britain and France agreed to respect the rights of U.S. citizens and vessels on the high seas. The Non-Intercourse Act replaced a prior, wider trade embargo, which had helped America stay out of war—but wound up damaging the economy.

1845: John Tyler signed the Texas Annexation Bill, admitting Texas to the Union as the twenty-eighth state. In doing so, the United States inherited Texas's border dispute with Mexico—which contributed to the Mexican-American War of 1848. The United States also inherited Texas's $10 million debt.

1872: Ulysses S. Grant established the national park system—and its first national park: Yellowstone. It is also believed to be the first national park in the world. In the summer of 1936, future president Gerald Ford worked as a park ranger at Yellowstone—the only president to ever work as a park ranger. Years later he recalled that time as "one of the greatest summers of my life."

1917: Woodrow Wilson told the American people of the "Zimmermann Telegram," the final straw in his decision to ask Congress to declare war against Germany. The German government, contemplating war against the United States, told Mexico in this communication that if it joined in the fighting, it would regain Texas, New Mexico, and Arizona—territory lost during the Mexican-American War seven decades before. Wilson would soon formally ask Congress to declare war (see April 2).

1961: President Kennedy signed an executive order establishing the Peace Corps. The president, who had brought up the idea during his 1960 campaign for the White House, saw the Peace Corps as part of the larger Cold War struggle with communism. He pointed out that the Soviet Union "had hundreds of men and women, scientists, physicists, teachers, engineers, doctors, and nurses … prepared to spend their lives abroad in the service of world communism." The United States had no such program.

Kennedy wanted young Americans to become more active in the cause of global democracy, peace, and economic development.

★ QUOTE OF THE DAY

For every young American who participates in the Peace Corps—who works in a foreign land—will know that he or she is sharing in the great common task of bringing to man that decent way of life which is the foundation of freedom and a condition of peace.

John F. Kennedy

March 2

1807: Thomas Jefferson signed a bill banning the importation of slaves. During his State of the Union address in 1806 (see December 12), the president—who over the course of his life owned more than 600 slaves himself—asked Congress to create the law, calling the international slave trade immoral and hurtful to America's reputation. The law went into effect on January 1, 1808.

1877: Just two days before inauguration day, Rutherford B. Hayes was declared the winner of the 1876 presidential election—even though he lost *both* the popular vote and the electoral college on election day. Why? On election day, Samuel Tilden, the governor of New York, received 184 electoral votes to Hayes's 165. But because of allegations of voter fraud and voter intimidation—primarily toward black voters, who generally supported Republicans—twenty additional electoral votes were in dispute in three states: Louisiana, South Carolina, and Florida. After a nasty, four-month standoff, all three states—and the White House—were awarded to Hayes. A deal (today called the "corrupt bargain") was made to make Hayes president in return for removing federal troops from the South and ending post–Civil War Reconstruction.

To this day, the election of 1876 remains one of the most controversial in American history. Others include the 1800 contest between Thomas Jefferson and John Adams (see February 17), the 1824 election between John Quincy Adams and Andrew Jackson (see February 9), and the 2000 election between George W. Bush and Al Gore (see December 12).

1965: Lyndon B. Johnson ordered Operation Rolling Thunder in Vietnam. The president's order began a three-and-a-half year U.S. bombing campaign against communist North Vietnam. It was regarded as the most intense air/ground battle waged during the half-century Cold War. Robust North Vietnamese air defenses, often provided by the Soviet Union and China, meant stiff losses for the United States: it's estimated that 922 American aircraft were lost—and 1,054 U.S. airmen killed, wounded, or captured.

☆ QUOTE OF THE DAY

Unjust attacks on public men do them more good than unmerited praise.

Rutherford B. Hayes

March 3

1845: Congress overrode a presidential veto for the first time—an appropriations bill on John Tyler's last full day in office. Tyler had previously vetoed ten bills sent to him by Congress, but this one was overturned by the required two-thirds majority in both the House and Senate.

The phrase "presidential veto" does not appear in the Constitution, by the way, but Article I requires that every bill, order, resolution, or other act of legislation by the Congress be presented to the president for his approval. The president can either sign it into law, return the bill to either the House or Senate with his objections to the bill (a veto), or neither sign nor return it to Congress after having been presented the bill for ten days exempting Sundays (if Congress is still in session, the bill becomes a law; otherwise, the bill does not become a law and is considered a "pocket veto").

1877: Amid fears of a coup, Rutherford Hayes was secretly sworn in as the nineteenth president. The ceremony occurred as rumors of a coup swirled about the nation's capital—after Hayes, just the day before, was declared the winner of the bitterly contested 1876 election (see March 2). To cover up the swearing in, President Ulysses S. Grant held a dinner party in Hayes's honor in the State Dining Room. At one point, the president and president-elect stole away for a few minutes to the room next door—the Red Room—where Morrison Waite, the chief justice of the Supreme Court, was waiting. There, in a room dimly illuminated by flickering gas lamps, and brimming with flowers, he administered the oath of office to Hayes. The president-elect, who declined to use a Bible, simply raised his hand and took the oath. It was the first time a president had been sworn in in the White House itself.

1931: Herbert Hoover signed legislation designating "The Star-Spangled Banner" as the U.S. national anthem. The song was written by Francis Scott Key in 1814, during the British siege of Fort McHenry in Baltimore Harbor.

★ QUOTE OF THE DAY

It is just as important that business keep out of government as that government keep out of business.

Herbert Hoover

On this day in 1963: John F. Kennedy, accompanied by his wife and a journalist friend, Charles Bartlett, toured Arlington National Cemetery in Virginia. Surveying the sweeping vista of Washington from Lee Mansion and environs, the President remarked "I could stay here forever." After his assassination eight months later, he would be buried near that same spot.

March 4

1797: The first presidential transition occurred, when John Adams was sworn in as the second president. The ceremony took place in the House of Representatives Chamber of Congress Hall in Philadelphia. In his inaugural address, the new president warned Americans not to lose sight of the ongoing threat to American liberty. Adams's inaugural was very colorful. It was the only time that outgoing president George Washington, Vice President Thomas Jefferson, who had been sworn in earlier that day, and Adams had ever appeared together at such a high-profile event. It was also the first time a president had been sworn in by the chief justice of the Supreme Court (Oliver Ellsworth). Before being sworn in, the president-elect told his soon-to-be first lady Abigail, that he was a nervous wreck, and that he felt as if he were on stage playing a part in a play. It was, he said, "the most affecting and overpowering scene I ever acted in."

Outgoing president George Washington, who declined to run for a third term, seemed relieved to relinquish the burden of the presidency; it was, historians said, as if a great weight had been removed from his shoulders.

1801: Thomas Jefferson was inaugurated as the third president of the United States. He would add the first water closets (bathrooms) to the White House and also colonnades (covered walkways) extending East and West.

1805: Thomas Jefferson's second inauguration featured the first inaugural parade ever.

1809: James Madison was inaugurated as the fourth president of the United States. He was president when the British attacked the White House and burned it down in 1814 (see August 24).

1817: James Monroe was inaugurated as the fifth president of the United States. He is the only person in American history to be a governor, senator, secretary of state, secretary of war (defense)—and president.

1825: John Quincy Adams was inaugurated as the sixth president of the United States. He was the son of John Adams—only one of two presidential sons to become president themselves. The other? George W. Bush.

1829: Andrew Jackson was inaugurated as the seventh president of the United States. He was nearly killed that very day during a wild party at the White House when he found himself pinned against a wall by well-wishers and unable to breathe. Aides reportedly had to evacuate him out a window to safety.

1837: Martin Van Buren was inaugurated as the eight president of the United States. He was the last sitting vice president to be elected president—until George H.W. Bush in 1988.

1841: William Henry Harrison was inaugurated as the ninth president of the United States. He would die after just a month in office—the shortest tenure of any president (see April 4). The first photograph of a sitting president was taken of Harrison. The portrait, using new daguerreotype technology (where an image forms on a highly polished silver surface), is missing.

1845: James Polk was inaugurated as the eleventh president of the United States. He is regarded as probably the most consequential one-term president in American history.

1853: Franklin Pierce was inaugurated as the fourteenth president of the United States. He did little to halt the slide toward a civil war and is regarded as one of the worst presidents.

1857: James Buchanan was inaugurated as the fifteenth president of the United States. Like Pierce, Buchanan was ineffectual in his efforts to avoid a civil war and is also regarded as one of the worst presidents.

1861: Abraham Lincoln was inaugurated as the sixteenth president of the United States. He is widely regarded as the greatest president, for successfully leading the United States through the Civil War.

1865: As Abraham Lincoln gave his second, towering, inaugural address, his future assassin stood just feet away, glaring. The Civil War would mercifully end in five weeks, and the president's speech was tinged with sadness and reflection—not of victory, but of the immense damage done to the country. Lincoln said that despite their bitter disagreement over the war's central issue, slavery, both North and South had erred in going to war. He had no way of knowing, of course, that in the crowd that day was the actor John Wilkes Booth, who would assassinate the president just six weeks later (see April 14).

1869: Ulysses S. Grant was inaugurated as the eighteenth president of the United States and took residence in the White House—after much disputation. By the time of his inauguration, the White House had become run down: some even considered it unfit for habitation. There was talk of building a new home at a new location for the president. In the end—and with the input of Grant himself—it was decided that the president's home would remain where it always was: 1600 Pennsylvania Avenue.

1881: James Garfield was inaugurated as the twentieth president of the United States. He would die of an assassin's bullet six months later (see September 19).

1885: Grover Cleveland was inaugurated as the twenty-second president of the United States. He soon became the first president to marry in the White House (see June 2).

1889: Benjamin Harrison was inaugurated as the twenty-third president of the United States. He was the only grandson of a president (William Henry Harrison) to become president himself.

1893: Grover Cleveland was inaugurated as the twenty-fourth president of the United States—the only person to serve two nonconsecutive terms as president.

With the Civil War about to begin, an incomplete U.S. Capitol seemed a metaphor for the country itself as Abraham Lincoln was first inaugurated on March 4, 1861. Library of Congress.

1897: William McKinley was inaugurated as the twenty-fifth president of the United States. He would become the third president to be assassinated (see September 14).

1905: Theodore Roosevelt was inaugurated for his own term as president. He had been the twenty-sixth president since taking over after William McKinley's assassination in 1901 (see September 14).

1909: William Howard Taft was inaugurated as the twenty-seventh president of the United States. He would later become the chief justice of the Supreme Court—the only person to head both the executive and judicial branches of government.

1913: Woodrow Wilson was inaugurated as the twenty-eighth president of the United States. He was the eighth president from Virginia—the state that has produced more presidents than any other.

1921: Warren Harding was inaugurated as the twenty-ninth president of the United States. His winning election margin over James Cox—26.17 percentage points—remains the biggest in American history.

This Day in Presidential History

1925: Calvin Coolidge was inaugurated for his own term as president. He had been the thirtieth president since taking over Warren Harding's death in 1923 (see August 2).

1929: Herbert Hoover was inaugurated as the thirty-first president of the United States. In his first year in office, the Great Depression began (see October 24) and the Oval Office burned down (see December 24).

1933: Franklin D. Roosevelt was inaugurated as the thirty-second president of the United States. Over the next twelve years—the longest tenure of any president—he would guide America through the Great Depression and World War II.

1987: Acknowledging a "mistake," Ronald Reagan took full responsibility for the Iran-Contra scandal. Iran-Contra—the trading of arms for hostages in Iran and funding of rebels in Nicaragua—led to the convictions of eleven Reagan administration officials (some were overturned on appeal). There was talk of impeaching the president, though no conclusive evidence ever emerged showing that Reagan (despite his taking responsibility for the scandal) actually authorized the Iran-Contra deal.

★ QUOTE OF THE DAY

With malice toward none; with charity for all, let us strive on to finish the work we are in; to bind up the nation's wounds.

Abraham Lincoln, March 4, 1865

FDR's 100 Days

Wasting no time—"this nation asks for action, and action now," Franklin D. Roosevelt said in his inaugural address—he skipped every inaugural ball thrown in his honor and got down to work. It was the beginning of a frantic 105 days in which he pushed 15 major pieces of legislation through Congress. It was a "presidential barrage of ideas and programs," historian Arthur Schlesinger Jr. observed, "unlike anything known to American history." The sense of urgency was palpable; save Abraham Lincoln, no president ever entered office amid such dire conditions, and to this day every new president's first "100 days" are compared with Roosevelt's.

This Day in Presidential History

March 5

When March 4 fell on a Sunday, several presidents were inaugurated on the following day, March 5.

1821: James Monroe was inaugurated for his second term as the fifth president of the United States.

1849: Zachary Taylor was inaugurated as the twelfth president of the United States. "Old Rough and Ready" would die less than a year and a half later (see July 9).

1877: Rutherford B. Hayes was inaugurated as the nineteenth president of the United States. He had actually been sworn in three days before, in a secret White House ceremony (see March 2). The term "First Lady" gained nationwide recognition and acceptance when Lucy Hayes was described that way in a newspaper article about her husband. The first known use of the term, however, may date back to 1838, when it was used in a profile of Martha Washington.

1917: Woodrow Wilson was inaugurated for his second term as the twenty-eighth president of the United States. His inaugural parade was the first one in which women participated.

1933: In one of his first moves to end the Great Depression, Franklin D. Roosevelt ordered all banks closed for four days in order to stop large amounts of money from being withdrawn. FDR thought the dramatic move (called a "bank holiday") was necessary, because in the prior four weeks, Americans had been withdrawing money from them at an alarming rate. The temporary closure helped the U.S. banking system maintain liquidity, while fundamental reforms shored up the system. In addition to the bank holiday, Congress also passed the Emergency Banking Act on March 9, and FDR used its emergency powers to encourage the Federal Reserve to create deposit insurance in the reopened banks, thus guaranteeing the safety of customer deposits.

1977: Jimmy Carter participated in a "Dial-a-President" radio show. With television anchor and journalist Walter Cronkite moderating, the president fielded calls from American citizens. Almost nine million people tried to call in. Carter said later that the questions were "the kind you would never get in a press conference."

Callers, not surprisingly, asked about a variety of subjects, such as the gasoline tax, relations with Cuba, and what the president was doing to create jobs. One caller asked why the president's son and daughter-in-law were living in the White House on the taxpayers' dime. Carter corrected the caller, saying, "all of the personal expenses of our family are paid for out of my own pocket or the pocket of my children."

★ QUOTE OF THE DAY

May the boldest fear and wisest tremble when incurring responsibilities on which may depend our country's peace and prosperity.

James Polk

March 6

1820: James Monroe signed the first Missouri Compromise, which admitted Maine to the Union as a free state. The second Missouri Compromise, signed into law April 6, admitted Missouri as a slave state but banned slavery in territories north of a line drawn at Missouri's southern boundary—except in Missouri itself. It was also an attempt to equalize the number of slave-holding states and free states in the country. Although the president did not support limiting slavery, he backed the Missouri Compromise because he thought it would help keep the Union together. The Missouri Compromise was largely the work of Kentucky senator Henry Clay, "the Great Compromiser."

1857: In a decision that helped lead to the Civil War—and propel Abraham Lincoln into the presidency—the Supreme Court issued its Dred Scott Decision. The verdict in *Dred Scott v. Sandford*, written by Chief Justice Roger Taney, said that neither slaves nor their descendants could ever become American citizens. The framers of the Constitution, Taney said, believed that blacks were "beings of an inferior order, and altogether unfit to associate with the white race, either in social or political relations, and so far inferior that they had no rights which the white man was bound to respect." President James Buchanan hoped that the decision would finally put the issue of slavery to rest. It had quite the opposite effect, of course.

1933: Eleanor Roosevelt held the first press conference by a First Lady— where only female reporters were invited to attend.

★ QUOTE OF THE DAY

We believe … in obedience to, and respect for the judicial department of government. We think its decisions on Constitutional questions, when fully settled, should control, not only the particular cases decided, but the general policy of the country, subject to be disturbed only by amendments of the Constitution as provided in that instrument itself. More than this would be revolution. But we think the Dred Scott decision is erroneous.

Abraham Lincoln, 1857

March 7

1977: In a meeting that paved the way for the Camp David peace talks, Jimmy Carter welcomed Israeli prime minister Yitzhak Rabin to the White House. Carter told Rabin, his successor, Menachem Begin, and Egyptian president Anwar Sadat that Mideast peace was a top priority. In November of that year, Sadat made his historic journey to Israel for talks with Begin, leading to the Camp David Accords. Sadat would be murdered by Islamic fundamentalists in 1981. Rabin—prime minister again in 1995—would also be murdered by an Israeli fundamentalist who was opposed to the Mideast peace process.

★ QUOTE OF THE DAY

Blessed are the peacemakers, for they shall be the children of God.

Jimmy Carter, paraphrasing scripture

March 8

1874: Millard Fillmore died at Buffalo, New York. He was the thirteenth president, serving from 1850 to 1853. Assuming office after Zachary Taylor died, Fillmore was the last Whig president and the last president not affiliated with either the Democratic or Republican parties.

Fillmore—America's sixth president in just nine years—is regarded as one of America's worst presidents for his failure to head off the deepening divide between North and South over the issue of slavery.

He also supported the Fugitive Slave Act (1850), which required that all escaped slaves, if captured, must be returned to their masters—and that officials and citizens of free states had to cooperate with this law. Abolitionists called it the "Bloodhound Law" for the dogs that were used to track down runaway slaves.

In his postpresidential years, Fillmore regarded the election of Abraham Lincoln and his desire to end the spread of slavery as a threat to the Union. He broke with Lincoln after the Emancipation Proclamation and supported Lincoln's opponent in the election of 1864.

1930: William Howard Taft died at Washington, D.C. He was the twenty-seventh president, serving from 1909 to 1913. After his presidency, Taft was appointed by President Warren Harding to became chief justice of the Supreme Court—the only person to serve in both roles. Taft considered the high court the more pleasurable and prestigious job. "I don't remember that I ever was President," he wrote.

1983: In one of the most famous speeches of his presidency, Ronald Reagan referred to the Soviet Union as an "Evil Empire." Speaking to a conference of Christian evangelicals in Florida, the president said that communism was morally corrupt because it repudiated God. In 1982, Reagan told the British Parliament "the march of freedom and democracy" would leave Marxism-Leninism on the "ash heap of history." Reagan later tempered his rhetoric, meeting frequently with Soviet leader Mikhail Gorbachev and entering into arms agreements with the Kremlin.

★ QUOTE OF THE DAY

I believe that communism is another sad, bizarre chapter in human history whose last pages even now are being written. I believe this because the source of our strength in the quest for human freedom is not material, but spiritual. And because it knows no limitation, it must terrify and ultimately triumph over those who would enslave their fellow man.

Ronald Reagan

March 9

1954: Dwight Eisenhower criticized Senator Joe McCarthy's anticommunist witch hunt—but only in private. Eisenhower was bothered by McCarthy's attacks on other Americans, but was reluctant to take on the controversial senator publicly. His failure to do so led to criticism from leading Democrats, like Adlai Stevenson, whom Eisenhower had beaten in the 1952 presidential election. Stevenson said that the president's silence on McCarthy's actions was tantamount to approval. But Eisenhower considered political mudslinging as beneath the presidency.

But that night, Edward R. Murrow, arguably the most prominent journalist in the United States, attacked McCarthy on his CBS program *See It Now*, warning that McCarthy was "treading a fine line between investigation and persecution."

1957: Dwight Eisenhower signed a bill authorizing U.S. military force to defend Middle East nations threatened by aggression. The president's decision to defend the Middle East from attack was clearly aimed at an aggressive and, some feared, expansionist U.S.S.R.

★ QUOTE OF THE DAY

How far you can go without destroying from within what you are trying to defend from without?

Dwight Eisenhower

March 10

1864: Abraham Lincoln promoted Ulysses S. Grant to lieutenant general, giving him command of all Union troops during the Civil War. The military rank had not been officially used since 1798, when President John Adams gave the rank to former president George Washington, in anticipation of a possible French invasion of the United States. General Grant went on to force the South's surrender at Appomattox in 1865. Four years later, he became the eighteenth president.

1982: Ronald Reagan banned oil imports from Libya. The Reagan administration charged that Libya was supporting terrorist activities and therefore was a threat to U.S. national security. Reagan's order also banned exports of high technology to Libya.

★ QUOTE OF THE DAY

I have never advocated war except as a means of peace.

Ulysses S. Grant

March 11

1862: Abraham Lincoln demoted his top Civil War general. General George McClellan was removed as general-in-chief. Lincoln was frustrated over what the president considered too much cautiousness about taking the battle to the enemy. McClellan would remain commander of the Army of the Potomac, but would be removed from that command in November after failing to decisively engage the Robert E. Lee's Confederate Army (see November 5).

1941: Franklin D. Roosevelt signed the Lend-Lease Bill, opening the door to military aid to countries fighting Nazi Germany and Japan. Between 1941 and the war's end in 1945, the United States shipped $50 billion in supplies (approximately $825 billion in 2016 dollars) to Great Britain, the Soviet Union, China, Free France, and other Allied nations. Formally titled "An Act to Further Promote the Defense of the United States," lend-lease effectively ended any American pretense of being neutral during World War II—which the United States would, of course, enter nine months later after Japan's attack on Pearl Harbor.

★ QUOTE OF THE DAY

Our country has determined to do its full part in creating an adequate arsenal of democracy. This great arsenal will be here in this country. It will be a bulwark of our own defense. It will be the source of the tools of defense for all democracies who are fighting to preserve themselves against aggression.

Franklin D. Roosevelt

March 12

1933: Franklin D. Roosevelt's first "Fireside Chat" changed the way presidents communicated with the American people. The president, in office just eight days, went on the radio to explain steps his administration had taken to shore up the nation's banks. Understanding the intimacy of the airwaves, he used simple, conversational words and addressed Americans as "my friends." Most Americans had never heard the voice of a president before—now there was one speaking in their very own home. The effect was electrifying. FDR, also knowing that less was more, kept his appearances to a minimum: there were just thirty such chats in his twelve years as president.

1947: The "Truman Doctrine." Harry Truman asked Congress to send $400 million in aid to Greece and Turkey, which he said were threatened by Soviet communism. "It must be the policy of the United States to support free peoples who are resisting attempted subjugation by armed minorities or by outside pressures," the president said.

1993: The first female attorney general—Janet Reno—was sworn in. Bill Clinton praised her swift Senate confirmation, saying Reno demonstrated to all "the qualities of leadership and integrity, intelligence, and humanity."

★ QUOTE OF THE DAY

It is your problem no less than it is mine. Together we cannot fail.

Franklin D. Roosevelt, from his first Fireside Chat

March 13

1868: Andrew Johnson's impeachment trial began. The seventeenth president had already been impeached by the House of Representatives on eleven counts of trying to fire War Secretary Edwin Stanton and for violating postwar Reconstruction Acts. After a dramatic two-month Senate trial, Johnson was acquitted by a single vote.

1901: Benjamin Harrison died at Indianapolis, Indiana. He was the twenty-third president, serving from 1889 to 1893. Harrison was the grandson of

This Day in Presidential History   **81**

William Henry Harrison. In the election of 1888, Harrison lost the popular vote by 90,596 votes to the incumbent, President Grover Cleveland. But by sweeping the largest states—New York, Pennsylvania, and Ohio, among others—Harrison won the Electoral College 233 to 168. Cleveland would turn the tables four years later.

1961: John F. Kennedy's "Alliance for Progress." U.S. relations with Latin America were in poor shape when Kennedy became president. The CIA had backed a coup in Guatemala in 1954. Vice President Richard M. Nixon had been attacked in Venezuela in 1958. Communism had taken hold in Cuba. Seeing the region as a Cold War test with the Soviet Union, the president proposed a ten-year, multibillion-dollar-aid program (Fidel Castro's Cuba was excluded, of course). But funds sent under the guise of the "AFP" were often misused by officials in those countries; by the time the program ended in the early 1970s, an estimated thirteen governments in Latin America had been replaced by military rule.

★ QUOTE OF THE DAY

We Americans have no commission from God to police the world.

Benjamin Harrison

March 14

1900: William McKinley signed the Gold Standard Act. It established gold—and no longer silver—as the sole basis for redeeming paper currency.

1907: Theodore Roosevelt banned Japanese laborers. The president's executive order was part of a "gentleman's agreement" that stopped Japanese workers from pouring into Hawaii and California. To defuse growing tensions, Japan agreed not to issue passports for Japanese citizens wishing to work in the United States, while the United States agreed to accept the presence of those immigrants who had already arrived, and their families.

1923: Warren Harding became the first president to pay income tax. The president paid about $17,000 of his $75,000 salary. The federal income tax had become law in 1913, but it didn't apply to the then president Woodrow Wilson, because of Article II, Section 1, of the Constitution, which said that the president's salary "shall neither be increased nor diminished during the Period for which he shall have been elected," and it was judged that a new tax diminished it (federal judges had a similar protection). In 1921, Harding said this was wrong—and that president should pay taxes like everyone else.

1967: The secret, second burial of John F. Kennedy. With Jacqueline Kennedy, Senators Robert F. Kennedy and Edward M. Kennedy, and President Lyndon B. Johnson on hand, Kennedy's coffin was reinterred at Arlington National Cemetery. It had been moved secretly from its November 25, 1963, burial site while a permanent gravesite was constructed just a few feet away. Also buried: Arabella Kennedy (informally named), who was stillborn to Mrs. Kennedy in 1956, and Patrick Kennedy, who died forty-eight hours after his birth in 1963. Arabella had originally been buried in Newport, Rhode Island, and Patrick in Brookline, Massachusetts, but after the president's assassination, the remains of both were transferred to Arlington.

★ QUOTE OF THE DAY

Our most dangerous tendency is to expect too much of government, and at the same time do for it too little.

Warren Harding

March 15

1767: Andrew Jackson was born in the Waxhaws area of the border of North and South Carolina. He was the seventh president, serving from 1829 to 1837. The era of "Jacksonian democracy" was characterized by a strong presidency and executive branch of government—at the expense of Congress. Jackson—"called Old Hickory" for his toughness—participated in thirteen duels and was shot twice. One bullet near his heart was never removed.

1913: Woodrow Wilson held the first presidential news conference. He asked reporters to gather, and more than 100 did. Prior to Wilson's formal news conference, reporters used to simply stand outside the White House gates, interviewing people who came and went. Theodore

Andrew Jackson. Library of Congress.

Roosevelt took pity on them one cold, rainy day and invited them in and set aside a room for them to work. TR's "news conferences" were usually one-way lectures and were often given while he sat in the barber's chair.

1965: Addressing Congress, Lyndon B. Johnson introduced the Voting Rights Act and called on white Americans to support it. "It is not just Negroes, but really it is all of us, who must overcome the crippling legacy of bigotry and injustice," Johnson said. And borrowing a phrase from the civil rights movement, he added, "We shall overcome." He told lawmakers that denying the right to vote for any one citizen cheapened the ideal of America for all citizens. It would be signed into law on August 5.

★ QUOTE OF THE DAY

For the life of this Republic, our people have zealously guarded their liberty against abuses of power by their governments. The one weapon they have used is the mightiest weapon in the arsenal of democracy—the vote.

Lyndon B. Johnson

March 16

1751: James Madison was born at Belle Grove Plantation in Port Conway, Colony of Virginia. He was the fourth president, serving from 1809 to 1817. Madison—one of America's Founding Fathers—is known as "Father of the Constitution," because he was its principal author. In 1788, he wrote more than a third of the *Federalist Papers*, still the most influential commentary on the Constitution itself. He later became secretary of state under President Thomas Jefferson. As president in his own right, Madison led the nation through the War of 1812, often referred to as America's "second war of independence." While the United States was victorious over Great Britain, the White House and Capitol building were destroyed in fires set by British troops. Before the White House was attacked, First Lady Dolley Madison distinguished herself by helping to save Gilbert Stuart's portrait of George Washington. The Madisons spent the remainder of their presidency living in Octagon House, while the White House was rebuilt.

1955: Dwight Eisenhower upheld the use of nuclear weapons. At a news conference, the president was asked whether the United States would use "tactical small atomic weapons" if necessary in wartime. Eisenhower, the former five-star army general, said yes: "In any combat where these things can be used on strictly military targets and for strictly military purposes, I see no reason why they shouldn't be used just exactly as you would use a bullet or anything else. I believe the great question about these things comes when you begin to get into those areas where you cannot make sure that you are operating merely against military targets. But with that one qualification, I would say, yes, of course they would be used."

1977: Jimmy Carter argued for a Palestinian homeland. At a Massachusetts town hall, the president—in office less than two months—laid the foundation for what would soon become the historic Camp David Accords. He said no lasting Middle East peace could be obtained without it. The issue of a so-called "two-state" solution between Israel and the Palestinians has yet to be resolved.

☆ QUOTE OF THE DAY

The advancement and diffusion of knowledge is the only guardian of true liberty.

James Madison

James Madison. Library of Congress.

March 17

1905: Perhaps the most consequential presidential marriage: Franklin D. Roosevelt wed his fifth cousin once removed, Eleanor Roosevelt. The two Roosevelts met when he was four and she was two; they saw each other at family events in ensuing years, and in 1903, FDR proposed. The bride was given away by President Theodore Roosevelt. The marriage was marred by FDR's unfaithfulness, but they remained together. When Roosevelt became president in 1933, Eleanor became a celebrity—and arguably the most influential First Lady—with her diligent work on civil rights and humanitarian issues, which she often promoted through radio broadcasts and a syndicated newspaper column. The president valued Eleanor's insight and frequently consulted her on presidential matters.

1960: Angry at Cuba's embrace of Soviet communism, Dwight Eisenhower approved a CIA plan to form an anti-Cuban Army. The plan called for Cuban exiles to attack their country and attempt to overthrow leader Fidel Castro. President John F. Kennedy inherited the plan, which went down in history as the Bay of Pigs (see April 17).

1983: Ronald Reagan and Tip O'Neill enjoyed a St. Patrick's Day lunch. Reaching out to the president in the spirit of friendship and bipartisanship, the House Speaker hosted the first St. Patrick's Day lunch at the U.S.

Capitol. "I'm going to cook you some Boston corned beef, and I'm going to have an Irish storyteller there," O'Neill said. "I'll have to polish up some new Irish jokes," the president quipped in response. It has since become an annual bipartisan event on Capitol Hill for guests of all ethnicities, with Irish-Americans playing the lead role.

★ QUOTE OF THE DAY

I'm very leery of ethnic jokes in my position—the only ones I can tell are Irish!

Ronald Reagan

March 18

1837: Grover Cleveland was born in Caldwell, New Jersey. He was the twenty-second president, serving from 1885 to 1889—and twenty-fourth president, serving from 1893 to 1897. Why the gap? He lost his reelection bid in 1888 to Benjamin Harrison, but turned the tables on him four years later, becoming the only man to hold the presidency at two different times.

Cleveland, a bachelor, was the first president to get married in the White House. First Lady Frances Folsom Cleveland, just twenty-one, was twenty-seven years younger than her husband. In his second term, the couple's second daughter, Esther, became the first child born to a president in the White House.

1969: As the Vietnam War continued, Richard M. Nixon ordered the bombing of neighboring Cambodia. The president believed Cambodia was being used as a staging area for attacks on U.S. troops. The administration was able to keep the bombings secret for two months. The bombing continued through April 1970.

2014: Barack Obama ordered the Syrian Embassy in Washington closed and expelled its diplomats. The president's move came amid rising tensions over Syria's civil war and what the United States said were "atrocities [that Syrian President Bashar al-Assad's] regime has committed against the Syrian people."

Grover Cleveland. Library of Congress.

★ QUOTE OF THE DAY

I would rather the man who presents something for my consideration subject me to a zephyr of truth and a gentle breeze of responsibility rather than blow me down with a curtain of hot wind.

Grover Cleveland

March 19

1919: A crushing setback for Woodrow Wilson—the Senate rejected the Versailles Treaty. The president hoped that the treaty, which ended World War I and formed the League of Nations (a precursor of the United Nations), would "make the world safe for democracy" (the phrase he used when asking for a declaration of war against Germany in 1917). But the Senate, then dominated by Republicans, determined that the treaty would infringe upon American sovereignty and tie the United States up in "entangling alliances."

This Day in Presidential History

2003: A United States-led coalition invaded Iraq. President George W. Bush said the goal of Operation Iraqi Freedom was to "disarm Iraq, to free its people and to defend the world from grave danger." The president said that Iraq possessed weapons of mass destruction, but none were found. In 2008, Bush announced that U.S. forces would leave Iraq by the end of 2011. During those 105 months of "official" war and various operations since, 4,827 Americans were killed (as of October 31, 2016) and more than 32,000 wounded. Direct spending on the Iraq war has been estimated at $757 billion, a figure that does not include interest on money borrowed to finance it or health care costs for veterans.

2011: Barack Obama ordered air strikes on Libya, as part of a U.N. Security Council decision to enforce a no-fly zone. The president told Congress that the attacks, which were undertaken with French, British, and other allies, would be limited in scope and duration, and that preventing a humanitarian disaster in Libya was in the best interest of U.S. national security.

★ QUOTE OF THE DAY

The dangers to our country and the world will be overcome. We will pass through this time of peril and carry on the work of peace. We will defend our freedom. We will bring freedom to others, and we will prevail.

George W. Bush

March 20

1965: Lyndon B. Johnson ordered U.S. troops to Alabama. During a news conference at his Texas ranch, the president explained that the troops were needed to keep order during a civil rights march from Selma to Montgomery. Alabama governor George Wallace—a staunch segregationist—refused to use state funds to protect the civil rights demonstrators. Johnson's announcement came two weeks after "Bloody Sunday"—March 7, 1965—when 600 demonstrators marched on Montgomery to protest intimidation of black voters and the earlier killing of a black man, Jimmie Lee Jackson, by a state trooper. In brutal scenes that were later broadcast on national television, state and local police attacked the marchers with billy clubs and tear gas. It was a key turning point in the civil rights movement.

2016: Barack Obama arrived in Havana, the first sitting president to visit Cuba in eighty-eight years. The president's move came three months after he said the United States and communist Cuba would resume diplomatic ties, after fifty-five years of estrangement (see January 3).

★ QUOTE OF THE DAY

The true strength of America lies not in arms and not in force and not in the might of the military or in the police, nor in the multitudes of marshals and State troopers but in respect and obedience to law itself.

Lyndon B. Johnson

March 21

1790: George Washington's first secretary of state was sworn in—Thomas Jefferson.

1915: This first movie ever shown in the White House caused political problems for Woodrow Wilson. The film was D. W. Griffith's *The Birth of a Nation*, a celebratory look at the Ku Klux Klan. The film, which sparked protests and riots across the nation, was a surprising choice for Wilson, the intellectual former president of Princeton University. His secretary Joseph Tumulty claimed, "the president was entirely unaware of the nature of the play before it was presented and at no time has expressed his approbation of it." That claim aside, some historians say Wilson's words and record on behalf of African Americans were not impressive (see February 23).

1947: Harry Truman ordered loyalty checks of federal employees. The president's move came as Cold War fears deepened, raising concerns about communist infiltration of the government. All departments and agencies set up "loyalty boards" to search for anyone who might be affiliated with any "totalitarian, fascist, communist, or subversive" organization. If "reasonable grounds" to doubt an employee's loyalty existed, he or she could be dismissed.

1973: Richard M. Nixon's lawyer warned him, "There is a cancer growing on the presidency." John Dean's dramatic comment, made during an Oval Office meeting, warned the president that the growing

Watergate scandal threatened Nixon's presidency. "It's growing daily. It's compounding, it grows geometrically now because it compounds itself," he said. Dean himself eventually pleaded guilty to obstruction of justice charges in connection with hush money payments to the burglars who broke into Democratic National Committee headquarters. During his incarceration, he testified against several other Watergate figures—and his testimony also was critical in providing information that eventually led to Nixon's resignation in 1974 (see August 8).

1980: Jimmy Carter told the U.S. Olympic team that he was ordering a boycott of the Summer games in Moscow. The president's move was part of his response to the Soviet Union's invasion of Afghanistan and the Kremlin's rejection of his demand for it to withdraw. Carter also cut off grain shipments to the Soviets and banned Soviet fishing boats from U.S. territorial waters. The Soviets retaliated for the U.S. boycott of the 1980 Moscow Olympics by boycotting the 1984 Summer Games in Los Angeles.

★ QUOTE OF THE DAY

Aggression unopposed becomes a contagious disease.

Jimmy Carter

March 22

1929: Herbert Hoover reluctantly signed a proclamation establishing U.S. immigration quotas for every country. The president, noting that Congress had not acted on immigration, said that while he favored strict and select immigration, he opposed limiting it on the basis of national origin.

1933: Franklin D. Roosevelt legalized the sale of beer and wine, signaling that Prohibition—the sales ban on alcohol—was coming to an end. The Beer and Wine Revenue Act meant that the federal government could tax booze—revenue that was badly needed during the Great Depression. The act meant that states could decide whether or not to sell alcohol; most quickly decided in favor of selling. In December 1933, the Twenty-first Amendment was passed, officially ending prohibition.

⭐ QUOTE OF THE DAY

Wisdom consists not so much in knowing what to do in the ultimate as knowing what to do next.

Herbert Hoover

FDR enjoyed holding cocktail parties in the White House. He often played bartender, mixing drinks for his guests—and martinis for himself. Roosevelt also drank during card games that he hosted. When he lost, he paid by check—knowing that the checks would be kept as souvenirs and never cashed!

March 23

1983: Ronald Reagan introduced his Strategic Defense Initiative (SDI)—designed to protect the United States from Soviet ballistic missiles. SDI—also known as "Star Wars"—was a shift from the prior, U.S. offensive-oriented strategy of mutual assured destruction with Moscow. Mutual Assured Destruction (MAD) was a Cold War theory that neither the United States nor the Soviet Union would attack the other because both knew they would be destroyed in return.

2010: Barack Obama signed the Affordable Care Act into law. The landmark health care reform bill—also known as "Obamacare"—was the product of a bitter, yearlong fight. It was the most sweeping and controversial piece of social legislation in decades. It was upheld by two separate Supreme Court rulings.

⭐ QUOTE OF THE DAY

Everybody should have some basic security when it comes to their health care.

Barack Obama

March 24

1949: Harry Truman approved aid for Palestinian refugees who were displaced following Israel's war of independence.

This Day in Presidential History

1977: Making good on a 1976 campaign promise, Jimmy Carter authorized direct diplomatic talks with communist Cuba. But the United States-Cuban talks went nowhere, resulting in nasty words between Washington and Havana—and the 1980 Mariel boatlift, in which Cuba's Communist leader, Fidel Castro, authorized the emigration of more than 100,000 Cubans to Florida. The exodus eventually hurt Carter when it was discovered that Castro used the boatlift to ship prison inmates and patients from Cuban mental hospitals. The Mariel boatlift was subsequently ended by mutual agreement between the two governments in October 1980.

1999: The United States and NATO allies began a bombing campaign against Serbia. The attacks, President Bill Clinton said, were meant to halt ethnic cleansing—the worst in Europe since World War II—being perpetrated by Serb forces in Kosovo and Albania.

★ QUOTE OF THE DAY

The best way to get a bad law repealed is to enforce it strictly.

Abraham Lincoln

March 25

1933: The navy's U.S.S. *Sequoia* became the official presidential yacht. Many presidents enjoyed this floating White House. The *Sequoia*, once called "America's equivalent to the Royal Yacht," has a rich and colorful history. Franklin D. Roosevelt and General Dwight Eisenhower planned the D-Day invasion of Europe, Harry Truman hosted poker games, Lyndon B. Johnson watched movies projected onto its white smokestack, and Richard M. Nixon decided to resign on it. After Nixon made his decision, he played "God Bless America" on the ship's piano. After he became president in 1977, Jimmy Carter, in a cost-cutting move, sold the *Sequoia*.

★ QUOTE OF THE DAY

Economy is the method by which we prepare today to afford the improvements of tomorrow.

Calvin Coolidge

A former navy secretary, Franklin D. Roosevelt loved the *Sequoia*, the presidential yacht. Guests included Winston Churchill and Dwight Eisenhower, with whom he planned D-Day. FDR also fished from the yacht. Library of Congress.

March 26

1790: Congress passed the first naturalization law—determining who could be an American citizen. It was limited to white people and excluded Native Americans, slaves, free blacks, and Asians. It also said that children born abroad to U.S. citizens "shall be considered as natural born citizens."

1804: Thomas Jefferson was given a "mammoth loaf" of bread—to go along with remnants of a 1,200 lb. chunk of cheese—a gift from a Baptist group for the president's support of religious tolerance. The "mammoth" bread and cheese were the centerpieces of a party in the Senate that Jefferson attended; a mammoth side of beef and booze also appeared; the president pulled out his pocketknife and cut the first slice of bread.

1979: Jimmy Carter's Camp David Accords. With the president looking on, Egyptian President Anwar Sadat and Israeli prime minister Menachem Begin signed a historic peace treaty at the White House. The Israeli-Egyptian treaty ended three decades of hostility between the two neighbors. For their brave efforts, Sadat and Begin won the Nobel Peace Prize. Sadat was murdered by Islamic terrorists in October 1981. To this day, Egypt and Israel remain at peace.

★ QUOTE OF THE DAY

We share a vision of a time when all the people of the Middle East may turn their energies back to the works of life, when young people can marry and start families and have a hope of seeing and knowing their own children's children, when the old can end their lives quietly after witnessing many a gentle spring. We pray for that time, and we shall continue to work for that time.

Jimmy Carter

March 27

1829: Washington's "society ladies" were shocked when Andrew Jackson named John Eaton to be his secretary of war. Eaton's wife was said to have had a "lurid" past, and his appointment as war secretary caused some to question the president's judgment. President Jackson didn't care, but Eaton and another supporter—Secretary of State Martin Van Buren—resigned to limit the "scandal."

★ QUOTE OF THE DAY

I will sink or swim with him, by God.

Andrew Jackson

March 28

1834: The Senate censured Andrew Jackson over his efforts to defund the Second Bank of the United States. Jackson earlier vetoed a bill that would have recharted the bank; he thought it was corrupt, benefited mostly rich Americans, and was a threat to liberty. Whig lawmakers were angry over Jackson's refusal to hand over documents in the matter; the public opposed Senate's censure of the president. To this day, Jackson remains the only U.S. president ever censured by Congress.

1969: Dwight D. Eisenhower died in Washington, D.C. He was the thirty-fourth president, serving from 1953 to 1961. Dwight David Eisenhower was christened David Dwight; he reversed his name when he enrolled at West Point. Before entering politics, Eisenhower spent decades in the Army, rising to the rank of five-star general during World War II. The wartime achievement that "Ike," as Eisenhower was known, will always be remembered for was leading the invasions of North Africa in 1942–43 and France on D-Day: June 6, 1944.

Eisenhower was a center-of-the-road Republican. He continued many New Deal programs launched by Franklin Roosevelt and oversaw an expansion of Social Security. He oversaw big government investment in everything from infrastructure (notably the Interstate Highway System) to science and technology (such as the Defense Advanced Research Projects Agency, or DARPA, which eventually led to the internet, among other things). Eisenhower also oversaw the creation of America's space agency, NASA, a response to the Soviet Union's aggressive space program.

On the foreign policy front, Eisenhower kept a campaign pledge and ended the Korean War (an uneasy truce still exists today). He also ordered a CIA coup in Iran, installing the Shah—creating resentment that, in some circles, still exists today. To counter rising Soviet power, he emphasized a rapid buildup of America's nuclear arsenal, though he reduced funding for conventional military forces. In 1956, Eisenhower refused to support three key allies—Israel, Britain, and France—when they invaded Egypt during the Suez Crisis; later that year he also refused to help Hungarian freedom fighters resisting the Soviets.

In terms of social policy, Eisenhower thought segregation was a state's rights issue, but after the landmark *Brown vs. Board of Education* Supreme Court decision ordering school desegregation, he sent federal troops to Little Rock, Arkansas, to support the enrollment of nine black students ("the Little Rock Nine"). He also signed civil rights legislation in 1957 and 1960 to protect the right to vote. He implemented desegregation of the armed forces in two years and made five appointments to the Supreme Court. He was the first term-limited president in accordance with the Twenty-second Amendment. In his last speech to the nation as president, in 1961, he warned of a military establishment that was too powerful and threatened America's economic prosperity.

☆ QUOTE OF THE DAY

A people that values its privileges above its principles soon loses both.

Dwight D. Eisenhower

March 29

1790: John Tyler was born in Charles City County, Virginia. He was the tenth president, serving from 1841 to 1845. Tyler served as vice president under William Henry Harrison, but when Harrison died after just one month in office, there was great controversy about whether Tyler should take over. The problem was that the constitution didn't explicitly state that the vice president would assume the presidency upon the death of the president. After two days of manuevering, however, Tyler—who became known as "His Accidency"—was sworn in.

Perhaps the best-known achievement of Tyler's administration was the annexation of the Republic of Texas in 1845. The Lone Star State became the twenty-eighth state in the Union. John Tyler was also elected to office in the government of the Confederacy during the Civil War. He died before actually assuming that office.

John Tyler. Library of Congress.

This Day in Presidential History

Widowed by the death of his first wife, Letitia, in 1842, Tyler married twenty-one-year-old Julia Gardner in 1844 at the age of fifty-four. Julia Tyler became the youngest first lady in history. Mrs. Tyler also became the first "Queen of the White House" to request that "Hail to the Chief" be played when the president entered the room.

1929: The Oval Office got its first telephone. It was one of the few good things to happen to Herbert Hoover that year. A massive stock market crash in October helped spark the Great Depression and the Oval Office was destroyed in a fire on Christmas Eve (see December 24).

1952: Harry Truman said he would not seek reelection. The president was deeply unpopular in 1952. Inflation and unemployment were rising. The Korean War seemed to be stalemated, and the president's firing of General Douglas MacArthur was widely criticized. Scandals—including a tax collection probe at the Internal Revenue Service—didn't help either. After being upset in the New Hampshire primary, the president withdrew.

2001: George W. Bush ordered the United States to abandon ratification of a global warming treaty. The Kyoto Protocol had been signed by 180 countries to reduce global warming that set limits on industrial emissions.

★ QUOTE OF THE DAY

I shall not be a candidate for reelection. I have served my country long, and I think efficiently and honestly. I shall not accept a renomination. I do not feel that it is my duty to spend another four years in the White House.

Harry Truman

March 30

1981: Ronald Reagan was shot in the chest as he left a Washington hotel. He soon collapsed and came within moments of death. His press secretary, James Brady, was shot in the head and barely survived; Secret Service officer Timothy McCarthy and Washington policeman Thomas Delahanty were also seriously wounded. A twenty-six-year-old man,

John Hinckley, was arrested but found not guilty by reason of insanity; he spent thirty-five years in a mental institution (see June 21). Reagan, a lifelong member of the National Rifle Association, later supported the Brady Bill (which mandated background checks on gun buyers) and the 1994 assault weapons ban.

★ QUOTE OF THE DAY

Honey, I forgot to duck.

Ronald Reagan to First Lady Nancy Reagan after he was shot

Ronald Reagan (elected in 1980) broke the streak—barely—which began in 1840, of every president elected in a year ending in "0" dying in office. William Henry Harrison (elected in 1840), Abraham Lincoln (elected in 1860), James Garfield (elected in 1880), William McKinley (elected in 1900), Warren Harding (elected in 1920), Franklin Roosevelt (elected in 1940), and John F. Kennedy (elected in 1960), all passed away while serving as president.

March 31

1933: Franklin Roosevelt's first big jobs program was passed by Congress. The Reforestation Relief Act created the Civilian Conservation Corps (CCC). The CCC gave immediate jobs to 250,000 men of ages eighteen to twenty-five. By 1941, when the program ended, it had employed more than two million Americans. It was part of the president's first, frantic, "100 Days" (see March 4).

1968: Lyndon B. Johnson stunned the nation by announcing that he would not seek reelection. In the spring of 1968, the president was overwhelmed by the war in Vietnam, and political rivals were nipping at his heels. He had barely won the New Hampshire primary over Eugene McCarthy a few weeks earlier, and then saw his archrival Robert Kennedy enter the race. In this speech on the war, at the very end, he made the surprise announcement that he would not seek reelection.

☆ QUOTE OF THE DAY

There is division in the American house now. There is divisiveness among us all tonight. ... And holding the trust that is mine, as president of all the people, I cannot disregard the peril to the progress of the American people and the hope and prospect of peace for all people. ... I do not believe that I should devote an hour or a day of my time to any personal partisan causes. ... Accordingly, I shall not seek, and I will not accept, the nomination of my party for another term as your President.

Lyndon B. Johnson

April

April 1

1953: Dwight Eisenhower signed a bill creating the Department of Health, Education, and Welfare (today's Department of Health and Human Services).

1970: Richard M. Nixon signed a bill banning cigarette advertising on radio and television to take effect after January 1, 1971. The president, who was an avid pipe smoker, indulging in as many as eight bowls a day, supported the legislation at the urging of public health advocates. There had been warnings about the dangers of smoking as far back as 1939, and by the end of the 1950s, all states had laws banning the sale of cigarettes to minors. In 1964, the Federal Trade Commission (FTC) and the Federal Communications Commission (FCC) agreed that advertisers had a responsibility to warn the public of the health hazards of cigarette smoking.

★ QUOTE OF THE DAY

When I do good, I feel good. When I do bad, I feel bad. That's my religion.

Abraham Lincoln

April 2

1917: Woodrow Wilson asked Congress to declare war on Germany. Four days later, Congress voted to do so and the United States formally entered World War I. Wilson's decision to go to war was prompted by Germany's anti-American aggression, including attacks on neutral shipping in the Atlantic and pledges to help Mexico regain Texas, New Mexico, and Arizona if it fought against America. Wilson learned of this promised help through the so-called Zimmermann Telegram (see March 1), and the resulting public anger against Germany was such that a declaration of war became inevitable. During World War I, 116,516 Americans would be killed and 204,002 others wounded. It was called the "war to end all wars."

1942: Franklin D. Roosevelt's War Production Board ordered wartime rationing of metal. Dozens of everyday items—kitchen utensils, razor blades, and bed springs to name but three—became hard to find. Americans learned to take care of what they had—or do without.

★ QUOTE OF THE DAY

Our motive will not be revenge or the victorious assertion of the physical might of the nation, but only the vindication of right, of human right, of which we are only a single champion.

Woodrow Wilson

April 3

1798: John Adams told Congress of the "XYZ Affair"—a dispute with France that nearly led to war with Napoleon. The "affair" began when a U.S. diplomatic delegation went to France in July 1797 to negotiate issues that were threatening to cause war. The diplomats, Charles Cotesworth Pinckney, John Marshall, and Elbridge Gerry, were approached by French officials (nicknamed X, Y, and Z by the United States) who demanded bribes and a loan before formal negotiations could begin. This was a common practice in those days, but the Americans were offended, and Pinckney and Marshall went home. But Gerry, seeking to avoid war, remained and with French foreign minister Talleyrand laid the groundwork for an eventual end to diplomatic and military hostilities.

1948: Harry Truman signed the Marshall Plan, which aimed to rebuild Europe after World War II. The $13 billion Marshall Plan ($130 billion in 2016 dollars) was named for Secretary of State George Marshall, who said that Europe, devastated during the war, needed assistance getting back on its feet. The Marshall Plan did just that, while checking growing Soviet power on the continent. The Soviet Union itself, also devastated during the war, was also offered help; Soviet leader Josef Stalin refused to accept it.

1974: The IRS ordered Richard M. Nixon to pay up. After investigating the president's finances, the Internal Revenue Service ordered him to pay $432,787 in back taxes and $33,000 interest.

★ QUOTE OF THE DAY

Few presidents have had the opportunity to sign legislation of such importance ... this measure is America's answer to the challenge facing the free world today.

Harry Truman on the Marshall Plan

April 4

1800: John Adams signed the Federal Bankruptcy Act, providing merchants and traders protection from debtors.

1841: William Henry Harrison died—just one month into his presidency. It is commonly believed—mistakenly—that the sixty-eight-year-old Harrison caught a cold while delivering his two-hour inaugural address in harsh weather with no hat or coat, which developed into pneumonia. In fact, Harrison did not become ill until three weeks after his March 4 inauguration. Historians now believe that an unsanitary water supply may have done Harrison in—another president, Zazhary Taylor may have died from the same cause nine years later (see July 9). Harrison died in a White House bedroom that is today the private second-floor dining room for First Families. His passing also sparked a debate over presidential succession, and whether Vice President John Tyler would officially become president—or merely an "acting president" until a new election could be held.

Death, Death in the White House?
Oh never before
Trod his skeleton foot on the President's floor.

Journalist Nathaniel P. Willis on the death of President Harrison

This Day in Presidential History

William Henry Harrison, 68, was the oldest president ever inaugurated—until Ronald Reagan, 69 years and 349 days, was sworn in on January 20, 1981. Donald Trump, who took office in 2017, was 70 years and 220 days old when he was sworn in.

1865: "You are free—free as air," Abraham Lincoln told slaves in Richmond, Virginia, in his first visit to the capital of the soon-to-surrender Confederacy.

1865: Ten days before his murder, Abraham Lincoln had a prophetic dream. In his dream, Lincoln heard people sobbing. He entered the East Room, saw a corpse and asked a soldier: "Who is dead in the White House?" Soldier: "The President. He was killed by an assassin." Lincoln later told a friend, Ward Hill Lamon, that the dream "strangely annoyed" him.

1882: Chester Arthur vetoed the Chinese Exclusion Act, which would have banned the immigration of Chinese workers for twenty years and denied American citizenship to Chinese residents already in the United States. The president's veto angered labor groups, who felt threatened by the influx of Chinese labor. The act would later be overhauled.

1949: Harry Truman signed the North Atlantic Pact, a mutual defense treaty among twelve nations. Known today as the North Atlantic Treaty Organization (NATO), twenty-eight nations are its members.

1968: Machine gun nests sprouted on the White House lawn as riots erupted in Washington and across the nation following the assassination of Dr. Martin Luther King, Jr. A shocked Lyndon B. Johnson addressed the nation, appealing for calm and an end to racial division.

☆ QUOTE OF THE DAY

We can achieve nothing by lawlessness and divisiveness among the American people. It is only by joining together and only by working together that we can continue to move toward equality and fulfillment for all of our people.

Lyndon B. Johnson

April 5

1792: George Washington issued the first presidential veto, rejecting a bill to give more House seats to northern states. Washington issued just two vetoes during his eight years in office. In 1797, he rejected a bill that would have reduced the number of army cavalry units.

1988: Ronald Reagan became the first cap-and-trade president by signing the Montreal Protocol—a global treaty to protect the ozone layer above the North and South Poles.

★ QUOTE OF THE DAY

The Constitution is the guide which I never will abandon.

George Washington

The first sixteen presidents—Washington to Lincoln—issued a combined 59 vetoes. Franklin D. Roosevelt issued 635 vetoes in his twelve years in office. Vetoes by recent presidents: George W. Bush 12, Clinton 37, Obama 12—the fewest in a century.

April 6

1841: A constitutional crisis was averted when Vice President John Tyler was sworn in as the tenth president, following the death of President William Henry Harrison. Harrison's death revealed a flaw in the Constitution. Article II, Section 1, did not explicitly say whether the vice president becomes president if the president dies in office, resigns, is removed from office, or is otherwise unable to discharge the powers of the office. The crisis centered around this question: Would Tyler be merely an "acting president"—until an election could be held—or the president, with all the powers normally granted to that office?

The late president Harrison's cabinet, most of whom were not supporters of Tyler, told him that he could not exercise the full powers of the presidency and that any decisions he made would be subject to their approval. Tyler rejected this, ultimately asking for the resignation of any cabinet member who disagreed. The crisis was ultimately resolved in his favor. The "Tyler Precedent" became the long-standing rule by which other vice presidents would take office upon the death of a president. It was ultimately codified in the Twenty-fifth Amendment to the Constitution—adopted in February 1967.

1917: At the request of Woodrow Wilson, Congress voted to declare war on Germany. During his reelection campaign of 1916, Wilson stressed that he had kept the United States out of World War I. But now, things had changed. Wilson realized that the United States could not remain neutral in the Great War (see February 26). The House of Representatives passed the war resolution by a vote of 373-50, the Senate vote was 82-6.

1971: Richard M. Nixon's voice-activated taping system became operational in the Executive Office Building (EOB), where the president often worked. Taping also began on phone conversations held in the Oval Office, the EOB, and the Lincoln Sitting Room. Other recording systems became operation earlier in the year (see February 16).

★ QUOTE OF THE DAY

I can never consent to being dictated to.

John Tyler

April 7

1922: The Teapot Dome scandal. Warren Harding's interior secretary, Albert Fall, leased government oil reserves (in California and Teapot Dome, Wyoming) to companies at low rates with no competitive bidding. Fall would later be convicted of accepting bribes and sent to prison. It was one of several scandals to stain the Harding administration (see January 29).

1954: During a news conference discussing the threat of Communism in Indochina, Dwight Eisenhower said, "Finally, you have broader considerations that might follow what you would call the 'falling domino' principle. You have a row of dominoes set up, you knock over the first one, and what will happen to the last one is the certainty that it will go over very quickly." This striking image morphed into one of the most famous Cold War-era coinages: the "domino theory." The president's domino metaphor warned that if one country in a region—say Vietnam—fell to Communism, that others would eventually follow. The domino theory influenced presidents John F. Kennedy and Lyndon B. Johnson (particularly Johnson) to increase U.S. military involvement in Vietnam.

1978: Jimmy Carter tabled production of the neutron bomb—a weapon designed to kill people but leave buildings standing.

★ QUOTE OF THE DAY

An enemy generally says and believes what he wishes.

Thomas Jefferson

April 8

1913: Woodrow Wilson broke a 113-year tradition by appearing personally before Congress. The president, who spoke to lawmakers about revising tariffs, was the first chief executive to appear before Congress since John Adams in 1800.

1952: Citing national security, Harry Truman ordered the Army to take control of the steel industry. Contract talks between steel workers and owners failed, and with the Korean War raging, the president determined that steel production was necessary for the war effort. A federal court ruled that Truman's actions were unconstitutional, a decision upheld by the Supreme Court.

★ QUOTE OF THE DAY

With American troops facing the enemy on the field of battle, I would not be living up to my oath of office if I failed to do whatever is required to provide them with the weapons and ammunitions they need for their survival.

Harry Truman

April 9

1865: An overjoyed Abraham Lincoln learned that the South had surrendered, bringing the Civil War to a close. The Civil War remains by far the bloodiest war in U.S. history: 750,000 Americans were killed—the equivalent of 7.6 million Americans in 2016. The president had less than a week to live (see April 14–15).

1962: John F. Kennedy threw out the first pitch at the season opener for the Washington Senators. The recently constructed sports arena—"District of Columbia Stadium"—would be renamed RFK Stadium after the 1968 murder of the president's brother, Robert F. Kennedy. JFK's ceremonial first pitch continued a tradition begun by President William Howard Taft in 1910. In 1950, Harry Truman dazzled the crowd by tossing two pitches—one right-handed, the other left-handed.

1996: Bill Clinton and the "line item veto." The president signed a bill giving him the power to veto (delete) specific items in spending and tax bills without vetoing the entire bill itself. Most governors have such authority, but the Supreme Court, in 1998, ruled it unconstitutional at the federal level.

★ QUOTE OF THE DAY

My first wish is to see this plague of mankind, war, banished from the earth.

George Washington

April 10

1790: George Washington signed the Patent Act. It protected "any useful art, manufacture, engine, machine, or device, or any improvement thereon not before known or used."

1933: Franklin D. Roosevelt created the Civilian Conservation Corps (CCC), a public works program which put millions of Americans to work on environmentally related projects. Workers planted an estimated three billion trees, built wildlife refuges, controlled soil erosion, and constructed facilities at more than 800 parks. At any given time, some 300,000 people were employed, and were given food, clothing, and shelter. Their wages were $30 a month, $25 of which had to be sent home to families. The CCC is regarded as one of the cornerstones of president's "New Deal"; it was wound down in 1942, after the United States entered World War II.

★ QUOTE OF THE DAY

The nation that destroys its soil destroys itself.

Franklin D. Roosevelt

April 11

1865: Abraham Lincoln's final speech—and his soon-to-be assassin was there. Appearing in the center window on the second floor of the White House, the president spoke of the end of the Civil War with typical humility: "We meet this evening, not in sorrow, but in gladness of heart….He from whom all blessings flow, must not be forgotten." Lincoln also said that blacks should have voting rights, a comment that incensed one man in the crowd: twenty-six-year-old actor John Wilkes Booth. Standing with his friend Lewis Paine (born Powell), Booth—who had been stalking Lincoln for weeks—growled, "That means nigger citizenship. That is the last speech he will ever make. ... By God, I'll put him through." He would assassinate Lincoln three days later.

1951: Harry Truman fired Gen. Douglas MacArthur, for what Truman considered insubordinate comments about the Korean War. MacArthur wanted to intensify the fight against China (which entered the war in November 1950) and the president refused. The firing of MacArthur was controversial. The general, a World War II hero who commanded Allied forces in the Pacific, and later put in charge if the occupation of Japan, was very popular, and many Americans disagreed with the president's decision.

★ QUOTE OF THE DAY

It sure is hell to be president.

Harry Truman

April 12

1861: The first shots of the Civil War were fired, when Confederate forces shelled Fort Sumter, South Carolina. Union forces held out for thirty-three hours before surrendering.

1945: Franklin D. Roosevelt died at the Little White House in Warm Springs, Georgia. He was the thirty-second president, serving from 1933 to 1945. Elected a record four times, President Roosevelt guided America through two grave crises: the Great Depression and World War II. After his death, the constitution was amended, saying a president could only be elected twice.

Roosevelt's "New Deal" coalition dominated American politics for two decades. Elected at the very depths of the Great Depression, FDR entered office under the campaign theme song "Happy Days Are Here Again." His first 100 days were a whirlwind of activity against which all subsequent administrations have been measured. Despite the polio that required him to use crutches or a wheelchair, Roosevelt's never-ending optimism revived the spirit of the nation. As Europe plunged into war in 1939, Roosevelt at first maintained neutrality but soon gave today's equivalent of $650 billion in aid to Great Britain, the Soviet Union, China, and other nations. After America entered the war itself in December 1941, Roosevelt oversaw the transformation of the United States into the "Arsenal of Democracy" that led to the defeat of Nazi Germany, Italy, and Japan.

1945: Harry Truman was sworn in as the thirty-third president, following the death of Franklin D. Roosevelt. He would serve the remainder of FDR's term, which ran until January 1949, then another four years after being elected himself in 1948. Truman's presidency was one of the most momentous in American history. He became president just as World War II was ending in Europe. He made the grave decision to drop two atomic bombs on Japan, which brought the Pacific war to an end. He oversaw the Marshall Plan (see April 3), Berlin Airlift (see May 1), Korean War (see June 25), and creation of NATO—the North Atlantic Treaty Organization (see April 4). The last president without a college degree, Truman was known for his honesty and accountability: a famous sign on his Oval Office desk said "The Buck Stops Here."

Thomas Jefferson. Library of Congress.

★ QUOTE OF THE DAY

The only limit to our realization of tomorrow will be our doubts of today. Let us move forward with strong and active faith.

Franklin D. Roosevelt

April 13

1743: Thomas Jefferson was born in Shadwll, Colony of Virginia. He was the third president, serving from 1801 to 1809. He also served as the second governor of Virginia, the first U.S. secretary of state, and the second U.S. vice president. Jefferson authored the Declaration of Independence and the Statute of Virginia for Religious Freedom.

1830: Andrew Jackson's clash with his vice president foreshadowed the Civil War. Vice President John Calhoun, who was from South Carolina, suggested that the state stop paying a federally imposed protective cotton tariff. Jackson threatened to send federal troops to the Palmetto state. At the Jefferson Day Dinner in Washington, Jackson denounced Calhoun, proclaiming, "Our Union—it must be preserved!" Calhoun's response:

This Day in Presidential History

"The Union, next to our liberty most dear!" The dispute over tariffs—in addition to slavery—would help split the South from the North.

★ QUOTE OF THE DAY

Commerce with all nations, alliance with none, should be our motto.

Thomas Jefferson

April 14

1865: The very day that he was shot Abraham Lincoln signed legislation creating the United States Secret Service. But it wouldn't have saved him: the original mission of the Secret Service was to prevent the creation of counterfeit money.

1865: Abraham Lincoln was shot as he watched the play *Our American Cousin* with wife Mary Todd Lincoln and a young couple at Ford's Theatre in Washington, D.C. He died early the next morning without regaining consciousness. His assassin, John Wilkes Booth, murdered the president to avenge the South's defeat in the Civil War. He had stalked the president for weeks, glaring at him during Lincoln's second inauguration ceremony, and coming within feet of him as the president strolled through the Capitol rotunda.

1910: William Howard Taft became the first president to toss the opening first pitch to the baseball season. Every president but one—Jimmy Carter—has thrown out the first pitch at least once during his presidency.

1912: A top military aide to William Howard Taft died when the *Titanic* sank. Archie Butt was forty-seven.

1950: Containment of communism became one of the guiding principles of the Cold War, when Harry Truman received a top secret National Security Council report (NSC-68) outlining what the United States could do to prevent Soviet and Chinese communism from spreading. The report predicted the eventual demise of communism and emergence of a "new world order" centered around American values.

★ QUOTE OF THE DAY

The ballot is stronger than the bullet.

Abraham Lincoln

April 15

1861: Following the Confederate shelling of Ft. Sumter, South Carolina, Abraham Lincoln called for 75,000 volunteers to join the Union Army. 92,000 did, and the Civil War—the most devastating war in American history—was on. Lincoln quickly adapted to the role of commander-in-chief, assuming vast powers. Supreme Court rulings declared some of Lincoln's wartime conduct unconstitutional, but the president ignored them, saying his priority was to preserve the Union.

1861: Needing cash during the Civil War, Abraham Lincoln signed the Revenue Act—imposing the first federal income tax. The president asked for the first federal income tax—a 3% surcharge on income—because he recognized that Americans needed to pay for their wars.

1865: Abraham Lincoln died of an assassin's bullet. He was the sixteenth president, serving from 1861 to 1865. Lincoln—the first of four presidents to be assassinated—had been shot in the head the night before while attending a play at Washington's Ford's Theatre. The mortally wounded president had been carried to the Peterson boarding house across the street from the theater to breathe his last. The president's body was taken back to the White House, where his autopsy and embalming were conducted in what is today the First Family's private dining room on the second floor.

1865: Andrew Johnson was sworn in as the seventeenth president, following the death that morning of President Abraham Lincoln.

1969: A U.S. spy plane was shot down by North Korea, killing all thirty-one Americans on board. Richard M. Nixon did not retaliate and ordered reconnaissance flights to resume three days later.

1986: Ronald Reagan ordered limited air strikes against Libya and the government of Muamar Qadhafi. "Operation El Dorado Canyon" was in retaliation for the Libyan bombing of a West Berlin nightclub that killed two American servicemen.

This Day in Presidential History

⭐ QUOTE OF THE DAY

We cannot escape history...the fiery trial through which we pass will light us down, in honor or dishonor, to the latest generation.

Abraham Lincoln

Four U.S. presidents have been assassinated:

Lincoln: 1865

Garfield: 1881 (see July 2)

McKinley: 1901 (see September 6)

Kennedy: 1963 (see November 22)

April 16

1789: Traveling by carriage, George Washington left his estate in Mount Vernon, Virginia, for New York, where he would be sworn in as the first president of the United States.

1862: Abraham Lincoln abolished slavery in the District of Columbia, an early step in his effort to end slavery during the Civil War. He would issue a preliminary Emancipation Proclamation later that year (see September 22).

1865: Abraham Lincoln, victim of an assassin's bullet, lay in state in the East Room of the White House. The catafalque that held the sixteenth president's coffin was later used for the caskets of, among others, presidents Franklin D. Roosevelt, John F. Kennedy, and Ronald Reagan. You can see it on display at the Capitol, in a room originally meant to be George Washington's tomb.

QUOTE OF THE DAY

I hope I shall possess firmness and virtue enough to maintain … the most enviable of all titles, the character of an honest man.

George Washington

April 17

1861: After Abraham Lincoln's decision to use force against the South, Virginia left the Union and joined the Confederacy. Three other states would soon follow: North Carolina, Tennessee, and Arkansas. In total, eleven states joined the Confederacy during the Civil War.

1961: John F. Kennedy's biggest foreign policy mistake: "Operation Zapata"—better known today as the Bay of Pigs Invasion. Planning for the attempted ouster of Cuba's Communist leader Fidel Castro began during the Eisenhower administration, but Kennedy gave the final go ahead. The plan was to invade Cuba using 1,400 Cubans who fled for the United States after Castro came to power. But after the invasion began, the U.S.-trained Cubans were quickly overwhelmed by a larger pro-communist force. After less than a day, 114 of the invaders were killed and 1,100 captured. The plan also tried to destroy Cuban airfields, using a squadron of American B-26 bombers—painted to look like stolen Cuban planes and flown by Cuban exiles. This, too, fizzled. The disaster sparked a round of finger-pointing in Washington, with both the White House and Central Intelligence Agency blaming each other for the debacle. The Bay of Pigs taught President Kennedy a valuable lesson, namely to be skeptical of military advice. It was a lesson that came in handy during the Cuban Missile Crisis a year and a half later.

★ QUOTE OF THE DAY

Victory has a thousand fathers, but defeat is an orphan.

John F. Kennedy

April 18

1878: Thomas Edison visited the White House, and his phonograph recorded a president's voice for the first time: that of Rutherford Hayes. Hayes, a high-tech president, invited inventors like Edison and Alexander Graham Bell (inventor of the telephone) to the executive mansion to demonstrate their wares, knowing the attention would help speed the integration of their inventions into the U.S. economy.

1977: Jimmy Carter called energy conservation the "moral equivalent of war," as he called for Americans to support his plans to reduce dependence on imported oil. Neither the public nor Congress had his sense of urgency, leading critics to call the speech by its acronym MEOW.

1983: Ronald Reagan denounced the "vicious terrorist bombing" of the U.S. Embassy in Beirut, Lebanon. The attack killed 63, including 17 Americans. But the president took no military action in response. Six months later, an even deadlier attack on a U.S. Marine base in Beirut killed 241 Americans (see October 23). Reagan ordered a U.S. military withdrawal from Lebanon in February 1984.

☆ QUOTE OF THE DAY

We must realize that no arsenal or no weapon in the arsenals of the world is so formidable as the will and moral courage of free men and women. It is a weapon our adversaries in today's world do not have. It is a weapon that we as Americans do have. Let that be understood by those who practice terrorism and prey upon their neighbors.

Ronald Reagan, from his 1981 inaugural address

April 19

1809: The father of the Constitution—President James Madison—purchased a slave to work in the White House. The seller: the father of the Declaration of Independence, former president Thomas Jefferson. Even more ironic, the slave Jefferson sold to Madison was named John Freeman.

1861: Abraham Lincoln ordered a naval blockade of Confederate ports. It was a tall order for the president. The navy only had forty-two ships when the Civil War began, and there were 3,550 miles of Confederate coastline to patrol. But the blockade eventually helped weaken the South by stopping the import of supplies from Europe.

1933: In his ongoing efforts to combat the Great Depression, Franklin Roosevelt took the United States off the gold standard. FDR did so because Americans had lost faith in the dollar, and "bank runs" were unloading them for gold. This run-on banks during the Depression took cash out of circulation, hurting the economy. Roosevelt's nationalizing of gold had another reason: he was planning a number of expensive social and economic programs, and he needed money to finance them.

1995: An angry Bill Clinton vowed to find the terrorists behind the bombing of a federal office building in Oklahoma City. The attack on the Alfred P. Murrah Federal Building killed 168 people, including 19 children, and wounded an estimated 680 others. Within days, Timothy McVeigh, a U.S. Army veteran, was captured. He said he was angry over what he considered the heavy hand of the federal government in fatally confronting a religious sect in Waco, Texas—on April 19, 1993—and a family in Ruby Ridge, Idaho, that was accused of possessing illegal weapons. McVeigh was convicted and, in 2001, executed. An accomplice, Terry Nichols, was sentenced to life in prison without the possibility of parole. A third man, Michael J. Fortier, was given twelve years for knowing about the plot but failing to warn authorities. The Oklahoma City bombing was the worst terror attack within the United States prior to September 11, 2001.

★ QUOTE OF THE DAY

If men were angels, no government would be necessary.

James Madison

April 20

1871: At Ulysses S. Grant's urging, Congress passed the Third Force Act, or Ku Klux Klan (KKK) Act, aimed at giving the government more power to protect voters. The KKK Act allowed the president to use federal troops to suppress Klan activities and to suspend the writ of habeas corpus to ensure that civil rights were upheld. Shortly after the law was passed, nine counties in South Carolina were placed under martial law and thousands of arrests were made. The law was declared unconstitutional by the Supreme Court in 1882.

1898: William McKinley asked Congress to declare war on Spain, two months after the U.S.S. *Maine* blew up in Cuba's Havana harbor. "Remember the *Maine!*" was the battle cry as America went to war with Spain. But the navy later determined that an onboard accident, not an attack, blew up the battleship. The Spanish-American War was fueled by sensationalist newspaper coverage from tycoons like William Randolph Hearst and Joseph Pulitzer.

1983: Ronald Reagan signed a $165 billion Social Security bailout bill. Funds for the retirement program came from increases in the U.S. payroll tax.

1999: Bill Clinton said he was "profoundly shocked and saddened" by a massacre at Colorado's Columbine high school. The massacre, which left fifteen people—including two student perpetrators—dead, sparked calls for stricter gun laws in the United States.

⭐ QUOTE OF THE DAY

That's all a man can hope for during his lifetime—to set an example.

William McKinley

Abraham Lincoln's funeral train made 180 stops during its seven-state, three-week long journey home to Illinois. This lithograph shows the assassinated president's remains being drawn to a service in Buffalo, New York, on April 27, 1865. Library of Congress.

April 21

1865: Abraham Lincoln's funeral train left Washington, D.C.; he would be buried in his hometown of Springfield, Illinois, thirteen days later. The train traveled 1,654 miles over twelve days, making numerous stops so grieving citizens could pay their respects. The train retraced the route Lincoln took when he came to Washington as president-elect in 1861. The martyred president's wife Mary Todd Lincoln remained at the White House because she was too distraught to make the trip.

★ QUOTE OF THE DAY

Be sure you put your feet in the right place, then stand firm.

Abraham Lincoln

April 22

1793: As tensions rose between France and Britain, George Washington said America would remain neutral. The president, who was wary of foreign entanglements, warned Americans to avoid aiding either side. He said that anyone who tried to undermine this policy would be prosecuted.

1994: Richard M. Nixon died in New York City. He was the thirty-seventh president, serving between 1969 and 1974. In 1968, Nixon promised to "bring us together" as a nation. But Watergate helped tear it apart; he became the only president to resign. Although Nixon is remembered for Watergate, he had notable successes both at home and abroad. He reached out to China, embarked on "détente" with the Soviet Union, and ended the Vietnam War.

At home, Nixon exempted nine million low-income citizens from paying taxes, while raising taxes on the rich. He fought for tougher workplace safety standards, sharply boosted Social Security benefits, created the Environmental Protection Agency, and fought for cleaner air and water.

Nixon was one of just two men to run on national tickets five times. He was Dwight Eisenhower's running mate in 1952 and 1956, the Republican presidential nominee in 1960, 1968, and 1972. Only the 1960 campaign was unsuccessful. (The other person? Franklin D. Roosevelt, of course, who was elected president in 1932, 1936, 1940, and 1944. FDR's only losing

This Day in Presidential History

appearance on a national ticket was in 1920, when presidential nominee James Cox asked him to be his vice presidential candidate.)

⭐ QUOTE OF THE DAY

I let the American people down.

Richard M. Nixon

April 23

1791: James Buchanan was born in Cove Gap, Pennsylvania. He was the fifteenth president, serving from 1857 to 1861. The only president who never married, Buchanan is considered one of the worst chief executives, largely for his failure to prevent the Civil War. As president-elect, Buchanan thought the crisis over slavery would dissipate if Americans would simply accept whatever the Supreme Court ruled on it. The Court was considering the legality of restricting slavery in the territories, and two justices hinted to Buchanan what the decision would be. In his inaugural address, the new president thus referred to the territorial question as "happily, a matter of but little practical importance" since the Supreme Court was about to settle it "speedily and finally."

James Buchanan. Library of Congress.

This Day in Presidential History

On March 6, 1857, two days after Buchanan was sworn in, the court issued its explosive *Dred Scott* decision. It said that neither slaves nor their descendants could become American citizens. Southerners were delighted, but the decision angered the North. The ruling helped spark Abraham Lincoln's rise to power in 1860—and the Civil War.

1898: With the United States gearing up for war with Spain, William McKinley called for 125,000 volunteers to fight. Among those who answered the call: Theodore Roosevelt, who resigned as secretary of the navy to serve.

★ QUOTE OF THE DAY

The Constitution expressly recognizes the right to hold slaves as property in states where slavery exists. This, then, is not a question of general morality, affecting the consciences of men, but it is a question of constitutional law. ... The southern states have rights guaranteed to them, and these rights I am determined to maintain, come weal, come woe.

James Buchanan

April 24

1800: John Adams approved $5,000 for the Library of Congress. The first books were ordered from London and arrived in 1801. The collection of 740 volumes and 3 maps was stored in the U.S. Capitol, the Library's first home.

1945: Harry Truman, president for just twelve days, was briefed on the Manhattan Project—the secret wartime effort to develop an atomic bomb. The president would soon order—after weeks of careful deliberation—two of them dropped on Japan. Worried that Nazi Germany would develop atomic weapons, Franklin D. Roosevelt had approved the crash project in 1939, which employed up to 130,000 people at its peak—only a handful of whom knew the actual objective of their labor. Truman knew that atomic weapons could accelerate the war's end, but worried about the death toll and the precedent it might set for the future. In the end, he determined that the bombs would save more lives than they ultimately took (see August 6 and 9).

This Day in Presidential History

1980: A disaster for Jimmy Carter and the nation: an attempt to rescue American hostages in Iran failed, killing eight U.S. servicemen. As Operation Eagle Claw unfolded, two helicopters went down in the Iranian desert with engine trouble; another crashed into a C-130, killing the servicemen. In the wake of the mission's failure, Secretary of State Cyrus Vance, who warned Carter against the mission, made good on his threat to resign.

★ QUOTE OF THE DAY

The atom bomb was no "great decision." It was merely another powerful weapon in the arsenal of righteousness.

Harry Truman

April 25

2001: George W. Bush said, explicitly, that the United States would defend Taiwan. Prior administrations had only hinted of defending the island from an attack by communist China. Since 1979, the United States has maintained an official "one China policy," recognizing only mainland China.

★ QUOTE OF THE DAY

It was my decision to attempt the rescue operation. It was my decision to cancel it when problems developed in the placement of our rescue team for a future rescue operation. The responsibility is fully my own.

Jimmy Carter

April 26

1865: Abraham Lincoln's assassin, John Wilkes Booth, was killed—twelve days after he had shot the president. After shooting the president at Ford's Theatre, Booth leaped to the stage from Lincoln's box seat. He broke his leg, but was able to escape to a waiting horse. But he was recognized by theatergoers—he was a famous actor after all—and the chase was on.

Twelve days later federal troops found Booth and an accomplice, David Herold, hiding in a barn in Virginia. The barn belonged to a man named Richard Garrett. Garrett, not knowing who Booth and Herold were, allowed his guests to sleep in the barn—but had the door locked from the outside so his horses wouldn't be stolen. When troops found Booth and Herold, they ordered them to surrender. Herald did, but Booth refused. Troops then set the building on fire. One soldier shot Booth, who died three hours later.

1984: Ronald Reagan arrived in China for a summit meeting with Chinese President Li Xiannian. The trip marked the second time a U.S. president had traveled to China since President Richard M. Nixon's historic trip in 1972 (Gerald Ford visited in 1975).

✯ QUOTE OF THE DAY

Freedom is never more than one generation away from extinction. We didn't pass it to our children in the bloodstream. It must be fought for, protected, and handed on for them to do the same.

Ronald Reagan

April 27

1822: Ulysses S. Grant was born at Point Pleasant, Ohio. He was the eighteenth president, serving from 1869 to 1877. Grant went to West Point (somewhat reluctantly) and graduated in the middle of his class. He fought in the Mexican War and was commanded by General Zachary Taylor, who went on to attain the presidency.

A Civil War hero who led smashing Union victories in key battles at Shiloh, Vicksburg, and Chattanooga, Grant won the admiration of President Abraham Lincoln. A colonel in 1861, Grant won promotion to major general in 1862 and lieutenant general in 1864. On April 9, 1865, Grant accepted the surrender of Confederate General Robert E. Lee's Army of Northern Virginia, ending the Civil War.

Ulysses S. Grant. Library of Congress.

Grant became the Republican candidate for president in 1868. He won, and would be reelected in 1872. Grant is generally regarded as a better general than president. He was regarded as an honest man, yet his administration was rocked by a series of scandals. Among the most notable was the "Black Friday Panic" of 1869 (see September 24), involving an attempt by three men—one of whom was the president's brother-in-law—to corner the gold market, and the "Whiskey Ring Scandal" (see May 10), which involved the president's private secretary.

★ QUOTE OF THE DAY

There never was a time when, in my opinion, some way could not be found to prevent the drawing of the sword.

Ulysses S. Grant

April 28

1758: James Monroe was born in Westmoreland County, Colony of Virginia. He was the fifth president, serving from 1817 to 1825. He is the only person in American history who has been a governor, senator, secretary of state, secretary of war (now defense), and president. Born in Virginia,

James Monroe. Library of Congress.

he fought alongside George Washington during the Revolutionary War, and sustained a near-fatal wound during the Battle of Trenton in 1776.

He was elected to the Senate in 1790. From 1794 to 1796 he was ambassador to France, an experience that would come in handy in1803, when he helped negotiate the Louisiana Purchase for President Thomas Jefferson. Elected to the presidency in 1816, he lived for the first few months of his administration in Octagon House—at 1799 New York Avenue NW—as restoration of the White House (destroyed during the War of 1812) was completed. He was reelected in 1820, despite a steep recession in 1819—the first in American history.

A key event in the pre–Civil War era occurred in 1820, when the president signed the Missouri Compromise. Missouri would join the Union as a slave state, while Maine would join as a free state—and slavery would be banned from north and west of Missouri forever.

Monroe will be best remembered for the doctrine that today bears his name. Fearful that governments in Europe might try to expand their influence in Latin America, the president endorsed a new policy: that "the American continents, by the free and independent condition which they have assumed and maintain, are henceforth not to be considered as subjects for future colonization by any European Power." Some twenty years after Monroe died in 1831, this became known as the Monroe Doctrine. In the two centuries since, the Monroe Doctrine has been invoked

This Day in Presidential History

by multiple presidents as a key part of American foreign policy. John F. Kennedy, for example, cited it during the Cuban Missile Crisis of 1962.

★ QUOTE OF THE DAY

The best form of government is that which is most likely to prevent the greatest sum of evil.

James Monroe

April 29

1974: Richard M. Nixon said he'd release transcripts of taped conversations related to the Watergate scandal. A congressional subpoena had been issued in July 1973, but Nixon ignored it, citing executive privilege. But with pressure mounting, he agreed to make public transcripts of forty-six White House conversations, and sent the House Judiciary Committee some 1,200 pages of transcripts. But Nixon said he had edited the transcripts to exclude material that was "irrelevant" to the Watergate investigation. The president also invited committee members to review the tapes to determine whether the transcripts omitted any incriminating evidence. "I want there to be no question remaining about the fact that the president has nothing to hide in this matter," Nixon said. He would, of course, resign a little more than three months later (see August 8 and 9).

1975: Gerald Ford ordered the evacuation of the U.S. Embassy in Saigon, South Vietnam, as communist North Vietnamese troops closed in. It was a humiliating end to the Vietnam War, in which the United States formally fought from 1964 (Gulf of Tonkin Resolution) to 1973 (Paris Peace Accord). Vietnam, once the longest war in American history, has since been surpassed by two wars fought simultaneously: Afghanistan, which began in October 2001, and the Iraq War, which ran from March 19, 2003, to December 18, 2011.

★ QUOTE OF THE DAY

This action closes a chapter in the American experience. I ask all Americans to close ranks, to avoid recrimination about the past, to look ahead to the many goals we share, and to work together on the great tasks that remain to be accomplished.

Gerald Ford

April 30

1789: George Washington was inaugurated as the first president of the United States. The ceremony took place at Federal Hall in New York, which was then the nation's capital. Washington was a reluctant president. At the age of fifty-seven, he wanted to stay retired. But he feared political factions were tearing the nation apart, and agreed to serve. He would serve two terms in office before retiring for good in 1798—the year before he passed away.

1803: The United States and France signed the Louisiana Purchase Treaty. It gave all of the Louisiana territory from the Mississippi River to the Rocky Mountains to the United States. It doubled the nation's size and is considered the greatest achievement of Thomas Jefferson's presidency.

1939: Franklin Roosevelt became the first president to appear on television. He did so while attending the New York World's Fair.

1970: Richard M. Nixon announced that U.S. troops were invading Cambodia—a nation being used by North Vietnam to wage war on South Vietnam. Nixon's public announcement came after a year of Cambodian bombing that the administration tried to keep quiet. The invasion sparked nationwide protests; four students at Kent State University in Ohio would be shot and killed by National Guard troops in May.

1973: Richard M. Nixon admitted responsibility for Watergate—but in a television address to the nation, he denied having any prior knowledge of the scandal. It was later established that the president was lying.

★ QUOTE OF THE DAY

I do solemnly swear (or affirm) that I will faithfully execute the Office of President of the United States, and will to the best of my ability, preserve, protect, and defend the Constitution of the United States.

The presidential oath of office—used by George Washington on April 30, 1789, and by every subsequent president of the United States

This Day in Presidential History

May

May 1

1931: With the push of a symbolic button, President Herbert Hoover dedicated the Empire State Building. Hoover wasn't in New York, he was at the White House, and when he pushed the button, someone else actually threw the switch that illuminated the iconic skyscraper. The Empire State Building, 102 stories and 1,250 feet high, was then the world's tallest structure—and took just one year and $40 million to build. Constructed during the depths of the Great Depression, it gave New York and the nation a renewed sense of pride.

1961: The Situation Room began operations on or about May 1. The "Sit Room" was requested by John F. Kennedy after the bungled Bay of Pigs operation in Cuba (see April 17). The president, frustrated with the quality and speed of information he received during that crisis, ordered that a bowling alley built for Harry Truman be replaced with a command post that brought in information from the CIA and the defense and state departments. It would prove valuable during the Cuban Missile Crisis a year and a half later (see October 16).

2003: Standing on the aircraft carrier U.S.S. *Abraham Lincoln* with a "Mission Accomplished" banner behind him, George W. Bush announced that "major combat operations in Iraq have ended." Bush was wrong. The war would continue for seven-and-a-half more years, ultimately claiming the lives of 4,486 Americans and countless Iraqis.

2011: Barack Obama announced that a U.S. raid had killed Osama bin Laden—the leader of al Qaeda and perpetrator of the September 11, 2001, terror attacks on New York and Washington, D.C. "Operation Neptune Spear," as the special forces operation that killed bin Laden was called, was among the most daring military missions in U.S. history. Bin Laden was killed early on May 2 in Abbottabad, Pakistan, which due to the time zone was still May 1 in the United States.

★ QUOTE OF THE DAY

To those families who have lost loved ones to al Qaeda's terror, justice has been done.

Barack Obama

May 2

2001: Warning that benefits might have to be cut and taxes raised to shore up Social Security, George W. Bush formed a commission to study options. One idea that was briefly considered was partially privatizing the retirement program—by allowing younger workers the option of investing a portion of their funds in the stock market, which, it was believed, would generate higher returns. Bush's idea didn't go anywhere.

★ QUOTE OF THE DAY

We in our time must rededicate ourselves to the great ideal Roosevelt defined 67 years ago: greater freedom and greater security for the average man than he has ever known before in the history of America. That's our charge, and we must keep it.

George W. Bush

May 3

1802: Washington, D.C. was incorporated as a city. The U.S. capital—home to an estimated 14,093 people, including President Thomas Jefferson and the newly relocated federal government—wasn't much of a city in 1802. Hogs and cattle ran free in the filthy, ramshackle streets. Historian David McCullough, in his grand biography of John Adams, noted that in 1800, Adams "could rightfully have fumed over the heat, the mosquitoes, the squalid shacks of the work crews ... there was no city as yet, only a rather shabby village and great stretches of tree stumps, stubble and swamp. There were no schools, not a single church."

1861: Lincoln asked for war volunteers: With the Civil War under way, Abraham Lincoln—president for just two months—issued an urgent call for 42,034 Army volunteers to serve for three years, and another 18,000 seamen to serve for "not less than one or more than three years."

Lincoln's Proclamation 83 said the volunteers were urgently needed because "existing exigencies demand immediate and adequate measures for the protection of the National Constitution and the preservation of the National Union by the suppression of the insurrectionary combinations now existing in several States for opposing the laws of the Union and obstructing the execution thereof."

1889: Benjamin Harrison invited a future president—Theodore Roosevelt—to head the Civil Service Commission. Roosevelt would be appointed days later, and over the next six years worked to improve and enforce civil service laws—clashing with politicians who wanted him to ignore those laws in favor of patronage. Roosevelt believed that (1) opportunities should be made available on an equal basis for all citizens, (2) federal jobs should be given on a merit-based system, and (3) public servants should not be punished for their political beliefs.

1994: Three presidents—including Ronald Reagan—called for an assault weapons ban. The former president coauthored a letter with former presidents Gerald Ford and Jimmy Carter asking the House of Representatives to ban such weapons, calling it "a matter of vital importance to the public safety." Reagan followed up with letters to individual lawmakers to get their backing. The measure passed and was signed into law by President Bill Clinton (see September 13).

★ QUOTE OF THE DAY

While we recognize that assault weapon legislation will not stop all assault weapon crime, statistics prove that we can dry up the supply of these guns, making them less accessible to criminals. We urge you to listen to the American public and to the law enforcement community and support a ban on the further manufacture of these weapons.

Ronald Reagan, Gerald Ford, and Jimmy Carter,
in a letter to Congress

May 4

1865: Three weeks after his murder, Abraham Lincoln was laid to rest in Springfield, Illinois. The site of the Lincoln Tomb, Oak Ridge Cemetery (now owned and managed as a state historic site), is marked by a 117-foot-tall granite obelisk with several bronze statues of Lincoln. Mary Todd Lincoln and three of their four sons are also buried there. Lincoln's most famous son, Robert Todd Lincoln, is buried in Arlington National Cemetery in Arlington, Virginia.

1970: Richard M. Nixon was stunned after four college students were shot and killed on the campus of Kent State University in Ohio. The president—in a statement read by his press secretary—said "that when dissent turns to violence, it invites tragedy." Nixon called on America's college campuses—administrators, faculty, and students—to stand "firmly for the right which exists in this country of peaceful dissent and just as strongly against the resort to violence as a means of such expression."

The shootings occurred when college campuses nationwide erupted in protest over news that U.S. forces had invaded the small southeast Asian nation of Cambodia. The invasion, Nixon announced on April 28, was to keep Cambodia from being used as a sanctuary by North Vietnamese troops, who were battling both American and South Vietnamese forces in South Vietnam.

★ QUOTE OF THE DAY

May our children and our children's children to a thousand generations, continue to enjoy the benefits conferred upon us by a united country.

Abraham Lincoln, in an October 4, 1862, speech

May 5

1960: Dwight Eisenhower denied that a U.S. spy plane had been shot down over the Soviet Union. The president was lying. The Soviets produced the U.S. pilot, Francis Gary Powers, and the president acknowledged the truth: that Powers, flying a U-2 aircraft high over Soviet territory on May 1, had in fact been shot down by a surface-to-air missile. At a later Paris peace conference with Soviet leader Nikita Khrushchev, Eisenhower refused to apologize; Khrushchev stormed out of the meeting and the Cold War got colder.

1961: John F. Kennedy congratulated the first American in space—Alan Shepard—after his fifteen-minute mission aboard his *Freedom* 7 capsule. The capsule, powered by a Redstone missile, propelled Shepard to an altitude of 116 miles. During his fifteen-minute mission (Shepard did not go into orbit), he was able to see the curvature of the earth, and described a view never seen by any American before. In May, the president announced to a joint session of Congress the goal of landing an American on the moon by the end of the decade.

1977: Discussing Watergate at length for the first time since resigning, Richard M. Nixon said he let the American people down. The former president's comments came during a series of extraordinary interviews he granted to British journalist David Frost for $600,000—and 20% of the profits from TV sales.

1985: Ronald Reagan angered Jewish leaders and Holocaust survivors by visiting a German military cemetery where Hitler's SS troops were buried. Before going to the Kolmeshöhe Cemetery in Bitburg, Reagan also visited the site of the Bergen-Belsen concentration camp, in which victims of Nazi persecution, mostly Jews, were exterminated.

☆ QUOTE OF THE DAY

We can let our pain drive us to greater efforts to heal humanity's suffering.

Ronald Reagan

May 6

1933: Franklin Roosevelt created the Works Progress Administration (WPA). The WPA put three million people to work in return for giving them financial assistance. FDR was opposed to welfare for people who were able to work; those getting assistance were required to help build schools, roads and hospitals; others restored theaters, wrote plays, etc.

This Day in Presidential History

Congressional opponents of the WPA scaled it back over time; it was suspended during World War II, when the United States economy quickly returned to full employment.

★ QUOTE OF THE DAY

The test of our progress is not whether we add more to the abundance of those who have much; it is whether we provide enough for those who have too little.

Franklin D. Roosevelt

May 7

1789: George Washington attended the first inaugural ball, which quickly became a tradition for new presidents. At the gala, which was held in lower Manhattan, the wife of Alexander Hamilton, Eliza, noted that the new president particularly enjoyed dancing the minuet.

Some presidents (Wilson, Harding) cancelled inaugural balls to save money. Others (Coolidge, Hoover, FDR) turned them into charitable events. One president, Rutherford Hayes, had no inaugural ball at all, owing to the fact that the contentious election of 1876 was decided only two days before inauguration day (see March 3).

1915: While golfing in Maryland, Woodrow Wilson was informed that RMS *Lusitania* had been torpedoed by a German U-Boat. The sinking of the *Lusitania* killed 1,198 people, including an estimated 128 Americans—pushing the United States closer to war with Germany. Until the ship was attacked, U.S. policy toward World War I had been neutral.

★ QUOTE OF THE DAY

I hope I shall possess firmness and virtue enough to maintain ... the most enviable of all titles, the character of an honest man.

George Washington

May 8

1884: Harry Truman was born in Lamar, Missouri. He was the thirty-third president, serving from 1945 to 1953. Truman became president when Franklin D. Roosevelt died suddenly in office. He retired with low approval ratings, but today is regarded as one of America's greatest presidents. He ordered the atomic bombing of Japan and oversaw the Marshall Plan, the Berlin Airlift, the Korean War, and the creation of NATO.

Each morning, Truman went on a brisk walk around Washington, D.C.—unthinkable today. He often played poker with White House reporters. He once threatened to punch a *Washington Post* reporter in the nose for writing a bad review about his daughter's singing. He was the last president without a college degree.

1945: Harry Truman, on his sixty-first birthday, announced the surrender of Nazi Germany. VE (Victory in Europe) Day meant the end of World War II in Europe, but the war against Japan would continue for four months.

1972: Richard M. Nixon said the United States would mine North Vietnamese ports to stem the flow of weapons to that communist nation. Nixon noted that the North Vietnamese had spurned American offers to end the war peacefully, and had actually stepped up its attacks in South Vietnam. "There is only one way to stop the killing," Nixon said. "That is to keep the weapons of war out of the hands of the international outlaws of North Vietnam."

Harry Truman. Library of Congress.

Intense feeling too often obscures the truth.

Harry Truman

May 9

1914: Woodrow Wilson signed a proclamation establishing Mother's Day. The president said an annual holiday would let Americans show "our love and reverence for the mothers of our country."

1974: The House Judiciary Committee began impeachment hearings against Richard M. Nixon, for his involvement in the Watergate scandal. It would vote to impeach him on three counts (see July 30). But before impeachment proceedings went to the full House itself, the president resigned.

2017: Donald Trump fired FBI director James Comey, saying that he had lost confidence in Comey's ability to lead the law-enforcement agency. Critics charged that the president was unhappy that Comey was pursuing an investigation into alleged collusion between Trump's 2016 presidential campaign and Russia.

★ QUOTE OF THE DAY

A full impeachment trial in the Senate, under our Constitution, comes only when the House determines that there is an impeachable offense. It is my belief that the House, after it conducts its inquiry, will not reach that determination. I do not expect to be impeached.

Richard M. Nixon, February 25, 1974

May 10

1815: James Madison ordered the Navy into battle against Mediterranean pirates. During the War of 1812, the North African Barbary states of Tripoli, Tunis, and Algeria often attacked American ships which did not pay tribute for right of safe passage. In June, a fierce U.S. attack led by Captain Stephen Decatur put an end to the practice. It was the second war against

This Day in Presidential History

the Barbary states, the first was waged by Thomas Jefferson between 1801 and 1805.

1875: Ulysses S. Grant and the "Whiskey Ring Scandal." A total of 238 people were indicted after distillers conspired with Treasury Department officials to defraud the government of millions of dollars in liquor taxes. The president's private secretary, Orville E. Babcock, would soon be indicted as well—an example of one of the poor personnel choices made by the president.

1877: The White House got its first telephone. The phone number was "1." But President Rutherford B. Hayes got few calls. The only other direct line to the White House at the time was from the Treasury Department next door (it wouldn't be for half a century, though, until a president—Herbert Hoover—had the first telephone line installed at the president's desk in the Oval Office). Hayes, who was interested in new technology, also had the first typewriter in the White House, and was personally given a briefing on the phonograph by Thomas Edison.

2005: An assassination attempt against George W. Bush. A man threw a hand grenade at the president during a visit to the former Soviet Republic of Georgia. It landed 65 feet away but failed to explode.

⭐ QUOTE OF THE DAY

The president of the United States should strive to be always mindful of the fact that he serves his party best who serves his country best.

Rutherford B. Hayes

May 11

1935: Americans in rural areas lacked electricity—until Franklin D. Roosevelt created the Rural Electrification Administration. REA crews would soon travel the country teaming up with states and local municipalities to provide power to farms and ranches. It helped rural America modernize and become more productive. It also helped create badly needed jobs during the Great Depression.

1961: John F. Kennedy upped United States involvement in Vietnam, sending 400 Special Forces and 100 military advisors to South Vietnam. He also ordered a secret warfare program to begin—to be conducted by

U.S.-trained South Vietnamese forces. Historians have always wondered what the United States might have done in Vietnam had Kennedy lived. Early in his presidency, JFK said he would continue the policy of his predecessor, Dwight Eisenhower, and support the Diem government in South Vietnam. Kennedy also adhered to Eisenhower's "Domino Theory," which said that if South Vietnam fell to communism, its neighbors would eventually follow. Kennedy gradually increased both aid and the number of American personnel in South Vietnam—but the war's major escalation, of course, would come during the administration of Lyndon B. Johnson.

★ QUOTE OF THE DAY

Now we have a problem in trying to make our power credible, and Vietnam looks like the place.

> John F. Kennedy, in a 1961 interview with the *New York Times*

May 12

1903: Theodore Roosevelt's trip to San Francisco was captured on film; it was the first time a sitting president was recorded in that medium. Roosevelt was shot on film during a parade.

1949: A big win for Harry Truman: Soviet dictator Stalin lifted his blockade of West Berlin. For eleven months the Soviets tried to force U.S. and British troops out of the divided city. When the blockade began, there were fears that West Berlin's two million people could starve. Truman: "We stay in Berlin. Period." And thus the Berlin Airlift (June 26, 1948–September 30, 1949). It was a symbol of American (and British) determination to stand up to communism; the president ordered 24/7 flights to feed and clothe West Berliners. It also led to the creation of NATO—the military alliance between the United States and allies in Europe.

1975: Gerald Ford was informed that a U.S. merchant ship, the *Mayaguez*, had been seized by the Cambodian Khmer Rouge. Ford ordered an attack on the small Cambodian island where the United States believed the crew of thirty-nine was being held. But by the time the attack began, the crew had already been released. Eighteen U.S. servicemen were killed in the subsequent attack and another twenty-three died in a helicopter crash.

Their names are the final ones inscribed on the Vietnam Veterans Memorial in Washington, D.C.

★ QUOTE OF THE DAY

When history says that my term of office saw the beginning of the Cold War, it will also say that in those eight years we have set the course that can win it.

Harry Truman, 1953

May 13

1846: At James K. Polk's urging, Congress approved a declaration of war against Mexico. The Mexican-American War would end in 1848 with the United States gaining 525,000 square miles of land.

But the war was somewhat controversial, and gave a future president—Abraham Lincoln—his first taste of the limelight. Lincoln, elected to Congress in 1846 (he would serve just one term), called the war unconstitutional, unnecessary, and expensive. He called President Polk "a bewildered, confounded, and miserably perplexed man." Polk ignored him.

Polk led the nation into the Mexican-American War, a conflict that made the United States a true continental power. Future president Zachary Taylor commanded U.S. forces at the Battle of Buena Vista, February 22-23, 1847. Library of Congress.

1954: Dwight Eisenhower signed the St. Lawrence Seaway Bill, connecting the Atlantic Ocean with the Great Lakes. Fulfilling an idea that dated back to the late 1800s, the United States worked with Canada to create a deep-water 114-mile navigation channel—that enabled ships to sail directly from the Atlantic Ocean to Duluth, Minnesota.

★ QUOTE OF THE DAY

With me it is exceptionally true that the Presidency is no bed of roses.

James K. Polk

May 14

1789: Congress officially approved the title of "President" for the leader of the federal government's executive branch. The United States didn't have a president for the first thirteen years of its existence (1776–1789). Resentful of England's King George III, America's founding fathers—among them Thomas Jefferson, James Madison, and George Washington—decided that America didn't need a powerful central figure; they feared a tyrant. But it didn't work. There was no clear leader to establish priorities, set the tone, or unify the fractious nation, and the Articles of Confederation—America's first Constitution—turned out to be weak. Congress could accomplish some initiatives, but in general, was feeble. Squabbling lawmakers couldn't collect taxes, finance an Army or Navy, or tackle large national issues. By the mid-1780s, the founding fathers had had enough. The nation was being torn apart by regional and partisan division; it was decided that the Articles of Confederation had to be replaced. A new Constitution was drawn up—providing for, among other things, a president of the United States.

1804: Fulfilling Thomas Jefferson's dream, Lewis and Clark began their expedition to explore the new Louisiana Territory. The territory, purchased the year before from French leader Napoleon Bonaparte, doubled America's size—the most important achievement of Jefferson's eight-year presidency.

1948: Harry Truman recognized the state of Israel. The United States was the first nation to do so (de facto recognition). Truman believed that in the wake of World War II and the Holocaust Jews needed a safe place, a homeland of their own.

This Day in Presidential History

1999: Bill Clinton apologized to China's president for the accidental NATO bombing of the Chinese embassy in Belgrade, Yugoslavia. Clinton told Jiang Zemin that the bombing—which killed three people and injured twenty—was a terrible mistake. China claimed it was a deliberate act.

★ QUOTE OF THE DAY

I felt that Israel deserved to be recognized and didn't give a damn whether the Arabs liked it or not.

Harry Truman

May 15

1800: John Adams ordered the federal government to leave Philadelphia and move to the new capital city: Washington, D.C., which stood for "District of Columbia." Washington officially became the U.S. capital on June 11, 1800. At the time the entire federal workforce numbered about 125. What is today known as the White House was still under construction, so when Adams arrived, he took a room over a Capitol Hill tavern, Tunnicliff's.

1911: The Supreme Court ordered the breakup of John D. Rockefeller's Standard Oil Company, pleasing William Howard Taft. The president had ordered the Justice Department to take on the company, arguing that it was a monopoly that restricted competition and therefore violated the Sherman Antitrust Act. The case originated in the prior administration of President Theodore Roosevelt. Other companies deemed monopolies would also be ordered to breakup.

1924: Calvin Coolidge vetoed a bill granting bonuses to veterans of World War I. The president claimed that "patriotism ... bought and paid for is not patriotism." Congress overrode his veto.

QUOTE OF THE DAY

There is danger from all men. The only maxim of a free government ought to be to trust no man living with power to endanger the public liberty.

John Adams

May 16

1868: The Senate came within one vote of removing Andrew Johnson from office. After being impeached by the House of Representatives on eleven counts of trying to fire Secretary of War Edwin Stanton, and for violating postwar Reconstruction Acts, the president's fate was up to the Senate. A two-thirds majority on any one count would have removed him from the presidency.

But the vote—thirty-five in favor of impeachment and nineteen against—was one vote short, and the president remained in office.

1918: Congress passed the Sedition Act, which, combined with the Espionage Act (see June 15) gave the Wilson administration greater power to limit freedom of expression during World War I. Among other things, it gave the postmaster general the right to ban the mailing of publications deemed subversive by the government.

1960: A summit meeting between Dwight Eisenhower and Soviet leader Nikita Khrushchev collapsed. Their Paris talks fell apart after Eisenhower refused to apologize for American U-2 spy flights over the Soviet Union. One U-2 pilot, Francis "Gary" Powers, was shot down (see May 5).

★ QUOTE OF THE DAY

Information is the oxygen of the modern age. It seeps through the walls topped by barbed wire, it wafts across the electrified borders.

Ronald Reagan

May 17

1954: Arguably the twentieth century's most important Supreme Court ruling: *Brown vs. Board of Education*, which ended school segregation. But *Brown vs. Board of Education* was not endorsed by Dwight Eisenhower; he also did not condemn segregation as morally wrong. Still, the president—fearing the ruling would spark racial unrest—enforced it with vigor, sending federal troops to Arkansas in 1957 to ensure the enrollment of the "Little Rock Nine" (see September 24).

★ QUOTE OF THE DAY

The Supreme Court has spoken and I am sworn to uphold the constitutional processes in this country; and I will obey.

Dwight Eisenhower

May 18

1917: At Woodrow Wilson's urging, Congress passed the Selective Service Act—allowing men to be drafted into the military. After the United States entered World War I in April 1917, the president asked for military volunteers. Only 97,000 signed up. He then asked for the draft. At peak strength, the United States had 4.3 million men under arms; the draft was canceled after the war's end in November 1918. It was America's first draft since the Civil War.

1933: Franklin Roosevelt signed the Tennessee Valley Authority (TVA) Act, a Depression-era economic development program. The TVA program brought navigation, flood control, electricity generation, fertilizer manufacturing, and economic development to the Tennessee Valley, a region particularly affected by the Great Depression.

QUOTE OF THE DAY

It is an unfortunate human failing that a full pocketbook often groans more loudly than an empty stomach.

Franklin D. Roosevelt

May 19

1828: In a move that widened the North/South divide, John Quincy Adams signed the Tariff Act of 1828. It protected northern industries that were being hurt by low-priced imports—but southern businesses were hurt, angering southern citizens. The Tariff Act, largely forgotten today, was one of many issues that together, caused southern resentment against the north to build—and eventually boil over into the Civil War thirty-three years later.

1921: Warren Harding signed the Emergency Quota Act into law, limiting immigration. Fears that the United States was being overrun by immigrants sparked the law, which limited the number of immigrants from any given country to 3% of that nationality already in the United States by 1910. It was followed by an even harsher anti-immigration law in 1924 (see May 26).

1943: Franklin Roosevelt and British prime minister Winston Churchill set May 1, 1944, as D-Day—the date for the Normandy landings against Nazi-occupied France. Weather delayed the actual invasion until June 6.

⭐ QUOTE OF THE DAY

He who knows best knows how little he knows.

Thomas Jefferson

May 20

1862: Abraham Lincoln signed the Homestead Act, giving 160 acres of land to family farmers ("homesteaders"). It was the first of a series of U.S. laws that gave an applicant ownership of land (called a "homestead") at little or no cost. The Homestead Acts were at first proposed as an expression of the "Free Soil" policy of northerners who wanted individual farmers to own and operate their own farms—in contrast to southern slave-owners who used slaves to operate farms.

1995: In the wake of the Oklahoma City bombing (see April 19), traffic on Pennsylvania Avenue in front of the White House was barred. President Bill Clinton and the Secret Service feared that a truck bomb, like the one used to destroy the Alfred P. Murrah Federal Building, could be detonated in front of the executive mansion as well. Today, that stretch of Pennsylvania Avenue is a pedestrian plaza.

⭐ QUOTE OF THE DAY

We cannot allow ourselves to be frightened or intimidated into a bunker mentality. We cannot allow our sacred freedoms to wither or diminish. We cannot allow the paranoia and conspiracy theories of extreme militants to dominate our society.

Bill Clinton

This Day in Presidential History

May 21

1961: After race riots broke out in Montgomery, Alabama, John F. Kennedy sent 300 federal marshals into the city. The president sent the marshals in after Alabama governor John Patterson said he could not guarantee that law and order would be maintained. The Montgomery riots were connected to the Freedom Rides, in which civil rights activists traveled the South by bus challenging segregation.

★ QUOTE OF THE DAY

Too often we ... enjoy the comfort of opinion without the discomfort of thought.

John F. Kennedy

May 22

1824: James Monroe signed the Tariff of 1824 into law, pleasing northern manufacturers but angering southern cotton growers, who feared retaliation from a major southern trading partner: Great Britain.

1947: Harry Truman signed a bill endorsing his "Truman Doctrine," which authorized aid to two nations—Greece and Turkey—that were threatened by Soviet communism. Some $400 million in aid was sent—an event that some historians say marked the beginning of the Cold War between the United States and Soviet Union.

1964: Lyndon B. Johnson unveiled his Great Society. In a speech at the University of Michigan, the president said its goals were to end poverty and racial injustice in the United States. It would ultimately encompass, among other things, civil rights, an expanded war on poverty, new education programs, Medicare and Medicaid, and cultural endeavors such as the National Endowment for the Arts and National Endowment for the Humanities.

1972: Richard M. Nixon arrived in Moscow, and became the first sitting president to visit the Soviet capital. But Nixon was not the first president to visit the Soviet Union itself: Franklin Roosevelt visited Yalta in the Soviet Crimea for the famous 1945 Yalta Conference with British prime minister Winston Churchill and Soviet premier Josef Stalin.

1977: Jimmy Carter said the United States had an "inordinate fear of communism" and instead human rights would be the focus of his foreign policy. The president's comments came during an address at Notre Dame University.

★ QUOTE OF THE DAY

I believe we can have a foreign policy that is democratic, that is based on fundamental values, and that uses [U.S.] power and influence … for humane purposes. I have a quiet confidence in our own political system. Because we know that democracy works, we can reject the arguments of those rulers who deny human rights to their people.

Jimmy Carter

May 23

1992: The end of the Cold War saw big reductions in nuclear weapons, when George H.W. Bush and the leaders of four former Soviet republics—Russia, Belarus, Ukraine, and Kazakhstan—agreed to the Lisbon Protocol. The United States and Soviet Union had signed the START I nuclear disarmament treaty in July 1991, but the U.S.S.R.'s collapse later that year left those arms reductions in doubt. Russia, as the successor state, would not be able to fulfill the treaty's terms until the other former Soviet republics had either destroyed those weapons or transferred them to Russian control. The United States and Russia applied diplomatic pressure to those new countries until they did so.

★ QUOTE OF THE DAY

I'm conservative, but I'm not a nut about it.

George H.W. Bush

May 24

1844: The first telegraph line in the United States—between Washington, D.C., and Baltimore—was completed; it would soon change the American

This Day in Presidential History

presidency. The telegraph would be used by President James Polk to manage the Mexican-American War, and it gave Abraham Lincoln an edge during the Civil War.

1883: Chester Arthur dedicated an American marvel: the Brooklyn Bridge. Along with New York governor and soon-to-be president Grover Cleveland, the president was astounded by the bridge, which connected the New York City boroughs of Manhattan and Brooklyn. Using new construction techniques, it was the longest suspension bridge in the world at the time—and one of the most revolutionary structures ever built.

1973: Richard M. Nixon hosted the largest dinner in White House history, welcoming newly freed prisoners of war from Vietnam. More than 1,200 guests attended.

2002: In the Kremlin, George W. Bush and Russian president Vladimir Putin signed a nuclear arms treaty, vowing to slash their nations' arsenals by two-thirds over the next ten years. SORT—the Strategic Offensive Reductions Treaty—would leave each country's nuclear arsenal to between 1700 and 2200 deployed warheads.

An engineering marvel then and now, and one of the great symbols of New York City: the Brooklyn Bridge. Dedicated by President Chester Arthur on May 24, 1883. Library of Congress.

★ QUOTE OF THE DAY

Am I not destroying my enemies when I make friends of them?

Abraham Lincoln

May 25

1961: John F. Kennedy called for the United States to land a man on the moon by the end of the decade. JFK's speech to Congress had a sense of urgency. Just six weeks earlier, the Soviet Union had put the first man in orbit—Yuri Gagarin. Kennedy saw the space program as a competition—of ideas, technology, and politics—between America and the U.S.S.R., and between democracy and communism. He said America should "go into space because whatever mankind must undertake, free men must fully share." Kennedy, of course, did not live to see his audacious goal achieved, but in July 1969, two astronauts—Neil Armstrong and Edwin "Buzz" Aldrin—walked on the moon.

★ QUOTE OF THE DAY

We stand, as we have always stood from our earliest beginnings, for the independence and equality of all nations. This nation was born of revolution and raised in freedom. And we do not intend to leave an open road for despotism.

John F. Kennedy

May 26

1868: The Senate acquitted Andrew Johnson on two impeachment charges. Ten days earlier, lawmakers had come within one vote or removing the president from office on another charge (see May 16).

1924: Calvin Coolidge signed an immigration law giving priority to those with education and job skills—particularly those from northern Europe. The law, coming in the wake of World War I, reflected the isolationist

This Day in Presidential History

desire of many Americans, who feared unfair competition for jobs from immigrants—even if those immigrants were mostly unskilled and uneducated.

The law also established quotas, limiting immigration to 2% of any given nation's residents already in the United States as of 1890. Japanese immigrants were completely barred from the quotas, while Canadians and Mexicans remained exempted. In 1927, the "two percent rule" was eliminated and a cap of 150,000 total immigrants annually was established.

1994: Bill Clinton said his administration would no longer link China's trade status with its human rights record. Echoing his predecessor George H.W. Bush, the president thought China's human rights record would improve if it wasn't linked to possible trade sanctions.

★ QUOTE OF THE DAY

Legislation can neither be wise nor just which seeks the welfare of a single interest.

Andrew Johnson

May 27

1921: Warren Harding agreed to raise trade tariffs—which wound up destabilizing the global economy. The president signed the Emergency Tariff Act, aimed at protecting American farm products from foreign competition. The protectionist legislation, with its heightening economic nationalism, ultimately hurt international commerce.

1929: A key presidential power—the pocket veto—was upheld by the Supreme Court. After a bill is passed, the Constitution gives a president ten days to review it. If the president has not signed the bill after those ten days, it becomes law without his (or her) signature. But if Congress adjourns during the ten-day period, the bill does not become law. The "Pocket Veto Case" (full name *Bands of the State of Washington v. United States* and *Okanogan, Methow, San Poelis, Nespelem, Colville, and Lake Indian Tribes v. United States*) concerned whether Native Americans in Washington State could sue the federal government for damages from the loss of their tribal lands.

This Day in Presidential History

1941: Alarmed by Nazi Germany's threats of world domination, Franklin D. Roosevelt declared a national emergency. In a radio address, the president warned Germany that the United States was prepared to go to war if necessary. FDR foresaw a frightening future if the Nazis weren't stopped, a future in which Americans would be enslaved, godless Nazis would outlaw freedom of worship, and America's children would be forced to goose-step. Roosevelt's comments were also aimed at isolationists who wanted to keep America out of the war. He reminded them that German submarines were attacking British shipping and threatening American shipping in the Atlantic and how brave British civilians were being ruthlessly bombed by the Nazis. The president repeated a famous line from his first inaugural address in 1933: "The only thing we have to fear is fear itself."

★ QUOTE OF THE DAY

When you see a rattlesnake poised to strike, you do not wait until he has struck to crush him.

Franklin D. Roosevelt

May 28

1830: Andrew Jackson signed the Indian Removal Act, giving him additional power to speed the forced removal of Native American communities from the eastern United States to territories west of the Mississippi River. Their removal cleared the way for white settlers to move in. The forced relocation of the Creek, Chickasaw, Cherokee, Choctaw, and Seminole tribes—on the "Trail of Tears"—resulted in thousands of deaths (including an estimated one-third of the Choctaw Nation).

1937: From the White House, Franklin D. Roosevelt pushed a button, allowing the first vehicles to cross the Golden Gate Bridge. The bridge, an engineering marvel that linked San Francisco to Marin County, was one of the great infrastructure projects not just of the Roosevelt era, but the twentieth century itself.

1972: The Watergate break-in you never heard about. Burglars associated with Richard M. Nixon's reelection team broke into Democratic National Committee headquarters. They didn't get all they wanted, so broke in again on June 17. This second time they were caught—setting in motion the scandal that toppled the president.

2011: Barack Obama became the first president to sign a bill without actually signing it. From Europe, he had an autopen sign an extension of the Patriot Act. The extension of George W. Bush's Patriot Act gave the federal government ongoing powers on roving wiretaps, surveillance of suspicious individuals, and more. (An early version of the autopen was invented by Thomas Jefferson.)

⭐ QUOTE OF THE DAY

They have neither the intelligence, the industry, the moral habits, nor the desire of improvement which are essential to any favorable change in their condition. Established in the midst of another and a superior race, and without appreciating the causes of their inferiority or seeking to control them, they must necessarily yield to the force of circumstances and ere long disappear.

Andrew Jackson, Fifth Annual Message, December 3, 1833, on the forced removal of Native Americans from their native lands

May 29

1917: John F. Kennedy was born in Brookline, Massachusetts. He was the thirty-fifth president, serving from 1961 to 1963. He was both the youngest president ever elected and—after his assassination on November 22, 1963—the youngest to die.

Kennedy's short-lived administration was marked by an energetic, restless approach to domestic and global challenges. In his inaugural address—regarded as one of the finest ever given—he told Americans, "Ask not what your country can do for you; ask what you can do for your country." He asked nations of the world to join together to fight what he called the "common enemies of man: tyranny, poverty, disease, and war itself," and added: "All this will not be finished in the first one hundred days. Nor will it be finished in the first one thousand days, nor in the life of this Administration, nor even perhaps in our lifetime on this planet. But let us begin."

Kennedy challenged the United States to land a man on the moon by the end of the decade (see May 25); he saw the space race as the ultimate competition with the Soviet Union, and between democracy and communism. But the United States and Soviets had serious confrontations on the ground: in Berlin, where the communists built a wall to keep its citizens from fleeing to the West, and in Cuba, where the presence of Soviet nuclear missiles nearly led to war between the two superpowers.

1988: Ronald Reagan arrived in Moscow—the capital of what he once called "The Evil Empire"—for a summit with Soviet leader Gorbachev. His landmark speech to students there (see May 31) is often overlooked, but is one of the finer Reagan addresses on the enduring allure of Western values.

★ QUOTE OF THE DAY

Let us not seek the Republican answer or the Democratic answer, but the right answer. Let us not seek to fix the blame for the past. Let us accept our own responsibility for the future.

John F. Kennedy

John F. Kennedy. Photographer unknown. Papers of John F. Kennedy. Presidential Papers. White House Staff Files of Dean F. Markham. John F. Kennedy Presidential Library and Museum, Boston.

This Day in Presidential History

May 30

1854: Buildup to the Civil War: Franklin Pierce signed the Kansas-Nebraska Act. It allowed people in the new territories of Kansas and Nebraska to decide for themselves whether or not to allow slavery. It repealed the Missouri Compromise of 1820 which prohibited slavery north of latitude 36°30′. The president feared it would make growing tensions over slavery worse—but signed it anyway, after senators threatened to block appointments. The Kansas-Nebraska Act was the most important piece of legislation of Pierce's presidency. His support in northern states faded, dealing his presidency a fatal blow (see June 16).

1922: The Lincoln Memorial, built to honor America's sixteenth president, was dedicated by Warren Harding. In attendance were William Howard Taft, who was president when the site for the memorial was chosen in 1913, and Lincoln's only surviving son, Robert Todd Lincoln. The building is in the form of a Greek Doric temple and contains a large seated sculpture of Abraham Lincoln and inscriptions of two well-known speeches by Lincoln: the Gettysburg Address and his second inaugural address.

1990: After the fall of the Berlin Wall, George H.W. Bush and Soviet leader Mikhail Gorbachev met to discuss the future of Germany. The Soviet Union had just lost its East European empire during a wave of revolutions in 1989, and the U.S.S.R. itself was showing increasing signs of strain. The future of Germany was of particular interest. The United States wanted a reunified Germany to be a member of NATO, while Moscow, mindful of being invaded by Germany during World War II, did not. In July 1990, Bush offered the Soviets economic aid and promised that Germany would not present a threat to the U.S.S.R.; Gorbachev relented, and in October 1990, a reunified Germany became a member of the Western military alliance.

★ QUOTE OF THE DAY

The dangers of a concentration of all power in the general government of a confederacy so vast as ours are too obvious to be disregarded.

Franklin Pierce

May 31

1790: George Washington signed the first U.S. copyright law. It was the first comprehensive attempt by the federal government to codify U.S. copyright protections.

1921: Teapot Dome—the biggest presidential scandal before Watergate—began during Warren Harding's presidency, when control of government oil reserves in Wyoming and California were transferred to the Interior Department. The department was run by the president's appointee Albert Fall (see April 7 and January 2).

1988: In Moscow, Ronald Reagan told Soviet students about freedom—and of his hope that they would be able to experience it. Reagan's speech—one of the last major addresses of his presidency—had a valedictory tone, as the Cold War wound down.

★ QUOTE OF THE DAY

Freedom is the right to question and change the established way of doing things. It is the continuing revolution of the marketplace. It is the understanding that allows us to recognize shortcomings and seek solutions. It is the right to put forth an idea, scoffed at by the experts, and watch it catch fire among the people. It is the right to dream—to follow your dream or stick to your conscience, even if you're the only one in a sea of doubters. Freedom is the recognition that no single person, no single authority or government has a monopoly on the truth, but that every individual life is infinitely precious, that every one of us put on this world has been put there for a reason and has something to offer.

Ronald Reagan

June

June 1

1812: Without explicitly asking for a declaration of war against Britain, James Madison made the case for it during a speech to Congress. Madison listed several grievances against Britain: it had been seizing American sailors and forcing them to serve in the Royal Navy; it was conducting illegal blockades, and it was renewing Indian warfare in the northwest. Madison told lawmakers that these acts constituted war and that for the United States to ignore them would undermine American sovereignty through an implicit acceptance of British actions. On June 4, the House of Representatives voted 79-49 for war, followed by a 19-13 Senate vote on June 17—and the War of 1812 was on.

Sandwiched between the Revolutionary and Civil Wars, the War of 1812 is often overlooked, but had enormous consequences for the United States. The United States would prevail, but not before invading British troops set fire to both the White House and Capitol (see August 24).

1868: James Buchanan died at Lancaster, Pennsylvania. He was the fifteenth president, serving from 1857 to 1861. Historians consider Buchanan one of the worst presidents, largely for his failure to prevent the Civil War.

1990: George H.W. Bush and Soviet President Mikhail Gorbachev agreed to stop producing chemical weapons and to destroy 25% and 40%, respectively, of their stockpiles.

★ QUOTE OF THE DAY

Whether the United States shall continue passive under these ... accumulating wrongs, or, opposing force to force in defense of their national rights, shall commit a just cause into the hands of the Almighty Disposer of Events ... is a solemn question which the Constitution wisely confides to the legislative department of the Government. In recommending it to their early deliberations I am happy in the assurance that the decision will be worthy the enlightened and patriotic councils of a virtuous, a free, and a powerful nation.

James Madison

June 2

1856: For the first time, a sitting president—Franklin Pierce—was denied his party's nomination for a second term. Democrats nominated former secretary of state James Buchanan instead. The president's standing had been irreparably damaged by his pro-Southern views, particularly on slavery—notably his support for the pro-slavery Kansas-Nebraska Act of 1854 (see May 30).

1886: Grover Cleveland became the first president to marry in the White House. The forty-nine-year-old president tied the knot with Frances Folsom, who was just twenty-one—the youngest first lady in U.S. history. The ceremony, attended by about forty people, was held in the Blue Room on the mansion's state floor.

1933: Franklin D. Roosevelt inaugurated the White House's indoor swimming pool. FDR had polio and the pool, with sterilized water, was a favorite retreat. It was converted in 1970, during the administration of President Richard M. Nixon, into what is today the press briefing room.

★ QUOTE OF THE DAY

As I would not be a slave, so I would not be a master. This expresses my idea of democracy.

Abraham Lincoln

June 3

1961: Cold War tensions rose—as a meeting between John F. Kennedy and Soviet leader Nikita Khrushchev went poorly. The president later said that Khrushchev bullied him on a variety of foreign affairs matters, such as threatening to cut off Western access to Berlin and fighting any country that tried to stop him. Within the next year and a half, Washington and

Moscow would confront each other over the building of the Berlin Wall (see August 13) and Cuban Missile Crisis (see October 16).

★ QUOTE OF THE DAY

Let us never negotiate out of fear. But let us never fear to negotiate.

John F. Kennedy

June 4

1800: John Adams became the first president to reside in Washington, D.C. The White House wasn't ready for him just yet (see November 1), so the president took a room at Union Tavern in Georgetown. The next day the president would move to a tavern, Tunnicliffe's, on Capitol Hill, where he would remain for the next five months.

1934: Franklin Roosevelt asked Congress for $53 million to battle the "Dust Bowl." Severe drought in much of the Great Plains dried the soil, and winds blew it away in vast clouds that reached as far as the East Coast. Millions of acres of farmland were destroyed, and hundreds of thousands of people were forced to abandon their homes. Many of these families migrated to California and elsewhere.

Pierre L'enfant's plan for Washington, D.C., in a 1792 revision by Andrew Ellicott.
Library of Congress.

This Day in Presidential History

1946: Harry Truman signed the National School Lunch Act—to provide healthy lunches for millions of American schoolchildren.

★ QUOTE OF THE DAY

No nation is any healthier than its children.

Harry Truman

June 5

1933: In another move to combat the Great Depression, Franklin Roosevelt took the United States off the gold standard. Bank failures had scared Americans into hoarding gold. FDR declared a bank holiday shortly after taking office, which helped stabilize and restore confidence in the banking system. The president followed up with this new policy on gold, which forbade banks from paying customers in gold or exporting it.

2004: Ronald Reagan died in Bel Air, California. He was the fortieth president, serving from 1981to 1989. Many historians credit Reagan—who was known as "The Great Communicator"—for helping to win the Cold War and for helping to revive the U.S. economy during his tenure. On a January 20 to January 20 basis, 5.3 million jobs were created during the president's first term and 10.7 million in his second term. But Reagan also presided over a tripling of the federal debt, an expanded government workforce, and taxes that were raised on gasoline and on businesses to the tune of $420 billion ($925 billion in 2016 dollars) by raising corporate taxes and closing loopholes.

★ QUOTE OF THE DAY

America is too great for small dreams.

Ronald Reagan

June 6

1833: Andrew Jackson became the first president to ride in a train. The president boarded a Baltimore & Ohio Railroad train for a pleasure trip to Baltimore.

This Day in Presidential History

1934: Franklin Roosevelt signed the Securities Exchange Act, which established the Securities and Exchange Commission (SEC), which helps ensure that U.S. financial markets are operated in a "fair, orderly, and efficient" manner. The following day, Congress passed the Corporate Bankruptcy Act, allowing corporations facing bankruptcy to reorganize if two-thirds of its creditors agree. Both bills addressed factors which had contributed to the Great Depression.

1944: D-Day. America held its breath as Allied forces landed in France on Normandy Beach. Franklin Roosevelt asked citizens to pray. The U.S.-led invasion of Nazi-occupied France—the third single bloodiest day in American history—hastened the end of World War II in Europe.

1968: After Senator Robert F. Kennedy's murder on this day, an angry Lyndon B. Johnson said, "Violence may bring down the very best among us." Kennedy, the brother of an assassinated president, was gunned down as he sought the presidency himself. Prior to Robert Kennedy's murder, presidential candidates were not given Secret Service protection. That policy changed.

2002: George W. Bush proposed a new cabinet agency: the Department of Homeland Security (DHS). The creation of DHS was part of a reorganization of the federal government in the wake of the September 11, 2001, terror attacks on the United States.

★ QUOTE OF THE DAY

Our sons, pride of our Nation, this day have set upon a mighty endeavor, a struggle to preserve our Republic.

Franklin D. Roosevelt's D-Day prayer to the nation

D-Day was the third single bloodiest day in American history. Second bloodiest day was September 11, 2001, when terrorists attacked New York and Washington, and first was the Civil War battle of Antietam, on September 17, 1862, which claimed almost 23,000 killed, wounded, or missing.

June 7

1892: Benjamin Harrison became the first president to attend a major league baseball game. The Cincinnati Reds beat the Washington Senators,

7-4. Even back then, baseball fans probably said of Washington: "First in war, first in peace. Last in the American/National league."

★ QUOTE OF THE DAY

There is no dignity quite so impressive, and no one independence quite so important, as living within your means.

Calvin Coolidge

June 8

1845: Andrew Jackson died at The Hermitage, Nashville, Tennessee. He was the seventh president, serving from 1829 to 1837. A hero of the War of 1812, Jackson's presidency became known as the era of "Jacksonian democracy," characterized by a strong assertion of executive powers— at the expense of the legislative branch. Jackson is also known for the founding of the Democratic Party.

Known as "Old Hickory" for his toughness (he participated in at least thirteen duels and was shot twice), and the "people's president" for his populist views, Jackson dismantled the Second Bank of the United States (see July 10)—which he viewed as corrupt, elitist, and bound to corporate interests—and backed policies that resulted in the forced migration of Native Americans from their homelands so white settlers could move in. The policy resulted in thousands of deaths (see May 28).

President Jackson also became the first president to use his veto power as a matter of policy—as opposed to rejecting legislation, as predecessors had, on the grounds that it was unconstitutional. And in a squabble that foreshadowed the Civil War, the president threatened to use force against South Carolina after the Palmetto state declared federal tariffs null and void and threatened to leave the Union (see December 10).

1956: Dwight Eisenhower was taken to Walter Reed hospital for an emergency operation to remove an intestinal blockage. Doctors feared that President Eisenhower might not survive the operation (he had suffered a heart attack nine months earlier), and his health became an issue during his reelection campaign. He went on to win a landslide reelection (see November 6).

This Day in Presidential History

1982: Ronald Reagan said communism would wind up on the "ash heap of history." In a speech to the British parliament, the president said that Soviet communism had failed, and that it would soon fade away. Seven years later, the Berlin Wall fell (see November 9), and, in 1991, the Soviet Union itself would collapse.

★ QUOTE OF THE DAY

I was born for a storm and the calm does not suit me.

Andrew Jackson

This is the birthday of Barbara Bush, who was born on June 8, 1925, in New York City. She is the wife of the forty-first president—George H.W. Bush, who served from 1989 to 1993—and the mother of the forty-third president—George W. Bush, who served from 2001 to 2009. The "silver fox," as her family calls her, focused on promoting literacy during her tenure as First Lady.

June 9

1886: Grover Cleveland asked Congress to approve an extradition treaty with Japan. The president asked Congress to consider legislation that allowed for Japanese immigrants who committed crimes—before fleeing home to Japan—to be extradited back to the United States for trial.

★ QUOTE OF THE DAY

A government for the people must depend for its success on the intelligence, the morality, the justice, and the interest of the people themselves.

Grover Cleveland

June 10

1801: Thomas Jefferson ordered U.S. forces into war against the Barbary Coast states of North Africa. Pirates from what are today Morocco, Libya,

Tunisia, and Algeria captured merchant ships and held crews for ransom. For years, the United States had paid either ransom or tribute—but now Jefferson sought an end.

Previously, a Muslim envoy told Jefferson that it was wrong for the United States not to acknowledge Muhammad—thus America had sinned. The envoy told Jefferson that because the United States was a sinner nation, "it was the right and duty of the faithful to plunder and enslave" it. The Muslim envoy didn't know of U.S. admiration of Muhammad, whose thoughts are cited as Constitutional precedent. John Adams praised him, and if you visit the Supreme Court, you'll see a frieze bearing an image of Muhammad; justices see it each day.

1921: Warren Harding signed the Budget and Accounting Act, requiring presidents to submit annual budgets to Congress. It was the first time a president would be required to submit spending plans for the entire federal government to Congress for approval.

1940: The United States edged closer to World War II. As Nazi Germany overran western Europe, Franklin Roosevelt, in a speech at the University of Virginia, announced that the United States stance toward the war would change from "neutrality" to "non-belligerency." The move meant that the United States would now openly support the Allies, notably Great Britain, without actually going to war against the Axis.

1963: Offering an olive branch to Moscow, John F. Kennedy called for the United States and Soviet Union to pursue peace. In a speech at American University, he pointed out that the United States and U.S.S.R. shared more similarities than differences, and should focus on them. The speech is regarded as one of Kennedy's finest.

1999: Bill Clinton ordered an end to "Operation Allied Force," the U.S.-led bombing campaign against Serbia, after Serb forces agreed to withdraw from Kosovo. American troops joined a 50,000-man peacekeeping force to enforce the agreement. The bombing campaign began on March 24, a response to Serbian aggression in Kosovo and Albania, and reports of ethnic cleansing.

★ QUOTE OF THE DAY

Let us not be blind to our differences—but let us also direct attention to our common interests and to the means by which those differences can be resolved. And if we cannot end now our differences, at least we can

This Day in Presidential History

help make the world safe for diversity. For in the final analysis, our most basic common link is that we all inhabit this small planet. We all breathe the same air. We all cherish our children's future. And we are all mortal.

John F. Kennedy

June 11

1800: The new city of Washington in the District of Columbia became the official capital of the United States, succeeding Philadelphia. It would not be until November that Congress convened in the new capital and President John Adams moved into the new Executive Mansion (see November 1).

1963: A day after sending National Guard troops to the University of Alabama, John F. Kennedy issued a proclamation forcing Governor George Wallace to let black students register for classes. Wallace—known for his cry "Segregation now! Segregation tomorrow! Segregation forever!"—literally stood at the door of the school's enrollment office, surrounded by state troopers, to defy federal orders. But he eventually gave in and let two African-American students—Vivian Malone and James A. Hood—enroll. The president vowed to send comprehensive civil rights legislation to Congress; his wishes were the basis for the 1964 Civil Rights Act, passed after his assassination (see July 2).

★ QUOTE OF THE DAY

The rights of every man are diminished when the rights of one man are threatened.

John F. Kennedy

June 12

1924: George H.W. Bush was born in Milton, Massachusetts. He was the forty-first president, serving from 1989 to 1993. Bush was the last U.S. president to have served in World War II. A navy pilot, he flew fifty-eight missions over the Pacific, and was shot down on September 2, 1944.

Before being elected to the presidency, Bush was a Texas congressman, ambassador to the United Nations, chairman of the Republican National Committee, head of the U.S. liaison office to China (not ambassador, since the United States did not have formal diplomatic ties with Beijing at the time), director of the CIA, and Ronald Reagan's vice president.

As president, Bush was known for his leadership during the collapse of communism and the end of the Cold War, and for his decision to go to war against Iraq in January 1991, after Saddam Hussein invaded neighboring Kuwait five months before. A mild recession contributed to Bush's failed reelection bid in 1992. Bush was the second president whose son (George W. Bush) also became president. The other pair? John Adams and John Quincy Adams. President Barack Obama awarded former president George H. W. Bush the Medal of Freedom in 2011.

1963: "Barbaric"—was an outraged John F. Kennedy's reaction to the murder of civil rights activist Medgar Evers, who was cut down today by a sniper at his home, with his two children watching.

1971: A White House wedding: Tricia Nixon, the eldest daughter of Richard and Pat Nixon, married Edward Finch Cox in the Rose Garden.

1987: In one of the most famous—and one of the last—speeches of the Cold War, Ronald Reagan, in front of the Berlin Wall, challenged Soviet leader Mikhail Gorbachev to "tear down this wall!" At the time, Reagan's dramatic speech was seen as a call for the Soviet Union to resume

George H.W. Bush.

This Day in Presidential History

negotiations on reducing nuclear weapons—and they did. But something even more dramatic occurred just two years later: the Wall did indeed fall, a symbolic end to the Cold War in Europe.

★ QUOTE OF THE DAY

America is never wholly herself unless she is engaged in high moral principle. We as a people have such a purpose today. It is to make kinder the face of the nation and gentler the face of the world.

George H.W. Bush

June 13

1807: Thomas Jefferson received a subpoena to testify before Congress in the treason trial of his former vice president, Aaron Burr. The president would tell lawmakers that Burr tried to split several states from the Union, create an independent nation in the center of North America, and make himself its ruler. Burr was eventually acquitted.

1898: William McKinley signed the War Revenue Act, to help pay for the Spanish-American War. The measure generated revenue from taxes levied on beer, tobacco, amusements, and some business transactions.

1967: Lyndon B. Johnson nominated Solicitor General Thurgood Marshall to be the first black justice on the Supreme Court. "I believe he earned that appointment; he deserves the appointment," the president said. "He is best qualified by training and by very valuable service to the country. I believe it is the right thing to do, the right time to do it, the right man and the right place."

1971: The Pentagon Papers, a secret history of the Vietnam War, were published, infuriating Richard M. Nixon. It was the name given to a secret Defense Department study of U.S. involvement in Vietnam dating from 1945 to 1967. In 1968, a Pentagon analyst named Daniel Ellsberg (who had worked on the study) grew to oppose the war. He secretly photocopied the report and in March 1971 gave it to the *New York Times*. The *Times*, followed by the *Washington Post*, published it. Even though the Pentagon Papers dealt with a period when Nixon wasn't president, he tried, and failed, to stop their publication, in hope that it would deter anyone from revealing secrets about his own administration in the future. The Supreme Court ruled in favor of the *Times* and *Post.*

★ QUOTE OF THE DAY

If one morning I walked on top of the water across the Potomac, the headline that afternoon would read: "President Can't Swim."

Lyndon B. Johnson

June 14

1922: Warren Harding became the first president to be heard on the radio—and the first to install a radio in the White House. The broadcast of Harding's speech dedicating a memorial site for Francis Scott Key began a revolutionary shift in how presidents communicated with Americans. But neither Harding nor his next two successors—Calvin Coolidge or Herbert Hoover—were very effective on radio; it took Franklin D. Roosevelt to truly leverage its vast power (see March 12).

1946: Donald Trump was born. The forty-fifth president, he has served since 2017. Before entering politics, Trump, the oldest person ever elected to a first term as president, spent decades in the real estate and construction business, running a company firm founded by his paternal grandmother. He also wrote several business books and hosted a popular reality TV show, *The Apprentice*, which aired on NBC from 2004 to 2015. In 2017, *Forbes* magazine estimated Trump's net worth at $3.5 billion, making him the wealthiest person ever elected president.

1954: Dwight Eisenhower signed a bill adding "under God" to the Pledge of Allegiance. Critics said it blurred the line between church and state.

★ QUOTE OF THE DAY

I don't like losers.

Donald Trump

This Day in Presidential History

Donald Trump. Official White House portrait.

June 15

1846: James Polk and the Oregon Treaty. As part of America's "Manifest Destiny" policy, the northern border of the United States was established at the forty-ninth parallel, giving the United States control of what is today Idaho, Washington, Oregon, and Montana. It also gave the United States access to the Pacific Ocean through the channel south of Vancouver Island and avoided a possible war with Britain.

1849: James K. Polk died of cholera at his home in Nashville, Tennessee. He was the eleventh president, serving from 1845 to 1849. Polk, just fifty-three, had left office three months before. His remains lie (with those of his wife, Sarah) at the Tennessee State Capitol in Nashville, after being moved from two prior resting places.

1863: Abraham Lincoln asked for 100,000 troops to protect Washington, D.C., from General Robert E. Lee's advancing Confederate Army. Lee's Army of Northern Virginia had advanced to the Potomac River, and the president—who could see enemy campfires from the White House—feared the nation's capital was in jeopardy. But Lee didn't attack Washington; his troops moved into Pennsylvania for a showdown at Gettysburg, regarded as the key turning point in the Civil War (see July 3).

1917: At Woodrow Wilson's request, Congress approved the Espionage Act, placing strict wartime limits on freedom of expression, and mandating that public criticism of the military or the government be punished by a $10,000 fine or up to twenty years in jail.

★ QUOTE OF THE DAY

Well may the boldest fear and the wisest tremble when incurring responsibilities on which may depend our country's peace and prosperity.

James Polk

June 16

1858: Future president Abraham Lincoln gave his famous "House Divided" speech, warning that slavery was tearing America apart. Along with the Gettysburg Address and his second inaugural address, the speech was the finest of Lincoln's career. Given in the wake of the Supreme Court's 1857 Dred Scott decision (which ruled that blacks were not American citizens and that the federal government had no power to regulate slavery in any territory acquired after the United States became a sovereign nation), Lincoln said that America could be one or the other: a nation where slavery was allowed everywhere—or nowhere at all.

1909: William Howard Taft proposed a constitutional amendment allowing the government to tax personal income. In a message to Congress, the president also asked for a 2% tax on all businesses except for banks. Four years later—and following the ratification of the Sixteenth Amendment—the Revenue Act of 1913 ushered in the first federal income tax since the Civil War.

1933: Franklin D. Roosevelt's "100 Days" (see March 4) ended with a flurry of legislation. The most important bill passed by Congress was the National Industry Recovery Act (NIRA). It established two important New Deal agencies: the Public Works Administration (PWA) and the National Recovery Administration (NRA). The PWA focused on providing jobs through the construction of roads, public buildings, and other projects; the NRA stimulated competition in the marketplace. Congress also passed the Banking Act of 1933, establishing the Federal Bank Deposit Insurance Corporation, and the Farm Credit Act.

1941: With war looming, Franklin D. Roosevelt ordered the closure of all German consulates in the United States. Six months later, Nazi Germany and the United States would declare war on each other (see December 11).

1992: The United States and Russia agreed to slash stocks of nuclear weapons. The Soviet Union had just dissolved, and George H.W. Bush and

This Day in Presidential History

Russian leader Boris Yeltsin agreed to reduce their country's arsenals of nuclear warheads to between 3,000 and 3,500 by the year 2003.

2004: The National Commission on Terrorist Attacks Upon the United States (9/11 Commission), set up to investigate the September 11, 2001, terror attacks on the United States, found "no credible evidence" of Iraqi involvement. The findings contradicted what some in the administration of George W. Bush believed and came a year after the United States invaded Iraq and ousted its leader, Saddam Hussein. Both Bush and his vice president, Dick Cheney, had insisted there were "long-established ties" between Iraq and the terror group al Qaeda. The report, later published in full on July 22, 2004, stated that while al Qaeda's leader, Osama bin Laden, had explored the idea of forging ties with Iraq, Baghdad never aided him.

★ QUOTE OF THE DAY

A house divided against itself cannot stand. I believe this government cannot endure, permanently, half slave and half free. I do not expect the Union to be dissolved—I do not expect the house to fall—but I do expect it will cease to be divided. It will become all one thing or all the other. Either the opponents of slavery will arrest the further spread of it, and place it where the public mind shall rest in the belief that it is in the course of ultimate extinction; or its advocates will push it forward, till it shall become lawful in all the States, old as well as new—North as well as South.

Abraham Lincoln, June 16, 1858

June 17

1930: Ignoring the advice of many economists, Herbert Hoover agreed to raise trade tariffs. The president hoped that signing the Smoot-Hawley Tariff Act would help pull the U.S. economy out of a deepening depression. But it caused other countries to raise their own tariffs as well; global trade fell as a result. Many historians believe this "economic nationalism" made both the international depression and nationalist tensions worse.

1972: The biggest political scandal in U.S. history—Watergate—began when five men were caught and arrested for breaking into Democratic National Committee headquarters in Washington's Watergate Office Building. It was actually the second break-in (see May 28). The scandal unraveled over the next two years, leading to the first-ever resignation of a president, Richard M. Nixon (see August 8–9). Watergate also resulted in the indictment, trial, conviction, and incarceration of forty-three people, including dozens of top Nixon administration officials.

★ QUOTE OF THE DAY

Let us begin by committing ourselves to the truth ... find the truth ... speak the truth ... live the truth.

Richard M. Nixon

June 18

1798: The first of the Alien and Sedition Acts was passed, sparking fierce criticism of John Adams. The acts put front and center the issues of free speech and the balance of power between states and the federal government. The president and the Federalist-dominated Congress signed off on four key pieces of legislation:

1. The Naturalization Act said anyone wanting to become an American citizen had to be a resident for fourteen years (previously, it had been five years).
2. The Alien Act authorized the president to deport any alien considered dangerous to national security.
3. The Alien Enemies Act allowed the president to deport aliens of an enemy country or restrict their freedom in times of war.
4. The Sedition Act targeted Americans themselves—by outlawing opposition to federal laws, and by making it illegal to publish criticism of the government.

The acts were passed in the wake of the chaotic French Revolution. Fearing similar unrest, Adams and his Federalist allies in Congress sought a strong central government. But political opponents—namely, the Democratic-Republican party and its most prominent leader Thomas Jefferson (who happened to be Adams's vice president)—thought the opposite: that the people were best served by a government with minimal power. Domestic opposition to the Alien and Sedition Acts wound up hurting Adams; in one of the nastiest campaigns in American history, he would lose to Jefferson in the presidential election of 1800.

This Day in Presidential History　　　　　　　　　　　　　　　**169**

1812: James Madison signed a congressional declaration of war against Great Britain—the War of 1812.

1979: Jimmy Carter signed a nuclear arms treaty with the Soviet Union. The second Strategic Arms Limitation Treaty (SALT II) was never ratified by the Senate, but both Washington and Moscow voluntarily complied with its terms.

★ QUOTE OF THE DAY

Remember Democracy never lasts long. It soon wastes, exhausts, and murders itself. There never was a Democracy yet, that did not commit suicide.

John Adams, in a December 17, 1814, letter

June 19

1934: Franklin D. Roosevelt signed the Communications Act of 1934. It launched the Federal Communications Commission (FCC), to regulate the nation's radio (and later television) airwaves. It also regulated the telephone industry.

1942: Franklin D. Roosevelt met with British prime minister Winston Churchill to plan the invasion of North Africa. On November 8, 107,000 Allied troops landed in Morocco and Algeria, under the command of General Dwight D. Eisenhower.

1964: A historic legislative victory for Lyndon B. Johnson: Congress approved the Civil Rights Act. The most sweeping domestic legislation in a century, the Civil Rights Act banned discrimination on the basis of race, religion, or national origin. It also gave the federal government new powers to enforce desegregation.

★ QUOTE OF THE DAY

You aren't learning anything when you're talking.

Lyndon B. Johnson

June 20

1803: Thomas Jefferson gave orders to Captain Meriwether Lewis to explore (with William Clark) the newly acquired Louisiana Territory. The territory—828,000 square miles—had been purchased from Napoleon that spring for $15 million. Lewis and Clark's journey, which would last from May 1804 to September 1806, would map the vast territory and take note of its plants, animals, geography, and other natural resources. The president also instructed Lewis and Clark to be friendly with native peoples in the territory and to establish trade ties with them.

1979: Jimmy Carter climbed onto the White House roof to celebrate the installation of solar power panels. As the United States was hit by oil shortages during the 1970s, Carter believed renewable energy could help the country ease its dependence on imports. The 32 solar panels cost $28,000 and generated enough energy to provide hot water for the entire 132-room mansion. President Ronald Reagan removed the panels in 1986, saying the energy crisis of the 1970s was a thing of the past.

★ QUOTE OF THE DAY

The energy crisis has not yet overwhelmed us, but it will if we do not act quickly.

Jimmy Carter

June 21

1982: A jury found John Hinckley, Jr., not guilty by reason of insanity in the shooting of President Ronald Reagan and three others (see March 30). Hinckley spent thirty-five years in a mental hospital before being released, in September 2016, to his family's custody in Williamsburg, Virginia.

★ QUOTE OF THE DAY

There's no more exhilarating feeling than being shot at without result.

Ronald Reagan, quoting Winston Churchill

The two women who tried to kill Gerald Ford in 1975 have also been freed from prison. Lynette "Squeaky" Fromme, who pulled a gun on Ford in Sacramento, California (see September 5), was released on parole in 2009, after serving thirty-four years in prison. Sara Jane Moore, who fired a shot at the president seventeen days later in San Francisco (see September 17), was freed in 2007. She later told NBC that she was tired of being criticized.

June 22

1877: Rutherford Hayes banned federal employees from engaging in political activities. The president's executive order—aimed at stopping corruption in the civil service—said that federal workers would neither be "required or permitted" to participate in "political organizations, caucuses, conventions, or election campaigns." Federal employees could still vote, of course.

1944: Franklin D. Roosevelt signed the GI Bill to provide financial aid to veterans returning from World War II. It gave returning service members low-interest home and business loans and college tuition. Giving veterans tuition assistance (plus living expenses, books, supplies, and equipment) transformed America. Before the war, only 10%–15% of young Americans went to college; by 1947, vets made up half of the nation's college enrollment, and by 1950 nearly 500,000 Americans had earned diplomas, compared with 160,000 in 1939.

2011: Barack Obama announced the first U.S. troop withdrawals from Afghanistan and pledged a pullout by the end of 2014. After peaking at about 100,000 troops in 2010–2011, troop levels declined to 16,000 by December 2014. In 2015, the president said conditions were too fragile to leave and that 9,800 troops would remain through most of 2016. In 2016, he said the security situation remained "precarious" and that 8,400 troops would remain through the end of his term on January 20, 2017.

★ QUOTE OF THE DAY

With the signing of this bill a well-rounded program of special veterans' benefits is nearly completed. It gives emphatic notice to the men and women in our armed forces that the American people do not intend to let them down.

Franklin D. Roosevelt

June 23

1972: Six days after the Watergate break-in, Richard M. Nixon ordered the FBI to back off on its investigation. The president's order was conveyed through his chief of staff H.R. Haldeman.

Transcripts of their conversation—released after an order from the Supreme Court two years later (see August 5)—became known as Watergate's "smoking gun" for proving that the president not only knew about the break in of Democratic National Committee headquarters (see June 17), but tried to cover it up.

☆ QUOTE OF THE DAY

You open that scab there's a hell of a lot of things and that we just feel that it would be very detrimental to have this thing go any further.

Richard M. Nixon

June 24

1853: Franklin Pierce signed the Gadsden Purchase—a treaty with Mexico that gave the United States approximately 45,000 square miles of territory that is today part of Arizona and New Mexico.

1908: Grover Cleveland died in Princeton, New Jersey. He was the twenty-second and twenty-fourth president, serving from 1885 to 1889 and from 1893 to 1897, respectively. Cleveland lost his reelection bid in 1888 to Benjamin Harrison, even though he won the popular vote (which also happened in 1824, 1876, 2000, and 2016). If he had won his home state (New York), he'd have been reelected. But Cleveland got his revenge on Harrison in 1892.

Cleveland was the only Democrat elected to the presidency between 1860 and 1912, an era thoroughly dominated by Republicans. He was a pro-business, free market president who hated subsidies and tariffs. He was an icon of American conservatives.

Cleveland was the only president to get married in the White House in 1886. His bride was Frances Folsom, the daughter of a close Cleveland friend. He was forty-nine. She was twenty-one.

This Day in Presidential History

A Cleveland biographer noted that "he possessed honesty, courage, firmness, independence, and common sense ... to a degree other men do not," though that didn't stop the president from being snared in a political scandal of his own making. In 1874, a lover gave birth to a boy. Both Cleveland and the woman, Maria Halpin, were single, and although Cleveland wasn't sure that the child was his, he claimed paternity and helped place the boy for adoption. It gave Republicans fodder to attack Cleveland during the campaign of 1884. The joke went: "Ma, Ma, where's my Pa?" to which a Cleveland supporter answered: "Gone to the White House, ha, ha, ha!"

1950: Harry Truman was informed by Secretary of State Dean Acheson that North Korea had invaded South Korea (it was June 25 in Korea itself). Two days after the North Korean attack, the president ordered U.S. forces to respond. America, he said, would contain communism.

★ QUOTE OF THE DAY

Above all, tell the truth.

Grover Cleveland

June 25

1798: Congress passed the Alien Act, giving John Adams the power to deport any alien he deemed potentially dangerous to the country's safety. It was the second of the controversial Alien and Sedition Acts—which sparked fierce criticism of the president (see June 18).

1845: James Polk ordered General Zachary Taylor to move his troops to the Mexican border in Texas—to discourage a Mexican invasion. Taylor's troops would soon invade Mexico itself, during the Mexican-American War.

1929: Herbert Hoover authorized the building of Boulder Dam, now known, of course, as Hoover Dam. Built during the Great Depression, the dam—the biggest in the world at the time of its completion in 1935—straddles the Colorado River on the border between Nevada and Arizona. It stores enough water in Lake Mead to irrigate two million acres and serves as a popular tourist destination.

1938: Franklin D. Roosevelt signed the Fair Labor Standards Act, establishing a forty-hour week and a minimum wage for American workers. In nominal terms, the first minimum wage, in 1938, was $0.25 an hour—equivalent to about $4.29 in 2016 dollars.

1997: Bill Clinton signed off on Environmental Protection Agency (EPA) regulations that sharply tightened air pollution controls in the United States. The president was caught between the EPA, which pushed for the stricter standards, and many big city mayors and corporations, who said that the tighter rules would cost money and jobs.

★ QUOTE OF THE DAY

I approved some strong new regulations today that will be somewhat controversial. But I think kids should be healthy.

Bill Clinton

June 26

1844: John Tyler, fifty-four, married Julia Gardiner, twenty-four, in a private ceremony in New York City. It was the first time a sitting president had gotten married. Julia became the youngest first lady (later eclipsed by Frances Folsom Cleveland, see June 2).

Tyler fathered fifteen children with his two wives. Some were fathered late in life—as late as seventy—and because several sons also fathered children late in their own lives, President Tyler—born in 1790—still has, as of spring 2017, two living grandchildren.

1934: Franklin D. Roosevelt signed the Federal Credit Union Act, establishing the first credit unions. Begun during the depth of the Great Depression, it made financial credit available to millions of Americans. Congress that day also passed the Federal Emergency Relief Act (FERA), which gave immediate grants to states for economic projects. It was designed to directly help some of the fourteen million Americans who were unemployed.

1948: On Harry Truman's orders, U.S. and British forces began the Berlin Airlift to supply their garrisons and the population of Berlin. The airlift became necessary after Soviet troops began a blockade of West Berlin, cutting off all road and rail access between the city and western Europe.

This Day in Presidential History

It was a contest of wills between Truman and Soviet premier Josef Stalin, and Truman was determined to win. Allied aircraft flew relief missions around the clock, delivering as many as 5,000 tons of supplies daily. Planes arrived every thirty seconds at multiple airports. Stalin lifted the blockade on May 12, 1949, but the airlift continued until the autumn of that year.

1963: In West Berlin, John F. Kennedy delivered his "Ich bin ein Berliner" ("I am a Berliner") address to an audience of 450,000. Condemning the Berlin Wall, which he said showed the failure of the communist system, the president made it clear that the United States would support West Berlin, an enclave of freedom that was surrounded on all sides by communist-controlled East Germany. The Berlin Wall was built in 1961 (see August 13) to keep its citizens from fleeing to the West. It was guarded around the clock by heavily armed soldiers, who were trained to shoot anyone trying to escape. During the twenty-eight years the wall stood, some 5,000 people attempted to escape; an estimated 600 were killed. The Berlin Wall was the most visible symbol of the Cold War and a hated symbol of communist oppression.

1990: George H.W. Bush's tax flip-flop. After famously declaring "no new taxes" during his 1988 campaign, the president, worried about deficits, issued a statement saying tax increases might be necessary in 1991. It would contribute to his failed reelection bid in 1992.

1993: Bill Clinton ordered an attack on Baghdad. The president ordered the navy to fire cruise missiles at Iraqi intelligence headquarters in the Iraqi capital—after learning that Iraqis had plotted to kill former president George H.W. Bush during his April 1993 visit to Kuwait.

☆ QUOTE OF THE DAY

There are many people in the world who really don't understand—or say they don't—what is the great issue between the free world and the Communist world. Let them come to Berlin.

John F. Kennedy

June 27

1950: Harry Truman ordered the Air Force and Navy to help defend South Korea after a North Korean invasion. U.S. ground forces would soon get into the Korean fight as well (see June 30); by the time a truce was signed in 1953, 36,516 Americans would be killed. The Korean War—"the forgotten war"—officially has not ended, and a state of war still exists today.

★ QUOTE OF THE DAY

The attack upon Korea makes it plain beyond all doubt that communism has passed beyond the use of subversion to conquer independent nations and will now use armed invasion and war.

Harry Truman

June 28

1836: James Madison died at his Montpelier plantation home in Orange, Virginia. He was the fourth president, serving from 1809 to 1817. Madison is known as "Father of the Constitution," because he was its principal author; in 1788, he wrote more than a third of the *Federalist Papers*, still the most influential commentary on the Constitution itself. He also wrote the Bill of Rights (the first ten amendments to the Constitution). Madison helped bring the capital to what is now Washington, D.C., saying it needed to be secure after citizens attacked Congress in Philadelphia in 1783. But the new capital wasn't secure. After vowing to defend "every inch" against the British in the War of 1812, President Madison fled; the city was torched. James and Dolley Madison spent the remainder of their presidency at a nearby mansion while the White House was rebuilt.

1934: In his continued efforts to rejuvenate the economy, Franklin D. Roosevelt signed two key bills. The Federal Farm Bankruptcy Act placed a moratorium on foreclosures of farms, and the Federal Housing Administration (FHA)—designed to stimulate homebuilding—was created.

1957: Dwight Eisenhower dedicated the Islamic Center in Washington. "I should like to assure you, my Islamic friends, that under the American Constitution, American tradition, and in American hearts, this Center, this place of worship, is just as welcome as could be a similar edifice of any other religion. Indeed, America would fight with her whole strength for your right to have here your own church and worship according to your own conscience."

This Day in Presidential History

★ QUOTE OF THE DAY

The truth is that all men having power ought to be mistrusted.

James Madison

June 29

1947: Harry Truman became the first president to address the NAACP—the National Association for the Advancement of Colored People. The president said it was his deep conviction that the United States had "reached a turning point in the long history of our country's efforts to guarantee freedom and equality to all our citizens." He said it was more important than ever to make sure that all Americans enjoyed those rights, and "When I say all Americans," Truman said, "I mean all Americans."

1956: The single largest public works program in U.S. history—the Interstate Highway Act—was signed into law by Dwight Eisenhower. The president didn't sign the 41,000-mile highway bill for the principal benefit of commuters. It was a primarily a defense project—designed to move troops and material quickly during wartime, and to evacuate citizens in the event of nuclear war. The federal government agreed to pay 90% of the cost, with funds coming from a 3-cents-a-gallon tax on gasoline.

★ QUOTE OF THE DAY

Many of our people still suffer the indignity of insult, the narrowing fear of intimidation, and, I regret to say, the threat of physical injury and mob violence. Prejudice and intolerance in which these evils are rooted still exist. The conscience of our Nation, and the legal machinery which enforces it, have not yet secured to each citizen full freedom from fear. We cannot wait another decade or another generation to remedy these evils. We must work, as never before, to cure them now.

Harry Truman

June 30

1812: With America at war again with Britain, James Madison issued an emergency declaration for new military officers. In 1812, the U.S. Army and Navy was an all-volunteer force (as it is today) and was considered weaker in both numbers and weaponry than Britain. There was a particular lack of officers who could lead. Madison urged Congress to increase emergency commissions of military officers, adjutants, quartermasters, inspectors, paymasters, and engineers.

Among the troops who would distinguish themselves in the War of 1812 (often called America's second war of independence) were two future presidents: William Henry Harrison and Andrew Jackson.

1882: James Garfield's assassin was executed. Charles Guiteau shot the twentieth president the year before (see July 2); Garfield lingered for eleven weeks before passing away. He was the second president to be murdered in sixteen years.

1906: Safer food was the goal of Theodore Roosevelt's Meat Inspection Act of 1906, signed this day. The president and lawmakers—moved after reading *The Jungle*, a 1906 novel that exposed unsanitary conditions and unfair labor practices in meatpacking plants by Upton Sinclair—designed the bill to provide better inspection and labeling of food processing plants in the United States.

1921: Warren Harding appointed former president William Howard Taft to be chief justice of the Supreme Court. Taft was easily confirmed by the Senate; he became the only person in history to head both the executive and judicial branches of government.

1950: Harry Truman ordered U.S. ground forces to Korea to help repel an invasion by communist North Korea (see June 25 and 27). He feared it was the beginning of World War III.

★ QUOTE OF THE DAY

Presidents come and go, but the Supreme Court goes on forever.

William Howard Taft

July

July 1

1862: Abraham Lincoln signed the Pacific Railroad Act, calling for the completion of a transcontinental railroad; it was completed on May 10, 1869. The government issued bonds to pay for the railroad; the president knew the investment would stimulate the economy and facilitate development of the western United States.

1863: A nervous Abraham Lincoln monitored the pivotal battle of the Civil War—Gettysburg. The Battle of Gettysburg lasted three days and produced the greatest number of casualties of the entire Civil War: 46,286 dead, wounded, or missing. The Union victory stopped Confederate General Robert E. Lee's invasion of the North; for the remainder of the war Lee would be in the defensive.

1893: Grover Cleveland's secret operation: In a parlor/"operating theater" of the yacht *Oneida,* anchored in Long Island Sound, physicians cut out a cancerous tumor, upper left palate, jawbone, and five teeth of the president of the United States. All aspects of the operation were kept secret because Cleveland feared that news of the risky surgery would spark financial and public panic. On July 5, Cleveland began his recuperation at his summer home and was later fitted with a prosthesis. The general public was none the wiser—official word was that the president had a toothache—until 1917, when an attending doctor on the *Oneida* broke his silence in a *Saturday Evening Post* article.

1944: The Bretton Woods Conference, also called the United Nations Monetary and Financial Conference, was held from July 1 to July 22, 1944. Having gained the upper hand over both Germany and Japan in World War II, the Allies began looking to the postwar era. A core belief of Franklin D. Roosevelt—borrowed from a prior wartime leader, Woodrow Wilson—was that free trade promoted not only international prosperity, but international peace. The 1930s, after all, with its trade barriers, currency devaluations, and other types of economic nationalism contributed to instability and geopolitical tensions—and ultimately war. This 1944 conference established two key pillars of the international monetary system: the International Monetary Fund (IMF) and the International Bank for Reconstruction and Development (IBRD).

2015: Barack Obama announced that the United States and Cuba would open embassies in each other's capitals, ending fifty-four years of diplomatic estrangement between the two neighboring nations.

★ QUOTE OF THE DAY

The probability that we may fail in the struggle ought not to deter us from the support of a cause we believe to be just.

Abraham Lincoln

July 2

1881: James Garfield was shot as he prepared to board a train in Washington, D.C. The bullet lodged in his back. The president didn't seem too concerned, telling bystanders who had seen the attack, "I don't think this is serious. I will live." But thanks in part to sloppy medical care, Garfield died seventy-nine days later (see September 19). Garfield had been in office just 119 days when he was shot; his assailant, a deranged office seeker named Charles Guiteau, was sentenced to death in January 1882 and hanged five months later.

> Robert Todd Lincoln, the president's son, was at the scene of three presidential assassinations: his father's in 1865, Garfield's in 1881, and William McKinley's in 1901. And another coincidence: Robert Todd Lincoln's life was once saved by Edwin Booth, older brother of his father's assassin, John Wilkes Booth.

1890: Benjamin Harrison signed the Sherman Anti-Trust Act. It was aimed at breaking up companies that had become, in the government's estimation, monopolies that hurt competition. The law would rarely be enforced, however, until the presidency of Theodore Roosevelt.

1964: Lyndon B. Johnson signed what is arguably the most important piece of legislation of the twentieth century—the Civil Rights Act. The Civil Rights Act outlawed racial and sexual discrimination, unequal voting requirements, and discrimination in the workplace and public facilities.

This Day in Presidential History

★ QUOTE OF THE DAY

If government is to serve any purpose it is to do for others what they are unable to do for themselves.

Lyndon B. Johnson

July 3

1894: Grover Cleveland sent troops to Chicago to put down a strike by railroad workers of the Pullman Company. Eugene Debs, president of the American Railway Union, organized the strike after George Pullman lowered worker wages during the depression of 1893. The strike spread throughout the country, affecting twenty-seven states and territories. U.S. troops arrested Debs and the strike ended.

1930: Herbert Hoover signed a bill creating the Veterans Administration. The Veterans Administration Act consolidated several federal agencies into a single department.

1938: On the seventy-fifth anniversary of the Battle of Gettysburg (see July 1), Franklin Roosevelt dedicated an Eternal Light Memorial—attended by 1,870 Civil War veterans (whose average age was ninety-four). The eternal flame at Gettysburg (now powered by electricity) inspired Jacqueline Kennedy a quarter-century later to have an eternal flame over her husband's grave at Arlington National Cemetery.

1979: Jimmy Carter signed a secret directive ordering aid to opponents of a pro-Soviet regime in Afghanistan.

★ QUOTE OF THE DAY

All of them we honor, not asking under which flag they fought then—thankful that they stand together under one flag now.

Franklin D. Roosevelt at the dedication of the Gettysburg Memorial

July 4

1803: Thomas Jefferson announced the Louisiana Purchase to the American people. The deal with Napoleon doubled the size of the United

This Day in Presidential History

States, encompassing what today are fifteen states. Napoleon, who needed the money for his war on Britain, said the Louisiana Purchase "affirms forever the power of the United States."

1826: On the fiftieth anniversary of American independence, two of its principal architects—the only presidents who signed the Declaration of Independence itself—died: John Adams and Thomas Jefferson. Adams, the second president, served from 1797 to 1801; Jefferson, the third President, served from 1801 to 1809. In addition to serving as president, Jefferson also served as vice president, secretary of state, and governor of Virginia. But Jefferson wanted none of these things mentioned on his tombstone. Instead, he wanted only three accomplishments listed: his authorship of the Declaration of Independence and of the statute of Virginia for religious freedom, and the foundation of the University of Virginia. You can, of course, see Jefferson's grave at the spectacular Monticello—his home near Charlottesville. It is covered with—what else—nickels.

Founding fathers and friends during the early years of the republic, Adams and Jefferson eventually grew into political rivals—facing off in the election of 1796, which Adams won, and in 1800, when Jefferson did. The two grew estranged from each other, only to rekindle their friendship late in life. When Adams passed, his last words were, "Thomas Jefferson still survives." Little did he know that his friend-turned-rival-turned-friend had passed away just a few hours earlier. Jefferson's last recorded words were more prosaic: "No, doctor, nothing more," though it has also been claimed that he asked from his death bed "Is it the Fourth?" or "This is the Fourth of July."

1831: James Monroe died in New York City. He was the fifth president, serving from 1817 to 1825 (for a review of his life, see April 28).

1872: Calvin Coolidge was born in Plymouth Notch, Vermont. He was the thirtieth president, serving from 1923 to 1929. He became president when Warren Harding died suddenly in 1923; he was sworn in in the middle of the night by his father, who was a notary.

A staunch Republican, a laissez-faire president who believed that "the business of America is business," Coolidge's 1920s are seen today as a golden era, a decade sandwiched between a great war and a great depression. Despite three downturns during that decade—including two on the president's watch—the economy expanded overall, with wages growing and unemployment remaining low. Americans prospered, connected as never before by electricity, automobiles, telephones, radio, and movies.

This Day in Presidential History   **183**

Life moved faster, though driven partly underground by Prohibition. It was an era of materialism, hedonism, and excess, depicted so wonderfully in F. Scott Fitzgerald's novel *The Great Gatsby*. In short, times were good, they were loud, and they were fun; the decade came to be known as the "Jazz Age," the "Roaring Twenties"—and the era of "Coolidge Prosperity."

The taciturn Coolidge was known as "Silent Cal." Once, a woman bet she could get three words out of him. Coolidge: "You lose."

Calvin Coolidge. Library of Congress.

★ QUOTE OF THE DAY

You will never know how much it has cost my generation to preserve your freedom. I hope you make good use of it.

John Adams

Most presidents had pets, of course. But Coolidge went above and beyond, maintaining a mini zoo that consisted of, among other things, six dogs, a bobcat, a goose, a donkey, a cat, two lion cubs, an antelope, and a wallaby. He even had a pygmy hippopotamus named Billy—a gift from Harvey Firestone, the tire magnate. Coolidge donated the animal—said to be six feet long and weighing 600 pounds—to the Smithsonian's National Zoo.

July 5

1865: The Secret Service began operations. Founded on April 14, 1865—the day of Abraham Lincoln's assassination—its original mission was to stop counterfeiting and was not involved in presidential security. It began informal, part-time protection of presidents in 1894 (under Grover Cleveland). It began official, full-time protection of presidents in 1902—after the assassination of President William McKinley (see September 6).

1865: Andrew Johnson signed an executive order allowing the execution of four people who conspired to kill President Abraham Lincoln and other top government officials. The Lincoln conspirators were tried by a military court because Lincoln had been commander in chief of the U.S. Army.

1935: Franklin D. Roosevelt signed the National Labor Relations Act, which set guidelines for business-labor ties, including collective bargaining by labor unions.

⭐ QUOTE OF THE DAY

By assuring the employees the right of collective bargaining it fosters the development of the employment contract on a sound and equitable basis … it seeks, for every worker within its scope, that freedom of choice and action which is justly his.

Franklin D. Roosevelt

July 6

1946: George W. Bush was born in New Haven, Connecticut. He was the forty-third president, serving from 2001 to 2009. Bush was the second son of a president to assume that office himself (the first was John Quincy Adams). Declared the winner of the presidency by the Supreme Court after one of the closest elections in American history (see December 12), Bush was in office for eight months when the United States was attacked (see September 11). Al Qaeda terrorists, using hijacked passenger jets, destroyed both towers of New York City's World Trade Center, hit the Pentagon with a third, and attempted to

George W Bush. Official White House portrait by Eric Draper.

attack another target in Washington, D.C.—probably the White House or Capitol—before that plane was downed after a counterattack by passengers.

The September 11, 2001, attacks defined the remainder of Bush's presidency. He declared a global war on terror, invaded Afghanistan—launching pad for the 9/11 attacks—and, more controversially, invaded Iraq. The president reorganized the federal government's vast intelligence gathering network, created the Department of Homeland Security, and signed the Patriot Act, which gave the government, among other things, the power to spy on American citizens without a search warrant.

On the domestic front, Bush pushed for and won large tax cuts. He signed the No Child Left Behind Act, the Partial-Birth Abortion Ban Act, and Medicare prescription drug benefits for seniors. He rejected the Kyoto Protocol—a global treaty to combat climate change.

Reelected in 2004, Bush's second term was marked—in addition to the war on terror—by his handling of Hurricane Katrina and, beginning in 2006, the collapse of the housing market and broader U.S. economy, which led to a series of economic bailouts in 2008. The president left office in 2009 a polarizing figure with some of the lowest approval ratings in American history.

★ QUOTE OF THE DAY

The wisest use of American strength is to advance freedom.

George W. Bush

July 7

1798: John Adams named George Washington commander in chief of the United States Army. A possible war with France loomed, and ever the patriot, Washington—who had retired a year earlier after two terms as president—wrote his successor: "Feeling how incumbent it is upon every person, of every description, to contribute at all times to his Countrys [*sic*] welfare, and especially in a moment like the present, when every thing we hold dear & Sacred is so seriously threatened, I have finally determined to accept the Commission of Commander in Chief of the Armies of the United States, with the reserve only, that I shall not be called into the field until the Army is in a Situation to require my presence, or it becomes indispensable [*sic*] by the urgency of circumstances."

1898: William McKinley signed a resolution that annexed Hawaii as a U.S. territory; it would become the fiftieth state in 1959.

1958: North to Alaska. Dwight Eisenhower signed a bill approving Alaskan statehood. Alaska had been a U.S. territory since its purchase from the Russians in 1867. The United States paid just $7.2 million, or 2.3 cents an acre (see October 18).

1981: Ronald Reagan nominated Sandra Day O'Connor to be the first female justice on the Supreme Court. She was Reagan's first appointee to the high court. O'Connor generally sided with the court's conservative bloc, but as the court edged to the right over the years, she often came to be regarded as a swing vote. She retired in 2005 and was replaced by another conservative, Samuel Alito.

★ QUOTE OF THE DAY

If we desire to avoid insult, we must be able to repel it; if we desire to secure peace, one of the most powerful instruments of our rising prosperity, it must be known, that we are at all times ready for War.

George Washington

This Day in Presidential History

July 8

1919: Woodrow Wilson returned from the Versailles Conference in France, which set peace terms at the end of World War I.

1950: After the United Nations Security council adopted a resolution calling on the United States to name a commander for U.N. forces in Korea, Harry Truman appointed General Douglas MacArthur. It was a move the president would soon regret. As the Korean War wore on, MacArthur went public with his proposal to bomb China, angering Truman. The president would eventually fire the general (see April 11).

★ QUOTE OF THE DAY

People call me an idealist. Well, that is the way I know. I am an American. America is the only idealistic nation in the world.

Woodrow Wilson

July 9

1850: Zachary Taylor died in Washington, D.C. Known as "Old Rough and Ready" for his forty years of military service, he was the twelfth president, serving from 1849 to 1850. Just sixteen months into his term, he fell ill on the fourth of July and died from an unknown intestinal affliction (his physician described it as "cholera morbus." "I am about to die," he said, "I expect the summons soon. … I have endeavored to discharge all my official duties faithfully. I regret nothing, but am sorry that I am about to leave my friends."

1868: The Fourteenth Amendment to the Constitution was ratified, granting citizenship to "all persons born or naturalized in the United States," which included former slaves recently freed.

2002: George W. Bush called for a crackdown on corporate financial corruption. Accounting scandals had rocked major companies like Enron and WorldCom. The president said laws were needed "to punish abuses, restore investor confidence, and protect the pensions of American workers."

★ QUOTE OF THE DAY

When abuses like this begin to surface in the corporate world, it is time to reaffirm the basic principles and rules that make capitalism work, truthful books and honest people and well-enforced laws against fraud and corruption. All investment is an act of faith, and faith is earned by integrity. In the long run, there's no capitalism without conscience; there is no wealth without character.

George W. Bush

The death of Zachary Taylor, probably from an intestinal affliction, and the death—nine years years earlier—of President William Henry Harrison may be linked. Contemporary reports suggested that Harrison contracted pneumonia from standing in cold, foul weather during his inaugural address, but this is not true (see April 4). Harrison probably died from typhus—possibly from human feces—in the White House water supply. Researchers think it may have also caused Taylor's death in 1850—and possibly James K. Polk's as well. Polk died just three months after his presidency ended, and researchers speculate that he might have been exposed to the same bacteria before leaving the White House.

July 10

1832: Andrew Jackson vetoed a bill that would have renewed the charter for the Second Bank of the United States. The Second Bank of the United States was created in the aftermath of the War of 1812 and had been controversial ever since. Many people—including the president—blamed it for the Panic of 1819, and Westerners and Southerners felt that the bank in general, and its lending policies in particular, favored Northern interests over their own.

1850: Vice President Millard Fillmore was sworn in as the thirteenth president. Only the second man to ascend to the presidency after the death of his predecessor (Zachary Taylor), Fillmore immediately began working to ease growing tensions over slavery. Unlike Taylor, who opposed the Compromise of 1850, Fillmore supported it, helping congressional titans of the day like Henry Clay, Daniel Webster, and Stephen Douglas get it passed (see September 18). Fillmore's swearing in capped a tumultuous time in the history of the American presidency: six presidents in nine years.

★ QUOTE OF THE DAY

The honor of my country shall never be stained by an apology from me for the statement of truth or for the performance of duty.

Andrew Jackson

July 11

1767: John Quincy Adams was born in Braintree, Province of Massachusetts Bay. He was the sixth president, serving from 1825 to 1829. Adams, the son of America's second president—John Adams—became president even though he lost both the popular vote and the electoral college vote to Andrew Jackson in the 1824 election (see February 9). Ironically, after Adams became president, he hated it, calling his time in the White House the "four most miserable years of my life." After the presidency, Adams served in the House of Representatives for seventeen years. He had previously been a U.S. senator as well.

John Quincy Adams. Library of Congress.

This Day in Presidential History

1995: Bill Clinton extended full diplomatic recognition of Vietnam, twenty-two years after U.S. participation in the Vietnam War ended.

★ QUOTE OF THE DAY

If your actions inspire others to dream more, learn more, do more and become more, you are a leader.

John Quincy Adams

July 12

1862: Abraham Lincoln signed a bill creating the Medal of Honor. It is the highest military decoration awarded by the U.S. government. It is given to those who have distinguished themselves in actual combat at risk of life beyond the call of duty. Since its creation, during the Civil War, more than 3,500 men and one woman have received the Medal of Honor for heroic actions in U.S. military conflicts.

1957: Dwight Eisenhower became the first president to fly in a helicopter. The president began using helicopters for convenience, but also because the Secret Service wanted a way to evacuate him from the White House quickly if needed. Eisenhower's first helicopter (a Bell H-13J flown by the Air Force) could only sit two comfortably, so the president sat with the pilot. It was also slow, with a top speed of about 100 mph. Eisenhower flew often from the White House to Camp David (named for his grandson) and to his farm in Gettysburg, Pennsylvania. The president himself had a pilot's license but wasn't allowed to fly.

Until 1955, the Secret Service refused to allow presidents on aircraft with less than four engines. Until 1976, presidential helicopters were flown by the Army ("Army One") or Marines ("Marine One"). The Marines assumed responsibility for all missions in 1976.

★ QUOTE OF THE DAY

Honor to the soldier and sailor everywhere, who bravely bears his country's cause. Honor, also, to the citizen who cares for his brother in the field and serves, as he best can, the same cause.

Abraham Lincoln

This Day in Presidential History

July 13

1973: A Watergate bombshell: Testifying before Senate investigators, a former Nixon administration official, Alexander Butterfield, confirmed the existence of an extensive White House taping system. Butterfield—who for a time was President Nixon's deputy chief of staff—was one of the few people who knew of the taping system, because he told the Secret Service to install it. Three days later, he gave more details before the Senate Watergate Committee itself—and the Nixon presidency began to unravel. Had it not been for Butterfield's revelation, the system might have stayed secret. A year later, the Supreme Court would order the president to turn over key tapes related to Watergate (see July 24).

1985: Ronald Reagan transferred his presidential power to Vice President George H.W. Bush for eight hours. Mr. Reagan did so after a cancerous polyp was discovered in his intestine, prompting surgery. Shortly before his operation, the president sent a five-paragraph letter to the president pro tem of the Senate and the speaker of the House transferring presidential power to Bush. During Reagan's surgery, Bush exercised no constitutional powers of the presidency, and at 7:22 p.m. that evening, Reagan signed another letter reclaiming his presidential authority. "I am able to resume the discharge of the constitutional powers and duties of the office of the President," the letter said in part.

★ QUOTE OF THE DAY

I like the dreams of the future better than the history of the past.

Thomas Jefferson, to John Adams in 1816

July 14

1913: Leslie Lynch King Jr.—who would change his name to Gerald Ford—was born in Omaha, Nebraska. He was the thirty-eighth president, serving from 1974 to 1977. Just two weeks after he was born, his parents Leslie Lynch King and Dorothy Ayer Gardner separated. In 1917, Dorothy married her second husband—Gerald R. Ford—and the couple began calling the boy Gerald R. Ford, Jr., though his name was not legally changed until December 3, 1935.

Known as the "Accidental President," Ford was named vice president by Richard M. Nixon after Vice President Spiro Agnew's resignation in October 1973 (see October 10). Ford would then succeed Nixon himself after Nixon resigned in August 1974 (see August 8-9). Thus, Ford was the only person in American history to become both vice president and president without being elected to either office.

A month after being sworn in, Ford pardoned Nixon, causing critics to charge that the two men made a deal. Ford denied it, but it contributed to his loss in the 1976 election. Ford also served on the Warren Commission, which investigated the assassination of President Kennedy, which concluded that Lee Harvey Oswald acted alone.

Because he made a few errant golf swings and slipped on the steps of Air Force One, Ford was depicted as a klutz by the media (and, famously, by Chevy Chase on *Saturday Night Live*). In fact, Ford was perhaps the most athletic president. Ford was center and linebacker on the University of Michigan football team that went undefeated and won back-to-back national championships in 1932 and 1933. Offered NFL contracts by both the Detroit Lions and Green Bay Packers; he chose to attend Yale Law School instead. He was a World War II naval officer and fought in

Gerald Ford. Official White House portrait.

This Day in Presidential History

the Pacific. He came home, married a fashion model, Elizabeth (Betty) Warren, and was elected to thirteen terms in Congress.

2015: Barack Obama announced that the United States, Britain, France, Russia, China, and Germany reached a deal with Iran to curb its nuclear program. The deal between the so-called "P5+1" and Iran called for a gradual lifting of energy/financial sanctions in return for Iranian limits on its nuclear production capability. The United States, which continued to name Iran on its list of nations that sponsored terror, said the deal would help ensure that "Iran's nuclear program is and remains exclusively peaceful."

★ QUOTE OF THE DAY

I have had a lot of adversaries in my political life, but no enemies that I can remember.

Gerald Ford

July 15

1971: A stunning announcement from Richard M. Nixon: he would visit communist China in early 1972. Nixon's journey to China—arguably the most dramatic trip ever taken by a president— opened the door for increased ties and competition between the two superpowers. It also marked China's emergence into the modern world, a development of monumental consequence.

1979: Jimmy Carter warned that the United States was threatened by a lack of "moral and spiritual confidence." He said that this lack of confidence was to blame for an ongoing recession—and was a "fundamental threat to American democracy." The speech is often referred to Carter's "malaise" address, though he never actually used that word.

★ QUOTE OF THE DAY

Associate with men of good quality if you esteem your own reputation; for it is better to be alone than in bad company.

George Washington

This Day in Presidential History

July 16

1790: George Washington signed the Residence Act, a bill authorizing the moving of the nation's capital from Philadelphia. The new location would be 130 miles to the south along the Potomac River, comprised of land donated by Maryland to the north and Virginia to the south. The area would be called the District of Columbia. It would include the preexisting settlements of Georgetown and Alexandria. In 1846, Congress would return the land originally donated by Virginia. On September 9, 1791, officials overseeing the capital's construction named the city in honor of President Washington.

1877: Rutherford B. Hayes sent troops to end the Great Railroad Strike of 1877. Workers on the Baltimore and Ohio (B&O) line in Maryland walked off the job after their pay was cut; the strike quickly spread to other states, threatening the economy. After some strikes became violent, the president sent in troops to ensure peace and protect mail delivery.

★ QUOTE OF THE DAY

Be courteous to all, but intimate with few, and let those few be well tried before you give them your confidence.

George Washington

The nation's capital was moved from Philadelphia to the new city of Washington for reasons of national security. In 1783, a group of unpaid soldiers attacked Congress in what came to be known as the Pennsylvania Mutiny of 1783. James Madison argued that the new federal government would need to be located in a new city that the government itself—not a state—controlled. Ironically, Madison would be president when British troops invaded that new city and burned the White House and Capitol to the ground (see August 24).

July 17

1945: Harry Truman, president for just three months, convened the Potsdam Conference with Soviet leader Josef Stalin and British prime minister Winston Churchill—until Churchill was replaced by new prime minister

Clement Atlee. The conference, held in a Berlin suburb, focused on the future of postwar Germany. The so-called "Big Three" determined how to administer punishment to the defeated Nazi Germany, which had surrendered on May 8 (V-E Day). The goals of the conference also included the establishment of postwar order, peace treaties issues, and countering the effects of the war.

★ QUOTE OF THE DAY

Though the United States wants no territory or profit or selfish advantage out of this war, we are going to maintain the military bases necessary for the complete protection of our interests and of world peace. Bases which our military experts deem to be essential for our protection, and which are not now in our possession, we will acquire. We will acquire them by arrangements consistent with the United Nations Charter.

Harry Truman, speaking to the American people on the Potsdam Conference (August 9, 1945)

July 18

1945: Harry Truman was informed of the successful test—two days before—of the first atomic bomb. The president learned of the test while in Germany at the Potsdam Conference (see July 17). He told Soviet premier Josef Stalin that the United States had "a new weapon of unusual destructive force." Stalin—who had learned of the bomb through his spies in America—replied through his translator that he hoped Truman would put it to good use against the Japanese. The president would soon do just that, bringing World War II to a close (see August 6 and 9).

1947: Harry Truman signed the Presidential Succession Act, which named the speaker of the House second in line to assume the presidency, after the vice president. The original order of presidential succession, signed by George Washington in 1792, said the president pro tem of the Senate followed the vice president. The original 1792 law was also revised in 1886, removing both the House speaker and president pro tem of the Senate from the presidential succession list.

Facts are stubborn things; and whatever may be our wishes, our inclinations, or the dictates of our passions, they cannot alter the state of facts and evidence.

John Adams

July 19

1884: Chester Arthur ordered the government to quarantine immigrants to avoid the spread of "pestilence." An economic depression gripped the United States during Arthur's presidency; citizens feared new immigrants would spread diseases like tuberculosis. Many states already had their own quarantine laws, but Arthur saw a need to widen the federal government's powers to intervene in a national health crisis. He advised cities along the coasts to "resist the power of the disease and to mitigate its severity" and urged citizens to report anyone suspected of carrying highly contagious diseases.

★ QUOTE OF THE DAY

The health of the people is of supreme importance. All measures looking to their protection against the spread of contagious diseases and to the increase of our sanitary knowledge for such purposes deserve attention of Congress.

Chester Arthur

July 20

1969: The most historic telephone call ever made by a president of the United States: Richard M. Nixon called two astronauts—Neil Armstrong and Buzz Aldrin—on the moon. *Apollo* 11's moon landing—a stunning display of American technological and economic prowess—attracted an estimated half-billion television viewers around the world, at the time, the largest audience in history. (The *Apollo* 11 crew included a third astro-

This Day in Presidential History   **197**

naut, Michael Collins, who orbited around the moon while Armstrong and Aldrin were on its surface.) Nixon's secretary recorded the phone call as an "interplanetary conversation."

1976: Gerald Ford hailed the landing on Mars by an American spacecraft— *Viking* I. The president saluted the landings of the twin robotic explorers, saying "Our achievements in space represent not only the height of technological skill, they also reflect the best in our country—our character, the capacity for creativity and sacrifice, and a willingness to reach into the unknown."

★ QUOTE OF THE DAY

Because of what you have done the heavens have become a part of man's world, and as you talk to us from the Sea of Tranquility, it inspires us to redouble our efforts to bring peace and tranquility to Earth. For one priceless moment in the whole history of man all the people on this Earth are truly one—one in their pride in what you have done and one in our prayers that you will return safely to Earth.

Richard M. Nixon to the crew of Apollo 11

July 21

1861: A Civil War setback for Abraham Lincoln: Union forces were routed in the Battle of Bull Run. The battle, near Manassas, Virginia, pitted Union General Irvin McDowell against Confederate Generals P.G.T. Beauregard and Thomas J. "Stonewall" Jackson. The defeat left Washington itself threatened—and uncertainty as to how to halt Confederate forces.

1954: The United States refused to sign an agreement that cut Vietnam in two. President Eisenhower instructed U.S. representatives not to sign the Geneva Accords, which established a ceasefire between a northern zone controlled by the predominately communist Viet Minh and a southern zone controlled by former emperor Bao Dai. An election was to be held in 1956 to create a unified Vietnam. But the president thought that the agreement gave too much power to the north, and in an irony, he feared that the communists might actually win the election.

2010: Barack Obama signed a bill to overhaul the financial industry. The Dodd–Frank Wall Street Reform and Consumer Protection Act was designed to better regulate the industry and curb excesses that helped contribute to the economic collapse of 2007–2009. It sought better transparency in the financial system, an end to the concept that banks were "too big to fail," to protect taxpayers from future bailouts (see October 3) and consumers from abusive practices of the financial services industry.

★ QUOTE OF THE DAY

I have never talked or corresponded with a person knowledgeable in Indochinese affairs who did not agree that had elections been held as of the time of the fighting, possibly 80 per cent of the population would have voted for the Communist Ho Chi Minh as their leader.

Dwight Eisenhower

July 22

1862: Abraham Lincoln told his cabinet of his Emancipation Proclamation. The president said he would issue the proclamation on January 1, 1863—setting a date for the freedom of three million black slaves (see January 1). It also redefined the Civil War itself as a fight against slavery. Up to that time, ending slavery had not been Lincoln's priority—putting down the Confederate rebellion was. The Emancipation Proclamation also did not free *all* slaves living in the United States—only slaves living in Confederate states that were beyond Union control. In practical terms, this meant two things: slaves in Confederate states would not truly be free unless the Union won the war. It also meant that slaves in states that were still loyal to the Union would not be freed; Lincoln feared antagonizing those states, whose contributions to the war effort were desperately needed.

★ QUOTE OF THE DAY

My paramount object in this struggle is to save the Union, and it is not either to save or to destroy slavery.

Abraham Lincoln, in an August 22, 1862, letter to Horace Greeley, editor of the *New York Tribune*

July 23

1885: Ulysses S. Grant died in Wilton, New York. He was the eighteenth president, serving from 1869 to 1877.

Grant encountered financial difficulties in his postpresidential years. A bad investment pushed him and wife Julia into bankruptcy. To make ends meet, he wrote his memoirs, which he finished just before he died of throat cancer. Friend Mark Twain published these memoirs to great fanfare, critical acclaim, and commercial success (providing much-needed funds to Grant's widow).

1973: Richard M. Nixon refused to release White House tape recordings related to the Watergate investigation. The Senate Watergate committee and special prosecutor Archibald Cox demanded that the president do so, saying that numerous tapes and documents were critical to their investigation. But the president, claiming executive privilege, refused. The battle would go for another year, before the Supreme Court ruled (see July 24) against Nixon.

Ulysses S. Grant was regarded as an honest and decent man, yet his presidency was tainted by corruption. Holding his administration together, at least according to this cartoon, was a high-wire act. Library of Congress.

★ QUOTE OF THE DAY

The friend in my adversity I shall always cherish most.

Ulysses S. Grant

July 24

1862: Martin Van Buren died at Kinderhook, New York. He was the eighth president, serving from 1837 to1841. Known as "Blue Whiskey Van" for his heavy drinking, Van Buren helped organize what today is the Democratic Party. The Van Buren presidency was largely characterized by the Panic of 1837 and the economic depression that followed. Critics attacked him, labeling him "Martin Van Ruin." Van Buren lost his reelection bid in 1840 to Whig candidate William Henry Harrison. (See December 5 for more about Van Buren.)

1897: William McKinley signed the Dingley Tariff Law, hiking tariffs on imported goods. Republicans said the high import tariffs helped keep the nation prosperous; Democrats said they helped spark inflation.

1955: Dwight Eisenhower presented his "Open Skies" proposal, allowing mutual air reconnaissance over the United States and Soviet Union. It was rejected by Moscow.

1967: Lyndon B. Johnson ordered 4,700 federal troops to Detroit after race riots erupted following a police raid on an unlicensed bar. An estimated 16 people were killed and 493 injured. It was the latest in a series of urban riots—such as the even deadlier riots in the Watts section of Los Angeles two years earlier—that tore through American cities during the decade. In his book *Reconstruction: America's Unfinished Revolution, 1863–1877*, writer Eric Foner said the scale of the rioting was probably surpassed only by draft riots that erupted in New York City in 1863 during the Civil War, and by the "Rodney King riots" in Los Angeles in 1992.

1974: The Supreme Court ordered Richard M. Nixon to turn over tape recordings to the Senate Watergate Committee. It was an 8-0 ruling. The tapes showed that the president not only knew about the Watergate break-in (see June 17), but tried to cover it up (see June 23). The disclosures shattered what was left of Nixon's political support. He would resign two weeks later (see August 8–9).

★ QUOTE OF THE DAY

The less government interferes with private pursuits, the better for general prosperity.

Martin Van Buren

July 25

1928: Calvin Coolidge recognized Chiang Kai-shek's Kuomintang (KMT) nationalist government of China. The United States also signed a tariff treaty with the Chinese.

1969: "The Nixon Doctrine." Looking to wind down American involvement in Vietnam, Richard M. Nixon stated that other nations (an obvious reference to Vietnam) should bear more responsibility for their own security.

1980: Carter signed Presidential Directive 59 ("PD-59") advocating "limited" nuclear war. Carter's order said that if nuclear deterrence with its enemies failed, the United States "must be capable of fighting successfully so that the adversary would not achieve his war aims and would suffer costs that are unacceptable." To make that feasible, PD-59 called for preplanned nuclear strike options and capabilities for rapid development of plans against "military and control targets."

★ QUOTE OF THE DAY

We will not learn how to live together in peace by killing each other's children.

Jimmy Carter

July 26

1918: In a proclamation, Woodrow Wilson denounced lynching. With violence against blacks on the rise, the president—who had resisted prior pleas to speak out—finally released a statement condemning mob violence and racial hatred. But Wilson was criticized for not making a public speech which would have had a greater impact.

1947: Harry Truman signed the National Security Act, a major overhaul of the U.S. national security establishment. It created the National Security Council, Central Intelligence Agency, the Department of Defense (which had been the War Department), and National Security Resources Board.

1948: Harry Truman desegregated the military. His Executive Order No. 9981 directed "equality of treatment and opportunity" in the armed forces. There was considerable opposition within the military to the president's order. Army chief of staff Omar Bradley, for example, declared that "the Army is not out to make any social reform."

1953: In a prime-time address to the nation, Dwight Eisenhower announced a truce to end the fighting in Korea. Three years after North Korea's surprise invasion of the south, igniting the Korean War, the president said that an armistice had been signed, bringing fighting to an end. A peace treaty was not signed, however—just an agreement to stop fighting. Officially, a state of war still exists on the Korean peninsula, and in 2017, 26,000 American troops remain based in South Korea. Sandwiched between World War II and Vietnam, the Korean War—"the forgotten war"—killed 36,516 Americans.

1990: George H.W. Bush signed the Americans with Disabilities Act (ADA). The president noted that despite the Civil Rights Act of 1964, people with disabilities were still victims of segregation and discrimination. It gave the same protections to the disabled as were given to others in 1964, which outlawed discrimination based on race, religion, sex, or national origin. The ADA covers employers with fifteen or more employees, including state and local governments, and applies to employment agencies and labor unions. At the bill signing, Bush invoked the Declaration of Independence: "Today's legislation brings us closer to that day when no Americans will ever again be deprived of their basic guarantees of life, liberty, and the pursuit of happiness."

★ QUOTE OF THE DAY

With special feelings of sorrow—and of solemn gratitude—we think of those who were called upon to lay down their lives in that far-off land to prove once again that only courage and sacrifice can keep freedom alive upon the earth. To the widows and orphans of this war, and to those veterans who bear disabling wounds, America renews tonight her pledge of lasting devotion and care.

Dwight Eisenhower

This Day in Presidential History

July 27

1965: Lyndon B. Johnson signed a bill requiring cigarette makers to print health warnings on all cigarette packages. A landmark report from the surgeon general in 1964 said that cigarette smoking caused lung cancer and probably heart disease.

1967: Lyndon B. Johnson appointed the Kerner Commission to investigate the causes of racial turmoil in the United States. Rioting had hit black neighborhoods in several big cities, like Los Angeles, Detriot, and Newark. The president asked the commission, named for its chair—Illinois governor Otto Kerner—to find out three things about the rioting: (1) "What happened?" (2) "Why did it happen? (3) "What can be done to prevent it from happening again and again?"

1974: Richard M. Nixon was charged with three counts of impeachment in the Watergate scandal. The president—who had refused to release tape recordings concerning the Watergate break in and cover up—was accused of obstruction of justice, abuse of power, and the unconstitutional defiance of its subpoenas.

☆ QUOTE OF THE DAY

Prosperity is only an instrument to be used, not a deity to be worshipped.

Calvin Coolidge

July 28

1932: Herbert Hoover ordered the Army to evict protesting veterans from Washington, D.C. Around 20,000 World War I veterans, demanding promised benefits and bonus money, had set up camps in the U.S. capital while trying to pressure Congress and the president to pay up. The president ordered General Douglas MacArthur and Major Dwight Eisenhower to force them, along with their families, out. They did so— with tanks and cavalry. Two veterans were wounded during the melee and later died.

1943: Franklin D. Roosevelt, who had heard rumors of mass executions of Jews in Nazi-controlled Europe, received a first-person account from a member of the Polish underground named Jan Karski. Karski, just twenty-eight years old, made his way out of Europe, through England—where Winston Churchill said he was too busy to meet him—and then to Washington, D.C. In an Oval Office meeting that lasted about an hour, Karski told the president what he had seen and the scale on which it was occurring. Roosevelt would later vow publicly to try top Nazis for their war crimes (see October 7).

1943: Franklin D. Roosevelt announced the end of coffee rationing; it had been in short supply in the early stages of World War II. Many things that we take for granted today were rationed to help the war effort: gas, sugar, meat, butter. Americans got by.

1965: Lyndon B. Johnson ordered 50,000 more U.S. troops to Vietnam, bringing the number to 125,000. But the U.S. buildup was just beginning. It would double, and then double again, peaking at 538,000 in 1968.

☆ QUOTE OF THE DAY

Always bear in mind that your own resolution to succeed is more important than any other.

Abraham Lincoln

July 29

1958: Vowing that the United States would lead the space age, Dwight Eisenhower signed an act creating the National Aeronautics and Space Administration—NASA. NASA was formed nine months after the Soviet Union beat the United States into space by launching the first satellite, Sputnik. Sputnik scared many Americans into thinking that the United States was falling behind foreign rivals; it spurred huge government investments in science, technology, engineering, and mathematics.

1975: Gerald Ford became the first sitting president to visit Auschwitz-Birkenau—the infamous Nazi death camp in Poland. An estimated 1.1 million men, women, and children, the majority of them Jews, were murdered in the camp during World War II.

★ QUOTE OF THE DAY

Power always thinks it has a great soul and vast views beyond the comprehension of the weak.

John Adams

July 30

1863: Abraham Lincoln issued his "eye-for-an-eye" order. It was described in the September 1863 issue of *Harper's New Monthly Magazine* as follows:

The law of retaliation is formally announced by both the National and the Confederate authorities. Two Confederate officers were executed in Tennessee, June 9, by order of General Rosencrans, as spies found within our lines. The Confederates chose by lot, from among our prisoners at Richmond, two officers, and set them apart for execution, when ordered, in retaliation. Two officers of the enemy in our hands were then placed in close confinement, to be executed if the threats of the enemy were carried out. President Lincoln has also issued a proclamation declaring, in effect, that no distinction will be recognized in the treatment accorded to our white and colored troops who may be captured by the enemy. Every case of ill-treatment will be retaliated in kind: hanging for hanging, shooting for shooting, imprisonment for imprisonment. If a colored soldier, taken prisoner, is sold into slavery, a Confederate prisoner will, in return, be confined at hard labor in some prison until the colored prisoner is set free.

Historians say Lincoln's order was intended primarily as a way to intimidate the Confederacy. It had a slight "restraining" influence on the Confederate government's voiced policy, but individual commanders and soldiers continued to murder captured black soldiers.

1956: Dwight Eisenhower signed a bill declaring "In God We Trust" to be the nation's official motto. The first paper money with that motto was printed in 1957; some critics say it violated the separation of church and state.

1965: Lyndon B. Johnson signed Medicare into law. It was (is) a single-payer, national social insurance program for Americans administered

This Day in Presidential History

through an expanded Social Security system. By the president's side for the bill signing was former president Harry Truman, who had called for a national health insurance program in 1945. Truman was unable to create such a health program himself, but continued to advocate for it. To honor his efforts, President Johnson presented Truman and his wife Bess with Medicare cards number one and two in 1966.

★ QUOTE OF THE DAY

I despise people who go to the gutter on either the right or the left and hurl rocks at those in the center.

Dwight D. Eisenhower

July 31

1875: Andrew Johnson died in Elizabethton, Tennessee. He was the seventeenth president, serving from 1865 to 1869. Johnson, who succeeded Abraham Lincoln after Lincoln's assassination, was the first U.S. president to be impeached. The House accused the president of hurling libelous "inflammatory and scandalous harangues" against congressional members. In a dramatic Senate trial, Johnson was acquitted by just one vote. Bill Clinton is the only other president to be impeached.

In 1874, five years after he left the White House, Tennessee elected Johnson to the Senate—he became the only president to win a Senate seat after serving as chief executive. Johnson suffered a stroke and died four months into his term.

1991: George H.W. Bush and Soviet leader Mikhail Gorbachev agreed to cut nuclear arsenals. The Strategic Arms Reduction Treaty (START I) was the first treaty to provide for deep reductions of both U.S. and Soviet/Russian strategic nuclear weapons. The breakup of the Soviet Union, which occurred later that year, complicated matters, given that it created several new nuclear powers: Russia, Belarus, Ukraine, and Kazakhstan. All four would soon agree to honor the arms reductions (see May 23).

★ QUOTE OF THE DAY

The goal to strive for is a poor government but a rich people.

Andrew Johnson

This Day in Presidential History

August

August 1

1882: Chester Arthur was informed by his physician, Brode Herndon, that he had Bright's disease, a fatal kidney ailment. "The President sick in body and soul," the doctor wrote in his diary. The diagnosis was kept secret from the American public. Arthur—who became president upon the death of the assassinated president James Garfield (see September 19)—would live for another four years before dying in 1886 (see November 18).

1946: Harry Truman signed the Fulbright Scholarship Program into law, named for Arkansas Senator J. William Fulbright. The last president to lack a college degree, Truman recognized the importance—particularly in the wake of World War II—of widening the knowledge and understanding of students around the world. Seven decades later, the Fulbright Program is the most widely recognized and prestigious international exchange program in the world. Supported each year by an annual appropriation from Congress and other nations, the Fulbright Program works with universities, schools, government agencies, nongovernmental organizations (NGOs), and the private sector to assist individuals of high achievement and potential who represent the full diversity of their respective societies. Nominees are chosen through open, merit-based competitions.

☆ QUOTE OF THE DAY

Without a strong educational system democracy is crippled. Knowledge is not only key to power. It is the citadel of human freedom.

Harry Truman

August 2

1923: Just two years into his presidency, Warren Harding died while visiting San Francisco, probably of a heart attack. He was the twenty-ninth president, serving from 1921 to 1923. Harding was extraordinarily popular while he lived—compared at times to George Washington—but after his death, reports of numerous and brazen affairs began seeping out. But infidelity was just one of Harding's many problems. He also had a gambling problem and lost some of the White House china—to Douglas MacArthur's first wife, Louise—in a poker game. Harding's administration was perhaps the most corrupt; the Teapot Dome scandal (see April 7) was the most notorious in U.S. history until Watergate.

1927: Calvin Coolidge stunned the nation by announcing that he would not seek reelection. The nation was prosperous and at peace, but the president—who served the final year and a half of his late predecessor Warren Harding's term before being elected himself in 1924—thought that voters might see another term as a third term in office. On vacation in South Dakota, he held a news conference and at the end, handed out slips of paper to reporters. The notes said: "I do not choose to run." As it happened, Coolidge died before that term would have been up—sparing the nation the trauma of another president dying in office (see January 5).

1939: Franklin Roosevelt was warned by the prominent physicist Albert Einstein of the "new phenomenon" of nuclear chain reactions and their power: "A single bomb of this type [i.e., a nuclear bomb], carried by boat and exploded in a port, might very well destroy the whole port together with some of the surrounding territory." Einstein also warned that Nazi Germany was trying to harness this power and mine uranium. He urged the United States to participate in the research. Roosevelt, worried by Einstein's warning, later signed off on the "Manhattan Project," the crash effort to build the bomb during World War II.

☆ QUOTE OF THE DAY

Our most dangerous tendency is to expect too much of government, and at the same time do for it too little.

Warren Harding

August 3

1923: Vice president Calvin Coolidge was sworn in as the thirtieth president, following the death of President Warren Harding. The ceremony took place in the middle of the night at the Coolidge home in Vermont, when the new president was sworn in by his father, a notary—the only time in American history when a president was administered the oath of office by a relative. President Coolidge then went back to bed.

His presidency coincided with the "Roaring 20s"—Coolidge would serve until 1929. But the president missed much of the "Roaring 20s" himself, as he routinely slept ten to eleven hours a night, plus long daily naps.

★ QUOTE OF THE DAY

If you see ten troubles coming down the road, you can be sure that nine will run into the ditch before they reach you.

Calvin Coolidge

August 4

1961: Barack Obama was born in Honolulu, Hawaii. He was the forty-fourth president, serving from 2009 to 2017. Obama, who grew up without a father, graduated from Columbia University and Harvard Law School, and became a community organizer in Chicago and later a law professor at the University of Chicago. He served in the Illinois State Senate before advancing to the U.S. Senate in 2004 and the presidency four years after that.

Obama became president amid the sharpest economic downturn since the 1930s. In his first month in office in 2009, the Democratic-controlled Congress passed a $787 billion tax relief and an economic stimulus plan (see February 17). A bill designed to reform Wall Street and better protect consumers—the Dodd–Frank Wall Street Reform and Consumer Protection Act—was passed the next year (see July 21). He emphasized renewable energy—used his powers to boost the development of wind and solar power—and supported efforts to combat climate change. During the president's eight years in office, the budget deficit fell sharply, yet the federal debt nearly doubled.

In foreign policy, the president honored the Bush-era agreement to pull U.S. troops out of Iraq, increased troop levels in Afghanistan—before withdrawing the vast majority of them—signed an arms control pact with Russia, ordered U.S. military involvement in Libya, and the military operation that resulted in the death of al Qaeda leader Osama bin Laden

Barack Obama. Official White House portrait by Pete Souza.

(see May 1). The United States joined Britain, France, Germany, Russia, and China in a deal with Iran that those six countries said would ensure that Tehran's nuclear program remained peaceful. He was sharply criticized for his inability to end a long and deadly civil war in Syria, or to better restrain an increasingly assertive Russia and China.

Obama was reelected in 2012—the first Democrat since Franklin D. Roosevelt to win two presidential elections with a majority of the popular vote. He won the Nobel Peace Prize in 2009.

⭐ QUOTE OF THE DAY

Americans ... still believe in an America where anything's possible—they just don't think their leaders do.

Barack Obama

August 5

1861: Abraham Lincoln signed the Revenue Act—creating the first federal income tax. The president and Congress—needing to pay for the Civil

War—agreed that all incomes over $800 would be taxed at a 3% rate. Lincoln knew that taxes would be unpopular.

1933: Franklin D. Roosevelt established the National Labor Board. It was created to enforce the right of organized labor to bargain collectively with employers.

1965: Lyndon B. Johnson signed the Voting Rights Act. The law guaranteed African Americans the right to vote—and made it illegal to impose restrictions on federal, state, and local elections that could deny that right. Despite passage of the law, it was often enforced loosely at the state and local level, particularly in the South. Still, it provided a legal foundation for African Americans—and the means to challenge voting restrictions.

1974: Richard M. Nixon reluctantly released tapes related to the Watergate scandal. One—the "smoking gun" tape from June 23, 1972—explicitly showed the president trying to obstruct the investigation. When the "smoking gun" tape was made public, Nixon's remaining political support collapsed.

1981: Ronald Reagan fired 11,359 striking air traffic controllers, saying they were violating federal law. Nearly 13,000 workers from the Professional Air Traffic Controllers Organization (PATCO) had walked off the job two days earlier, after contract talks with the Federal Aviation Administration broke down. The president ordered them to return to work; those who did not were dismissed.

★ QUOTE OF THE DAY

Republicans are for both the man and the dollar, but in case of conflict the man before the dollar.

Abraham Lincoln

August 6

1850: Millard Fillmore said he would support the Compromise of 1850. After the Mexican-American War, there was fierce debate between free states and slave states about whether slavery would be allowed in territory won during the war. A series of bills that would soon pass Congress helped defuse those tensions. The compromise, drafted by Senators

Henry Clay of Kentucky and Stephen Douglas of Illinois, left both the pro- and anti-slave sides satisfied over some of its provisions and dissatisfied over others. Among its key provisions: California was admitted as a free state, the new Utah and New Mexico territories were allowed the right to determine what they wanted themselves, and the slave trade—but not slavery altogether—was banned in the District of Columbia. A stricter fugitive slave law—with stiff provisions for returning runaway slaves to their owners—was also enacted.

1945: On Harry Truman's orders, an atomic bomb was dropped on the Japanese city of Hiroshima. The president—who called the weapon "the most terrible bomb in the history of the world"—ordered the attack after being told an invasion of Japan could cost up to one million American casualties. Truman knew that U.S. and Allied casualties in two recent battles—Iwo Jima and Okinawa—were horrendous: approximately 77,469 killed and wounded. A second atomic bomb was dropped three days later on Nagasaki (see August 9). Between the initial blast, burns, and exposure to radiation, the atomic bombings of Hiroshima and Nagasaki killed 210,000 people by the end of 1945 and 340,000 within five years—mostly civilians. Horrific as they were, the bombs appeared to do what the president and his advisors determined they would do: save more lives than they took, and hasten the end of World War II (see August 14).

★ QUOTE OF THE DAY

I did what I thought was right.

> Harry Truman, in *Memoirs: Years of Trial and Hope 1946–1952*,
> on the use of atomic bombs against Japan

August 7

1794: George Washington and the Whiskey Rebellion. With "the deepest regret," the president said he would order federal troops to western Pennsylvania to put down a rebellion by farmers who refused to pay a tax on whiskey—if the farmers did not disburse by September 1. The tax was a part of Treasury Secretary Alexander Hamilton's attempt to pay debts left over from the Revolutionary War. The president himself would lead troops into the field (see October 1). The incident showed the power and ability of the new federal government to suppress violent resistance to its laws.

1953: Dwight Eisenhower signed the Refugee Relief Act of 1953—admitting 214,000 more immigrants into the United States than were permitted under existing immigration quotas.

1964: Congress passed the Gulf of Tonkin Resolution—giving Lyndon B. Johnson the authority to use military force in Vietnam. The resolution came about after the U.S. destroyer *Maddox* (conducting electronic espionage) was fired on by North Vietnamese torpedo boats. Further attacks were later reported (the validity of which has since been questioned by some historians), prompting the president to seek military action.

1990: After Iraq's invasion of Kuwait, George H.W. Bush ordered Operation Desert Shield. Operation Desert Shield was the beginning of the U.S. military buildup that culminated in Operation Desert Storm, which freed Kuwait. U.S. troops briefly crossed into Iraq for tactical purposes, but the United States did not consider occupying it: Defense Secretary Dick Cheney said it wasn't worth the casualties or "getting bogged down."

1998: Bill Clinton vowed revenge after al Qaeda bombed U.S. embassies in Kenya and Tanzania. Twelve Americans were among the 224 killed. It was the first time that most Americans had heard of the terror group and its leader, Osama bin Laden. Bin Laden, a Saudi national, had declared war on the United States in 1996—upset that the United States had been allowed to station troops in Saudi Arabia as part of its effort to oust Iraqi troops from neighboring Kuwait.

★ QUOTE OF THE DAY

Always vote for principle, though you may vote alone, and you may cherish the sweetest reflection that your vote is never lost.

John Quincy Adams

August 8

1974: Richard M. Nixon resigned, the first—and only—U.S. president to ever step down. His resignation was the climax of America's worst political scandal: Watergate (see June 17). He quit after being told, bluntly, by Republican leaders that his political support had vanished and that he would not survive a Senate impeachment trial. The House Judiciary Committee had already voted for three articles of impeachment concerning the president's involvement in the Watergate scandal and his use of government agencies to cover it up. Nixon, the thirty-seventh president, had been in office since 1969; his resignation, made official the next day, thrust Vice President Gerald Ford into the presidency.

★ QUOTE OF THE DAY

I have never been a quitter. To leave office before my term is completed is abhorrent to every instinct in my body. But as president, I must put the interest of America first. America needs a full-time president and a full-time Congress, particularly at this time with problems we face at home and abroad.

To continue to fight through the months ahead for my personal vindication would almost totally absorb the time and attention of both the president and the Congress in a period when our entire focus should be on the great issues of peace abroad and prosperity without inflation at home.

Therefore, I shall resign the presidency effective at noon tomorrow. Vice President Ford will be sworn in as president at that hour in this office.

Richard M. Nixon

August 9

1945: A second atomic bomb was dropped on Nagasaki, Japan. The bombing, ordered by President Harry Truman, came three days after a similar bomb was dropped on Hiroshima (see August 6). The obliteration of two cities in three days helped convince the Japanese to surrender on August 14, bringing World War II to an end.

1974: Gerald Ford was sworn in as the thirty-eighth president, following the resignation of Richard M. Nixon. Ford, a longtime Michigan congressman, had been appointed vice president by President Nixon the previous fall (see October 12) after Spiro Agnew's resignation (see October 10). Nixon's resignation—the first and only time a president has quit—demonstrated the power of Congress, the Supreme Court, and the

Constitution itself. It underscored the system of checks and balances that the Founding Fathers had envisioned. After his swearing in—in a somber East Room ceremony—the new president told the nation, "I believe that truth is the glue that holds government together, not only our government but civilization itself."

1989: George H.W. Bush signed a bill to bail out the nation's savings and loan banks. In the late 1980s, more than 1,000 S&Ls—about a third of the national total—failed for a variety of reasons. The damage rippled across key sectors of the economy, including the mortgage and car loan industry. The Financial Institutions Reform, Recovery, and Enforcement Act gave $166 billion in aid to troubled S&Ls and created a new government entity—the Resolution Trust Company—to oversee the merger or liquidation of troubled banks.

2001: George W. Bush said the federal government would fund stem cell research. The new policy permitted funding on already-extracted stem cells but banned the extraction of additional stem cells from human embryos. Such research, it was hoped, would improve care—and ultimately speed cures—for diseases such as diabetes, Parkinson's disease, Alzheimer's disease, heart disease, stroke, burns, cancer, and osteoarthritis.

★ QUOTE OF THE DAY

My fellow Americans, our long national nightmare is over. Our constitution works; our great Republic is a government of laws and not of men. Here the people rule.

Gerald Ford

August 10

1846: The world's biggest series of museums was created when James K. Polk signed the Smithsonian Institution Act. The Smithsonian, tourists to Washington are often surprised to learn, consists of not one museum, but twenty-eight museums, galleries, research facilities, and the National Zoo. The Smithsonian today contains more than 142 million artifacts and specimens.

1874: Herbert Hoover was born in West Branch, Iowa. He was the thirty-first president, serving from 1929 to 1933. Seven months after Hoover

Herbert Hoover and First Lady Lou Hoover. Library of Congress.

was inaugurated, the stock market collapsed. The Dow fell 89% between 1929 and 1932, helping spark the Great Depression. The Great Depression saw unemployment rise from 3% in 1929 to 23% in 1932; income fell by half, millions lost everything. As the situation deteriorated, bread lines were common; many Americans were forced to live in squalid shantytowns—known as "Hoovervilles." The president sought reelection in 1932, but was crushed by New York Governor Franklin D. Roosevelt.

★ QUOTE OF THE DAY

Freedom is the open window through which pours the sunlight of the human spirit and human dignity.

Herbert Hoover

August 11

1943: The Quadrant Conference: Meeting secretly in Quebec, Franklin D. Roosevelt and British prime minister Winston Churchill agreed, among other things, that the Allied invasion of Nazi-occupied France would occur in the spring of 1944. Their conference would run through August 24.

1984: Ronald Reagan's hot mic joke set off alarms in the Kremlin. Testing a microphone prior to making a radio address, the president joked about attacking Russia. "My fellow Americans, I'm pleased to tell you today that I've signed legislation that will outlaw Russia forever. We begin bombing in five minutes." But the microphone was on and he was being recorded. The recording was later leaked to the public. A Japanese newspaper reported that the Soviet Union placed some of its forces on heightened alert; a Soviet news agency said, "The U.S.S.R. condemns this unprecedented and hostile attack by the U.S. president" and that "this kind of behavior is incompatible with the great responsibility borne by heads of nuclear states for the destinies of their own people and mankind."

★ QUOTE OF THE DAY

Peace is not absence of conflict, it is the ability to handle conflict by peaceful means.

Ronald Reagan

August 12

1867: In what would eventually lead to his impeachment Andrew Johnson asked Secretary of War Edwin Stanton to resign. Stanton and the president disagreed sharply over reconstruction of the South following the Civil War. But Stanton refused to step down. The president then suspended him and appointed Ulysses S. Grant—the Civil War general—as interim secretary of war.

1898: With William McKinley looking on, the United States and Spain signed a protocol ending the Spanish-American War. Spain agreed to grant Cuba its independence and cede Puerto Rico and Guam to the United States. The fate of the Philippines, site of a U.S. victory, would be determined at a later date. The pact was signed in a room overlooking the White House's South Lawn, which served as the Cabinet Room between 1867 and 1902. The Spanish-American war thrust the United States—already the world's biggest economic power—onto the global stage as a military power as well.

1941: FDR and Churchill's Atlantic Charter: Meeting on a warship off the coast of Newfoundland, Franklin D. Roosevelt and British prime minister Winston Churchill established the framework for what would justify the seemingly inevitable entry of America into World War II—and the post-war order. The two leaders said that the Allies were determined to fight, among other things, to "ensure life, liberty, independence and religious freedom and to preserve the rights of man." Roosevelt and Churchill's Atlantic Charter was the foundation for what would become, four years later, the United Nations charter.

★ QUOTE OF THE DAY

Let us ever remember that our interest is in concord, not in conflict; and that our real eminence rests in the victories of peace, not those of war.

William Mckinley

August 13

1961: John F. Kennedy criticized construction of the Berlin Wall: seeking to prevent its citizens from fleeing, Communist East Germany began building the wall, which ran between East and West Berlin. Communist troops guarded the wall around the clock and for the next twenty-eight years shot at anyone trying to escape. Some 5,000 people did try to escape; an estimated 600 were killed. The Berlin Wall was the most visible symbol of the Cold War and a hated symbol of communist oppression.

Still, President Kennedy realized that a wall dividing the city meant that the Soviet Union would not attempt to seize West Berlin. He concluded at the time that the wall lowered the chance of war.

Kennedy visited West Berlin two years later (see June 26), and in a rousing speech, noted that the wall represented the failure of communism.

★ QUOTE OF THE DAY

A wall is a hell of a lot better than a war.

John F. Kennedy

August 14

1935: Franklin Roosevelt signed the Social Security Act. Initially created to provide guaranteed income for unemployed and retired Americans, it was later expanded to include the disabled. When the president launched Social Security, the United States was mired in the Great Depression and the poverty rate for seniors was estimated to be over 50%. In 1937, Social Security paid out $1.28 million to 53,236 recipients. In 2013, it paid approximately $813 billion—the largest source of federal spending—to some sixty-six million Americans.

1945: Harry Truman announced the surrender of Japan, bringing World War II to an end. The surrender of Japan came within days of two atomic bombs being dropped on the cities of Hiroshima (see August 6) and Nagasaki (see August 9). In his surrender proclamation, Japanese Emperor Hirohito cited "a new and most cruel bomb," overriding the objection of others who wanted to fight on.

★ QUOTE OF THE DAY

We can never insure one hundred percent of the population against one hundred percent of the hazards and vicissitudes of life, but we have tried to frame a law which will give some measure of protection to the average citizen and to his family against the loss of a job and against poverty-ridden old age.

Franklin D. Roosevelt

August 15

1914: The Panama Canal opened, fulfilling the vision of former president Theodore Roosevelt. The United States would return control of the canal to Panama on December 31, 1999—while reserving the right to defend it for national security reasons.

1971: The "Nixon Shock." Richard M. Nixon announced that the United States would no longer be on the gold standard—ending convertibility between the dollar and gold. Nixon also announced a ninety-day freeze on wages, prices, and rents—designed to combat inflation, which was heating up.

1973: Richard M. Nixon denied involvement in the Watergate cover-up. During a nationwide TV address, the president took "full responsibility" for the "abuses [that] occurred during my administration," but claimed he had no prior knowledge of the Watergate break-in. Nixon added that he neither participated in nor knew about efforts to cover it up. It was later established that the president was lying.

★ QUOTE OF THE DAY

Because the abuses occurred during my Administration, and in the campaign for my reelection, I accept full responsibility for them. I regret that these events took place, and I do not question the right of a Senate committee to investigate charges made against the President to the extent that this is relevant to legislative duties.

However, it is my constitutional responsibility to defend the integrity of this great office against false charges.

Richard M. Nixon

August 16

1841: John Tyler was burned in effigy outside the White House—by members of his own Whig party. A states' rights president, Tyler believed that the Constitution placed narrow parameters around what the federal government could and could not do. This led to a series of vetoes of bills passed by the Whigs—including one that would have started a new national bank of the United States. As the vetoes mounted, the Whigs rebelled against who they thought had been their president. A mob believed to consist of angry Whigs marched to the White House, where they threw rocks, fired guns, and hung the president in effigy. It was probably the most violent demonstration to ever occur at the mansion, and as the melee continued, First Lady Letitia Tyler—in poor health due to a stroke—lay in her bed shaking and crying in fear.

★ QUOTE OF THE DAY

In matters of style, swim with the current; in matters of principle, stand like a rock.

Thomas Jefferson

August 17

1998: Bill Clinton became the first sitting president to testify as the subject of a grand jury investigation. The president's testimony was related to his affair with an intern, Monica Lewinsky, which Clinton initially denied. The testimony capped a four-year investigation into the president and First Lady Hillary Clinton's purported involvement in a series of alleged scandals. As the investigation unfolded, an independent prosecutor, Kenneth Starr, learned of the affair. When questioned about the affair, Clinton denied it, which led Starr to charge the president with perjury and obstruction of justice. The president was later impeached by the House, but acquitted by the Senate.

★ QUOTE OF THE DAY

Indeed, I did have a relationship with Miss Lewinsky that was not appropriate. In fact, it was wrong. It constituted a critical lapse in judgment and a personal failure on my part for which I am solely and completely responsible.

Bill Clinton

August 18

1795: George Washington signed the Jay Treaty with Britain—possibly preventing war. The president, aware of reports that Britain—at war with France—was interfering with American trade with that country, and violating parts of the 1783 Treaty of Peace that ended the American Revolution, sent an envoy—Supreme Court Chief Justice John Jay—to London to smooth things over. The resulting treaty eased tensions. President Washington said it showed America's "reluctance to hostility." But the pact was opposed by two future presidents—Thomas Jefferson and James Madison—who claimed it made too many concessions to the British.

1991: George H.W. Bush learned of a coup that toppled Soviet leader Mikhail Gorbachev.

Soviet hardliners, alarmed with Gorbachev's reforms, detained Gorbachev at his vacation home and said that they had taken the reins of power. The coup, poorly organized and half-hearted, was resisted by Soviet citizens and fell apart after three days. But the Soviet Union, irreparably weakened, would peacefully dissolve four months later—the final chapter of the Cold War.

★ QUOTE OF THE DAY

Observe good faith and justice toward all nations. Cultivate peace and harmony with all.

George Washington

August 19

1946: Bill Clinton was born William Jefferson Blythe III at Hope, Arkansas. He was the forty-second president, serving from 1993 to 2001. A five-term governor of Arkansas, he became the second-youngest person ever elected president, after John F. Kennedy. Clinton was the first post–Cold War president, leading a United States that had no major geopolitical rivals. His focus, therefore, was on domestic affairs. He signed the North American Free Trade Act—negotiated by his predecessor George H.W. Bush—which created a free trade zone between the

Bill Clinton. Official White House portrait by Bob McNeely.

This Day in Presidential History

United States, Canada, and Mexico. With his wife, he tried and failed to pass a massive overhaul of the nation's healthcare system. Republicans seized control of Congress in 1994, but as the economy boomed, voters reelected the president in 1996 (in a three-man race) with 49.2% of the vote and 379 electoral votes. The federal budget deficit was eliminated during the Clinton presidency.

On the foreign policy front, Clinton helped broker the Oslo Accords—a peace deal between Israel and the Palestine Liberation Organization. He ordered the bombing of Serbia to end its "ethnic cleansing" of Kosovo, signed an arms reduction pact with Russia, and eased China's entry into the World Trade Organization—which occurred after he left office. The Islamic terror group al Qaeda launched three major attacks against American targets overseas during his presidency, while a homegrown terrorist killed 168 people after destroying a federal office building in Oklahoma City (see April 19).

Clinton also became the second president to be impeached (see December 19)—after being charged with perjury and instruction of justice in connection with an affair he had with a White House intern. The Senate acquitted the president, who completed his second term and left office with a Gallup approval rating of 67%.

1953: Dwight Eisenhower authorized a CIA-backed coup in Iran. It succeeded and a pro-American regime, led by Shah Mohammad Reza Pahlavi, was installed. The Shah would rule until his overthrow by Islamic hardliners in 1979.

1974: Gerald Ford selected Nelson Rockefeller, the former New York governor, to be his vice president. Ford had ascended to the presidency ten days earlier after the resignation of Richard M. Nixon. Rockefeller's selection was allowed by the Twenty-fifth Amendment, enacted in 1967, which said that a vice presidential vacancy could be filled. It was invoked in October 1973 for the first time, when President Nixon himself picked Ford to fill the vacancy left by the resignation of Spiro Agnew (see October 10).

★ QUOTE OF THE DAY

We are all in this together. If we have no sense of community, the American dream will wither.

Bill Clinton

August 20

1833: Benjamin Harrison—the only grandson of a president to become president himself—was born in North Bend, Ohio. He was the twenty-third president, serving from 1889 to 1893. Harrison is best remembered for signing the Sherman Anti-Trust Act of 1889, which set the precedent for breaking up industrial monopolies. His grandfather was William Henry Harrison ("Old Tippacanoe"), who served as the ninth president for one month in 1841.

★ QUOTE OF THE DAY

I pity that man who wants a coat so cheap that the man or woman who produces the cloth or shapes it into a garment shall starve in the process.

Benjamin Harrison

The White House was wired for electricity in 1891, but President Harrison and First Lady Caroline Harrison—concerned about being shocked—were afraid to turn anything on or off! They had aides or servants do so.

Benjamin Harrison. Library of Congress.

This Day in Presidential History

August 21

1858: The first Lincoln-Douglas debate. Perhaps the most famous political debates in American history pitted two men from Illinois—Senator Stephen Douglas, "the Little Giant," who was defending his seat against former congressman Abraham Lincoln. Slavery was the principal issue during their seven encounters. The Supreme Court's infamous Dred Scott decision had recently been handed down (see March 6), and Lincoln used it to reinforce his long-held opposition to slavery. For his part, Douglas argued that U.S. territories could refuse to pass laws necessary to support slavery. The debates generated enormous newspaper coverage, and while Lincoln lost the Senate race, they helped vault him into the national spotlight. He would win a far greater prize—the presidency—two years later.

1959: Dwight Eisenhower signed a bill making Hawaii the fiftieth state. Hawaii, which had been annexed by the United States in 1898 in the wake of the Spanish-American War, was considered vital to national security. Some Democratic lawmakers from southern states expressed concern about letting Hawaii into the Union because it had a predominantly non-white population.

★ QUOTE OF THE DAY

I hate it because of the monstrous injustice of slavery itself. I hate it because it deprives our republican example of its just influence in the world—enables the enemies of free institutions, with plausibility, to taunt us as hypocrites—causes the real friends of freedom to doubt our sincerity, and especially because it forces so many really good men amongst ourselves into an open war with the very fundamental principles of civil liberty—criticizing the Declaration of Independence, and insisting that there is no right principle of action but self-interest.

Abraham Lincoln on slavery

August 22

1862: Abraham Lincoln said that ending slavery was not his main Civil War goal—preserving the Union was. The president told the *New York Tribune* that "If I could save the Union without freeing any slave I would do it, and if I could save it by freeing all slaves I would do it." Lincoln made the comments in a letter to Horace Greeley, the prominent editor of the *New York Tribune*, who had criticized the president for what he considered soft treatment of slaveholders. Greeley also said that Lincoln was lax in enforcing the Confiscation Acts, which called for the seizure of property, including slaves, of Confederates when their homes were captured by Union forces. But Lincoln also hinted to Greeley of a coming policy change—that would soon be known to the world as the Emancipation Proclamation. "I intend no modification of my oft-expressed personal wish that all men everywhere could be free," he said.

1996: Bill Clinton signed a "Welfare to Work" bill. The Personal Responsibility and Work Opportunity Reconciliation Act, which fulfilled a 1992 campaign pledge to "end welfare as we know it," required welfare recipients to work or participate in job training programs. It also set a five-year limit for federal assistance. The act also made many legal immigrants ineligible to receive public benefits. It also cut spending on the Food Stamp Program and disability benefits for children.

★ QUOTE OF THE DAY

If I could save the Union without freeing any slave, I would do it; and if I could save it by freeing all the slaves, I would do it; and if I could save it by freeing some and leaving others alone, I would also do that.

Abraham Lincoln

August 23

1940: Franklin D. Roosevelt signed two bills to protect investors. The Investment Company Act and Investment Advisers' Act, both of which passed Congress unanimously, gave the Securities and Exchange Commission greater power to regulate investment trusts and investment counselors. It was the latest in a series of steps taken by the president to restore confidence in the economy.

1958: Military crisis with China. Dwight Eisenhower ordered the reinforcement of the navy's seventh fleet, which stepped up patrols near Taiwan, after communist China shelled two islands, Quemoy and Matsu. The battle between Taiwan—an American ally—and China lasted for a month and killed hundreds on both sides.

1977: Jimmy Carter defended plans to return the Panama Canal to Panama. Polls showed most Americans opposed giving up control of the waterway, but the president, in a news conference, noted that talks had begun thirteen years earlier during the administration of Lyndon B. Johnson. He added that a proposed treaty had the backing of his predecessor, President Gerald Ford. Carter pointed out that that the United States would retain control of the canal through the end of the twentieth century—and would have "no constraints on the action that we can take as a nation" in time of emergency.

★ QUOTE OF THE DAY

We are cleaning house, putting our financial machinery in good order. This program is essential, not only because it results in necessary reforms, but for the much more important reason that it will enable us to absorb the shock of any crisis.

Franklin D. Roosevelt

August 24

1814: The White House and Capitol were burned to the ground by invading British troops—the low point of the War of 1812. In one of the darkest days in American history, President James Madison, who earlier in the day had gone to the front in Bladensburg, Maryland, returned to the White House to find it deserted. He fled as well, never to live in the mansion again. Just before the president's retreat, First Lady Dolley Madison helped save Gilbert Stuart's famous portrait of George Washington.

Before the British arrived, the White House had another set of invaders—local citizens who did some looting; "a rabble," one servant called them.

Within hours, British troops entered the city, burned the Capitol and other federal buildings before entering the White House itself. They ate and drank the president's food and wine before setting the mansion ablaze. It was said to be done in revenge for an earlier American attack on the city of York (now Toronto), in which the Canadian Parliament was burned. The president and Secretary of State Monroe, watching the fires from Virginia, were nearly captured by British forces. The fires that destroyed the White House and Capitol were put out by a massive storm—possibly a tornado—that caused yet more damage.

The shell of the White House was all that remained after the British set it on fire in 1814. It took three years to rebuild, forcing James and Dolley Madison and then James and Elizabeth Monroe, to live elsewhere. Library of Congress.

The destruction of the White House was a spectacular and humiliating defeat for Madison; the president and first lady lived in a nearby mansion until Madison left office in 1817. James Monroe, who became president in March of that year, would move into the rebuilt White House later that year (see September 17). The Stuart portrait was there—and still is.

After the attack on Washington, there was talk of moving the nation's capital further inland for security reasons. Cincinnati was mentioned as one possibility before the decision was made to stay put.

★ QUOTE OF THE DAY

It is a universal truth that the loss of liberty at home is to be charged to the provisions against danger, real or pretended, from abroad.

James Madison

August 25

1950: Harry Truman ordered the Army to take control of the railroads, ahead of a threatened strike by civilian workers. Because the Korean War

This Day in Presidential History

had just broken out, the president said the railroads had to keep operating to move troops and material.

★ QUOTE OF THE DAY

It is essential to the national defense and the security of the nation, to the public health, and to the public welfare generally that every possible step be taken by the government to assure to the fullest possible extent continuous and uninterrupted transportation service. Accordingly, I intend to take all steps necessary to assure the continued operation of the railroads.

Harry Truman

August 26

1794: George Washington told Virginia Governor Henry "Light Horse Harry" Lee that he would subdue the "Whiskey Rebellion." And the president would do just that—with force (see September 19).

1987: Ronald Reagan proclaimed September 11 as 9-1-1 Emergency Number Day. The president urged Americans to remember the number, which he said would save numerous lives in times of emergency.

★ QUOTE OF THE DAY

Protecting the lives and property of citizens is one of government's fundamental responsibilities. In times of emergency, citizens must have a quick and easy way to summon police and other rescue services. The 9-1-1 emergency telephone number fulfills this need and proves its value hundreds of times every day throughout our country.

Ronald Reagan

August 27

1908: Lyndon Baines Johnson was born in Stonewall, Texas. He was the thirty-sixth president, serving from 1963 to 1969. "LBJ" became president after one of the most tragic events in American history—the assassination of President John F. Kennedy (see November 22). Johnson was the only president to witness the slaying of his predecessor. The president would be elected in a landslide the next year.

Johnson's years were momentous. He was determined to build what he called a "Great Society," and leveraging his legislative skills—he had been a Texas congressman and Senate majority leader before being tapped as Kennedy's vice president—he shepherded the Civil Rights Act, the Voting Rights Act, Medicare, and the War on Poverty, among other things, through Congress. LBJ was also a staunch supporter of the space program, which landed a man in the moon six months after he left office.

But Johnson's domestic achievements were offset by the Vietnam War. On his watch, the number of troops in Vietnam ballooned from about 16,000 in late 1963 to 538,000 by 1968. Growing public opposition to the war—which at its height was killing forty-six Americans per day—weighed heavily, and the president decided not to seek reelection.

★ QUOTE OF THE DAY

Being president is like being a jackass in a hailstorm. There's nothing to do but to stand there and take it.

Lyndon B. Johnson

Lyndon B. Johnson signing the 1968 Civil Rights Bill. Warren K. Leffler. Library of Congress.

August 28

1894: An income tax became law—without the president's signature. The Wilson-Gorman Tariff Bill included an income tax of 2% on all personal income greater than $4,000 and on all corporate income above operating expenses. But President Grover Cleveland refused to either sign or veto the measure—so it became law.

1917: Leaving the White House, Woodrow Wilson was hounded by women suffragists demanding the right to vote. Ten were arrested and thrown in jail—where they went on hunger strikes and were force-fed. The resulting publicity upset the president, who agreed to back the Nineteenth Amendment (see September 30). In 1920, that amendment was passed, officially giving women the right to vote.

1981: Ronald Reagan's attempted assassin pled not guilty. John Hinckley, Jr., was later found not guilty by reason of insanity in the shooting of the president (see March 30). Hinckley would spend thirty-five years in a mental institution before being released (see June 21).

2005: Hurricane Katrina devastated New Orleans and the Gulf Coast—sparking fierce criticism of George W. Bush. The category 5 storm (category 3 at landfall)—one of the deadliest natural disasters in American history—killed at least 1,245 people and caused, in 2017 terms, some $130 billion in damage. The president and his administration, along with various state and local officials along the Gulf Coast—were widely castigated for what was perceived as a slow and inadequate response to the disaster.

★ QUOTE OF THE DAY

The folks on the Gulf Coast are going to need the help of this country for a long time. This is going to be a difficult road. The challenges that we face on the ground are unprecedented. But there's no doubt in my mind we're going to succeed.

George W. Bush, August 31, 2005

August 29

1862: The second Battle of Bull Run was a Union disaster—leaving Washington D.C. vulnerable to attack. A year after Union forces were routed at present-day Manassas, Virginia (see July 21), a second battle yielded the same result. President Abraham Lincoln was told that the capital city was exposed to possible attack. But Confederate General Robert E. Lee, leading his troops across the Potomac, would march not into Washington—but to the Maryland town of Sharpsburg, where the titanic battle of Antietam would soon occur (see September 17).

1945: With World War II finally over, Harry Truman signed an order allowing for voluntary military enlistments. Some 16 million citizens—out of a population of about 130 million—had served in the African, European, and Pacific theaters. The president that day also ordered the Navy to seize control of oil refineries, to head off a planned strike by civilian workers; Truman said the oil was needed to help with the military's massive demobilization that was under way.

1972: Richard M. Nixon downplayed the growing Watergate scandal. In a news conference, the president said that an internal investigation into the June break-in of Democratic National Committee headquarters (see June 17) showed that no one on the White House staff, in the administration, or anyone "presently employed" was involved in the Watergate break-in.

★ QUOTE OF THE DAY

Whenever a man has cast a longing eye on offices, a rottenness begins in his conduct.

Thomas Jefferson, 1799

August 30

1963: John F. Kennedy established a direct phone line (a "hotline") to the Kremlin in Moscow. During the 1962 Cuban Missile Crisis (see October 16), in which a nuclear war between the Soviet Union and United States was barely averted, the president was frustrated that he could not communicate quickly enough with Soviet premier Nikita Khrushchev. Each used encrypted messages that had to be relayed by telegraph or radioed between the Kremlin and the Pentagon. Kennedy feared that such a cumbersome system might lead to misunderstandings or delays in communicating during a future crisis. The hotline would allow the president to call the Pentagon with the message, which would be immediately typed into a teletype machine and fed into a transmitter. The message could reach the Kremlin within minutes, as opposed to hours. In 1963, it was regarded as a communications marvel.

★ QUOTE OF THE DAY

I have seen enough of one war never to wish to see another.

Thomas Jefferson

August 31

1935: Franklin D. Roosevelt signed the Neutrality Act, which banned the shipment of arms to belligerents during a state of war. The Act was clearly aimed at two countries in Europe that were rapidly arming and talking in increasingly belligerent terms: Adolph Hitler's Germany and Benito Mussolini's Italy. Roosevelt also said that the United States would increase its patrol of foreign submarines lurking in American waters—it was a clear response to Hitler's declaration that Germany would no longer abide by the terms of the Treaty of Versailles. That treaty, written after Germany's defeat in World War I, banned Germany from rebuilding its military.

★ QUOTE OF THE DAY

The policy of the Government is definitely committed to the maintenance of peace and the avoidance of any entanglements which would lead us into conflict. At the same time it is the policy of the Government by every peaceful means and without entanglement to cooperate with other similarly minded Governments to promote peace.

Franklin D. Roosevelt

September

September 1

1802: A Federalist newspaper in Richmond, Virginia, published the first in a series of articles accusing Thomas Jefferson of fathering several children with a slave, Sally Hemings. The president ignored the allegations.

In January 2000, a study of available DNA, original documents, and written and oral historical accounts reported "a high probability" that Jefferson was the father of all six of Sally Hemings' children listed in Monticello records. But a subsequent study, reviewing "essentially the same material," reached a different conclusion, calling it "very unlikely" that Jefferson fathered any of them. It suggested that Jefferson's younger brother Randolph was "more likely the father of at least some" of Hemings' children.

1954: Dwight Eisenhower signed a major expansion of Social Security. The Social Security Amendments of 1954 added some ten million more Americans to the program, and raised payments to all retired workers by at least five dollars a month. It also raised benefits for future retirees to as much as $4,200.

★ QUOTE OF THE DAY

These ... Social Security amendments I have approved today will bolster the health and economic security of the American people. They represent one of the cornerstones of our program to build a better and stronger America.

Dwight Eisenhower

September 2

1862: Abraham Lincoln put General George McClellan back in command of the Army of the Potomac. The president had previously demoted McClellan for failing to capture the Confederate capital, Richmond—

accusing him of having a "case of the slows." But the general hadn't changed—and would soon be fired by his commander in chief for a second and final time.

1940: Franklin Roosevelt, fearing the collapse of Britain in its life-and-death struggle with Nazi Germany, gave it fifty mothballed U.S. Navy destroyers. In September 1940, Britain stood alone against Germany, and the Nazis were gearing up for an invasion. Britain desperately needed help, but was running out of money to buy military goods, food, and raw materials that only the United States—the "arsenal of democracy"—could provide. Thus, FDR signed the "Destroyers for Bases" agreement, giving Britain the ships. In return, the United States received ninety-nine-year leases to bases in Newfoundland and the Caribbean. This so-called "Lend-Lease" program was extended to other allies as well. British prime minister Winston Churchill later called it "the most unsordid act" that one nation had ever done for another.

1958: As the United States tried to catch up to the Soviet Union in the space race, Dwight Eisenhower signed the National Defense Education Act. It gave loans to students studying math, science, and foreign languages—disciplines that were deemed critical to national security. There was a growing fear that America, technologically, was falling behind the U.S.S.R., which had launched the first satellite, *Sputnik*, into space the year before.

★ QUOTE OF THE DAY

Preparation for defense is an inalienable prerogative of a sovereign state. Under present circumstances this exercise of sovereign right is essential to the maintenance of our peace and safety. This is the most important action in the reinforcement of our national defense that has been taken since the Louisiana Purchase. Then as now, considerations of safety from overseas attack were fundamental.

Franklin D. Roosevelt

September 3

1919: Woodrow Wilson began a cross-country tour to win support for the League of Nations and the Treaty of Versailles. It would end badly. The president, stung by fierce Republican opposition to the treaty, which was drawn up by the United States and its European allies at the end of World War I, took to the road to explain its merits to the American people. Speaking at town halls, fairgrounds, arenas, hotel luncheons and dinners, and from the platform of his railroad car, Wilson made forty speeches in twenty-two days, traveling through the Midwest and up and down the West Coast. But the 8,000-mile journey was too much for the president. He collapsed from exhaustion in Colorado, sped back to Washington, and later suffered a near fatal stroke (see October 2).

1964: Lyndon B. Johnson signed the Wilderness Act, protecting nine million acres of federal land.

The president praised Congress for its efforts to protect the land from development, and for working to ensure that future generations would have clean air to breathe and water to drink. "No single Congress in my memory has done so much to keep America as a good and wholesome and beautiful place to live," he said.

★ QUOTE OF THE DAY

A wilderness, in contrast with those areas where man and his own works dominate the landscape, is hereby recognized as an area where the earth and its community of life are untrammeled by man, where man himself is a visitor who does not remain.

From LBJ's Wilderness Act

September 4

1951: Harry Truman made the first coast-to-coast TV broadcast. CBS said that the president was seen on eighty-seven stations in forty-seven markets. Truman delivered a speech that focused on the Treaty of San Francisco that the United States and forty-seven other nations would sign four days later. The treaty officially ended America's post–World War II occupation of Japan and outlined settlement details of various war-related issues. Truman said that since Japan's surrender in 1945, the new threat of communism now necessitated an alliance between the United States and Japan. The president added that he hoped Japan would become a strong, democratic nation.

2002: George W. Bush made his case for war with Iraq. Meeting with congressional leaders, the president said that Iraqi president Saddam Hussein was a threat to America's national security, and brought up the concept of regime change. The United States would lead an invasion of Iraq six months later (see March 19).

★ QUOTE OF THE DAY

Saddam Hussein is a serious threat. He is a significant problem. And it's something that this country must deal with.

George W. Bush, September 4, 2002

September 5

1905: Theodore Roosevelt ended a war between Russia and Japan: With the president acting as a mediator, both countries signed the Portsmouth Treaty, ending hostilities and allowing the United States to maintain a balance of power in the Far East. It also preserved America's "Open Door Policy" with respect to a neighbor of both Russia and Japan: China. The Open Door Policy concerned the protection of equal privileges among nations trading with China; it also supported China's territorial and administrative integrity. The Open Door policy would remain a key pillar of American foreign policy in Asia through 1949, when China fell to communism.

1975: An assassination attempt against Gerald Ford: Visiting Sacramento, California, the president was walking near the state capitol when a woman standing behind a rope line—just two feet away—pulled a gun. Ford saw the gun and recalled a frantic moment when he was shielded and rushed away to safety while agents subdued the suspect, who was identified as Lynette "Squeaky" Fromme, a member of the Manson cult. Fortunately her gun never fired and no one was injured. Fromme spent thirty-four years in prison before being released in 2009. There would be another attempt on the president's life two weeks later (see September 17).

★ QUOTE OF THE DAY

I am only an average man but, by George, I work harder at it than the average man.

Theodore Roosevelt

September 6

1901: William McKinley was shot. Accompanied by three bodyguards, the president attended a public reception in Buffalo, New York. Despite pleas from his secretary that security was inadequate, McKinley stood at the head of a receiving line and, at about 4:00 p.m., began greeting citizens.

Well-wishers were usually instructed to approach the president with their hands open and empty. But it was a hot day and many in line held handkerchiefs to wipe their brows. Within minutes, Leon Czolgosz, a twenty-eight-year-old Polish-American anarchist, approached the president. His right hand was wrapped in a handkerchief, as if he was injured. Seeing this, the president reached for his left hand instead. As their hands touched, Czolgosz shot McKinley twice with a .32 revolver that was hidden under the handkerchief. One bullet lodged in the president's stomach while the other ricocheted off a button. As the crowd pounced on the assassin, beating him, McKinley said, "Go easy on him, boys." Looking into the face of his killer, the collapsing McKinley said, "May God forgive him."

Asked if he felt much pain, the president put his hand into an opening on his shirt, near his heart and replied, "This wound pains greatly." He removed his hand, fingers covered in blood. His head dropped to his chest. The president was conscious as he was rushed to a hospital. On the way, he felt in his clothing and pulled out a metal object. "I believe this is a bullet." He lingered for eight days before succumbing to his wounds (see September 14).

★ QUOTE OF THE DAY

Let us ever remember that our interest is in concord, not in conflict; and that our real eminence rests in the victories of peace, not those of war.

William McKinley

William McKinley had an unusual superstition: If he wore a red carnation in his lapel, it would bring him good luck. He wore one as usual on September 6, 1901, when he arrived at an exhibition hall in Buffalo, New York to greet well-wishers.

A twelve-year-old girl, Myrtle Ledger, stepped forward to meet the president. McKinley, promptly gave her his good luck carnation. "I must give this flower to another little flower," he said.

Moments later he was shot.

September 7

2008: As the housing industry continued to collapse, George W. Bush unveiled a $200 billion bailout of Fannie Mae and Freddie Mac, the government-sponsored mortgage companies. The mortgage giants, which backed some $5 trillion in home loans, were placed under direct federal control in an attempt yet to shore up the nation's housing market, which had been battered since 2006 by soaring foreclosures and plunging prices.

★ QUOTE OF THE DAY

These housing mortgage companies cannot continue to operate safely and soundly and fulfill their public mission, posing an unacceptable risk to the broader financial system and our economy … putting these companies on sound financial footing and reforming their business practices is critical to the health of our financial system and to making further progress with the housing correction that today is weighing heavily on our economy.

George W. Bush

September 8

1954: The United States signed the SEATO—South East Asian Treaty Organization—pact, designed to thwart communist expansion. Dwight Eisenhower had ordered Secretary of State John Foster Dulles to form an alliance to prevent aggression in Vietnam, Laos, and Cambodia, or Southeast Asia in general. Signatories, including France, Great Britain, Australia, New Zealand, the Philippines, Pakistan, Thailand, and the United States, pledged to "act to meet the common danger;" but SEATO did not contain a mutual defense clause like the better-known North Atlantic Treaty Organization (NATO) pact had (see April 4).

1974: Gerald Ford pardoned Richard M. Nixon. The new president told Americans he wanted the nation to move beyond Watergate—the scandal that had brought Nixon down (see August 8-9).

Speaking to the nation, Ford said he granted "a full, free, and absolute pardon unto Richard M. Nixon for all offenses against the United States which he, Richard M. Nixon, has committed or may have committed or taken part in during the period from January 20, 1969, through August 9, 1974." Critics smelled a deal between the two men. Ford denied it. His approval ratings fell and the pardon likely cost him votes in his unsuccessful 1976 presidential bid.

★ QUOTE OF THE DAY

I feel that Richard M. Nixon and his loved ones have suffered enough and will continue to suffer, no matter what I do, no matter what we, as a great and good nation, can do together to make his goal of peace come true.

Gerald Ford

September 9

1850: Road to the Civil War: Millard Fillmore signed the Compromise of 1850—a series of bills meant to defuse tensions between pro-slave and antislave states of territory acquired during the Mexican-American War of 1846–1848. The compromise, drafted by Whig Senator Henry Clay of Kentucky and Democratic Senator Stephen Douglas of Illinois, helped ease those tensions. The most controversial of these bills was the Fugitive Slave Act (see September 18).

1893: The only presidential child born in the White House—Esther Cleveland—was born to President Grover Cleveland and First Lady Frances Cleveland. It was the couple's second child (they would have five).

1957: Dwight Eisenhower signed the Civil Rights Act of 1957. The first civil rights legislation passed by Congress since 1875, the act was intended to strengthen voting rights for blacks in the South. The act prompted the longest one-person filibuster in American history, when South Carolina senator Strom Thurmond, then a Democrat, spoke for twenty-four hours and eighteen minutes in an attempt to keep it from passing.

★ QUOTE OF THE DAY

I would rather try to persuade a man to go along, because once I have persuaded him, he will stick. If I scare him, he will stay just as long as he is scared, and then he is gone.

Dwight Eisenhower

September 10

1833: The "Bank War." Andrew Jackson shut down the Second Bank of the United States, saying it had too much power. Jackson also disliked its lending practices and political ties. The president removed all federal funds from the bank. The following March, Jackson would be censured by the Senate, which said he was abusing his presidential powers.

President George Washington and his treasury secretary Alexander Hamilton first created a national bank in 1791. They believed the government needed a central bank to hold its money. The Second Bank of the United States was founded in 1816, five years after this first bank's charter had expired. Traditionally, the bank had been run by a board of directors with ties to industry and manufacturing, and therefore was biased toward the urban and industrial northern states. Jackson, the epitome of the frontiersman, resented the bank's lack of funding for expansion into the unsettled western territories. Jackson also objected to the bank's unusual political and economic power and to the lack of congressional oversight over its business dealings.

1842: Letitia Tyler died September 10, 1842—the first sitting first lady to pass away.

★ QUOTE OF THE DAY

Any man worth his salt will stick up for what he believes right, but it takes a slightly better man to acknowledge instantly and without reservation that he is in error.

Andrew Jackson

This Day in Presidential History

While Jackson is the only U.S. president to have been censured by the Senate, the House of Representatives has formally reprimanded two presidents. In 1842, lawmakers accused John Tyler of abusing his powers after vetoing several bills he had originally promised to support. Six years later, in 1848, James K. Polk was reprimanded for starting the Mexican War without formally obtaining congressional approval.

September 11

1841: John Tyler's entire cabinet, with one exception, resigned. The Cabinet was angry that the president vetoed a second bill for the establishment of a National Bank of the United States.

Anger at Tyler from within his own Whig party had boiled over to the point that a few weeks earlier, Whig protestors descended upon the White House in protest, throwing rocks, firing guns—and hanging the president in effigy (see August 16). The only Cabinet member who did not resign was Secretary of State Daniel Webster, who said, "If you leave it up to me, Mr. President, I will stay where I am."

1970: Thirty-one years before September 11, 2001, Richard M. Nixon ordered the creation of what became known as the sky marshals program, in which armed federal agents would begin serving on U.S. flights.

The president's order came in the middle of a weeklong crisis that began when four passenger jets bound for New York were hijacked on September 6. The planes, originating in Frankfurt, Zurich, and Amsterdam were taken by members of the Popular Front for the Liberation of Palestine (PFLP). Three of the planes were forced to land in Jordan, while the fourth landed in London after the plot was foiled. Three days later a fifth plane, bound from Bahrain to London, was also hijacked and forced to land in Jordan. The crisis played out over a week before being resolved; two hijackers were killed and, miraculously, all 608 passengers and crew survived.

Nixon had originally ordered Dawson's Field, the Jordanian airstrip where four of the planes had landed, to be bombed, sparking a dispute with the British government, which favored negotiating with the hijackers.

2001: George W. Bush vowed revenge after Islamic terrorists hijacked four U.S. passenger jets and used them to attack New York and Washington.

This Day in Presidential History

Two jets smashed into the twin towers of New York's World Trade Center; both would collapse within two hours. A third jet smashed into the Pentagon. A fourth jet, believed headed for either the White House or U.S. Capitol, was brought down in western Pennsylvania after passengers fought back. The president, in Florida when the hijackings began, was taken, for security reasons, to military bases in Louisiana and Nebraska before the Secret Service allowed him to return to White House that evening. The terror attack killed an estimated 2,977 people from sixty-five countries. It was the second–single bloodiest day in American history, only behind the Civil War battle of Antietam (see September 17).

★ QUOTE OF THE DAY

Make no mistake: the United States will hunt down and punish those responsible for these cowardly acts.

George W. Bush

September 12

1994: A stolen airplane crashed onto the White House grounds in middle of night—just below the presidential bedroom. Because of maintenance work being done to the White House ventilation system, President Bill Clinton, First Lady Hillary Clinton, and daughter Chelsea were sleeping at Blair House, just down the street from the mansion. The pilot, thirty-eight-year-old Frank Corder, stole the plane—a two-seater Cessna 150—from a Maryland airport late on September 11. He was killed on impact. No one tried to stop the plane; the incident prompted a sweeping review of security procedures by the Secret Service.

★ QUOTE OF THE DAY

In times of war and peace, in hard times and good, the White House is an enduring symbol of our democracy. It tells our people and those around the world that the mission of America continues, as it does on this happy and important day. So let me assure all Americans, the people's house will be kept safe, it will be kept open, and the people's business will go on.

Bill Clinton

This Day in Presidential History

September 13

1993: As Bill Clinton looked on, Israel and the Palestine Liberation Organization signed a peace deal on the White House's South Lawn. Israeli prime minister Yitzhak Rabin and the PLO's Yasser Arafat—bitter enemies—even shook hands after they signed, a stunning image.

Under the so-called Oslo Accord, Israel would withdraw from the two occupied territories—the Gaza Strip and West Bank—by April 1994, and elections would be held to form a new Palestinian government. Rabin would be assassinated two years later by a far-right Zionist who opposed his peace initiative.

1994: Bill Clinton signed an assault weapons ban. Known formally as the Public Safety and Recreational Firearms Use Protection Act, the bill—supported by three prior presidents including Ronald Reagan (see May 3)—prohibited civilian use of certain semiautomatic firearms and "large-capacity" ammunition magazines. The bill passed by a 52-48 margin in the Senate, applied only to weapons made after the bill was signed. The bill was also good for only ten years. After its expiration on September 13, 2004, it has not been renewed.

★ QUOTE OF THE DAY

The peace of the brave is within our reach.

Bill Clinton

September 14

1901: William McKinley died. The president had been shot eight days earlier while greeting well-wishers in Buffalo, New York (see September 6). Rushed to a hospital, it looked like he would recover. But gangrene soon set in. The president, a Civil War hero who had seen more than his share of death, knew he was dying. "It is useless, gentlemen," he said bravely. "I think we ought to have a prayer." On the evening of September 13, he said: "Good-bye, all, good bye. It is God's way. His will be done." At 2:15 on the morning of September 14, with First Lady Ida McKinley holding his hand, William McKinley died. He was fifty-eight. He was the third president of the United States to have been assassinated in thirty-six years.

1901: In Buffalo, New York, Theodore Roosevelt was sworn in as the twenty-sixth president upon the death of William McKinley. Roosevelt was just forty-two years old—the youngest person ever to become president. Energetic and restless, he led a confident and rapidly growing nation into what would become known as the American century. Roosevelt quickly and with a sense of urgency made his mark on everything from business (breaking up monopolies like John D. Rockefeller's Standard Oil and E. H. Harriman's Northern Trust Railroad) and foreign policy (building the Panama Canal and brokering an end to a war between Russia and Japan—for which he won the Nobel Peace Prize) to conservation (protecting vast swaths of land and expanding America's national park system). Roosevelt also oversaw an expansion of the White House itself, ordering the construction of today's East and West Wings.

★ QUOTE OF THE DAY

That's all a man can hope for during his lifetime—to set an example—and when he is dead, to be an inspiration for history.

William McKinley

September 15

1857: William Howard Taft was born in Cincinnati, Ohio. He was the twenty-seventh president, serving from 1909 to 1913. Taft also served as chief justice of the Supreme Court, the only person to lead both the executive and judicial branches of government. In fact, he wanted to be chief justice more than president. But his wife Helen (nicknamed "Nellie"), a bit of a social climber, thought the presidency more prestigious.

Weighing at times as much as 340 pounds, Taft was the heaviest president—and also the last to have facial hair. Taft ate so much that a White House housekeeper, Elizabeth Jaffray, noted in her diary that she had a conversation with the president and Mrs. Taft about his ever-expanding waistline. In it, she detailed a typical breakfast consumed by the president: "two oranges, a twelve-ounce beefsteak, several pieces of toast and butter and a vast quantity of coffee with cream and sugar." When she and Helen commented on his eating habits, he jovially responded that he was planning to go on a diet, but lamented the fact that "things are in a sad

William Howard Taft. Library of Congress.

state of affairs when a man can't even call his gizzard his own." According to his biographers, he had to have his shoes tied by his valet and often got stuck in the White House bathtub and had to be lifted out by two or more men. Once, while visiting the czar of Russia, Taft split his pants seam while descending from a carriage.

1979: While jogging at Camp David, Jimmy Carter collapsed. The president had been participating in a grueling 6.2-mile mountain run at Camp David—the presidential retreat in Maryland—when he began to wobble. "His legs couldn't support him, his mouth hung open, he was moaning and his eyes had a glazed look," one fellow runner said. "It was very scary." It was feared that the president was having a heart attack and the Situation Room was notified. It turned out that Carter was suffering from heat exhaustion, a common problem among runners. Even so, the incident, when it became known to the public, fueled public perception that the president was a weak leader.

2008: The financial services firm Lehman Brothers collapsed. With Lehman Brothers holding $600 billion in assets, it was the largest bankruptcy in American history. And it was arguably the most dramatic moment in a flurry of economic and financial events that caused the near-collapse of the U.S. economy.

This Day in Presidential History

The economic crisis had begun in the first half of 2006, when the housing market began collapsing, and in autumn 2007, when the stock market fell. Both problems led to a cascade of bank failures and federal bailouts of mortgage giants Fannie Mae and Freddie Mac in August 2008 (see September 7), big banks (see October 3), and automakers General Motors and Chrysler (see December 19). The crisis changed the tenor of the 2008 presidential campaign. For much of the race, the war in Iraq and national security had been the principal issue; these security concerns gave way to economic concerns—and gave Barack Obama, the Democratic candidate for the White House, a considerable boost.

★ QUOTE OF THE DAY

Politics, when I am in it, makes me sick.

William Howard Taft

September 16

1940: Franklin D. Roosevelt signed the Selective Service and Training Act—requiring men aged between twenty-one and thirty-five to register for draft. America moved toward the draft as World War II engulfed Europe. Nazi Germany had overrun Western Europe and was now bombing London and other British cities (in attacks known as the Blitz) ahead of a planned invasion (which never occurred). The United States itself would enter the war in December 1941 (see December 7–8) and by war's end, more than 16 million Americans (out of a population of about 133 million) would serve in the military.

1974: Gerald Ford announced a conditional amnesty for Vietnam War deserters—if they agreed to work for up to two years in public service jobs. The president said he wanted America to move beyond Vietnam, which had badly divided the country. In his proclamation, Ford said that "desertion in time of war is a major, serious offense," and that draft evasion "is also a serious offense." Such actions, he said, need not "be condoned." "Yet," he continued, "reconciliation calls for an act of mercy to bind the nation's wounds and to heal the scars of divisiveness."

Jimmy Carter, who became president in 1977, would issue a full pardon for Vietnam-era draft dodgers (see January 21).

My sincere hope is that this is a constructive step toward calmer and cooler appreciation of our individual rights and responsibilities and our common purpose as a nation whose future is always more important than its past.

Gerald Ford

September 17

1787: The final draft of the Constitution was signed in Philadelphia, replacing the Articles of Confederation. It devised a system of checks and balances among three separate but coequal branches of the federal government: executive, legislative, and judicial. One debate the Founding Fathers had concerned the representation of states: should big states and small states be represented in Congress equally—or by size? It was decided that the answer was both. States would be represented equally in the Senate—but proportionally in the House of Representatives.

1817: James Monroe moved into the rebuilt White House. Burned to the ground during the War of 1812 (see August 24), it took three years to construct a new mansion.

1862: A nervous Abraham Lincoln waited for news on what remains the single bloodiest day in U.S. history—the Battle of Antietam. The clash near the Maryland town of Sharpsburg left 23,000 soldiers dead, wounded, or missing (both sides) after just twelve hours of savage fighting. The outcome is generally seen as a strategic victory for the Union, ending the Confederate Army's first invasion of the North. It also led to the president's issuance of the preliminary Emancipation Proclamation (see September 22).

1975: Visiting San Francisco, Gerald Ford was the target of an assassin for the second time in two weeks. Sara Jane Moore fired at him and missed. Moore spent 32 years in prison.

1978: Jimmy Carter's Camp David Accords were signed in the White House. The momentous agreement ended decades of hostility and several wars between two bitter enemies—Israel and Egypt. The president helped broker the pact over fourteen months of difficult diplomacy, including twelve days of negotiations at Camp David, between Israeli prime minister Menachem Begin and Egyptian president Anwar Sadat. Begin and Sadat would win the Nobel Peace Prize. Sadat was murdered by Islamic terrorists in 1981. The Israeli-Egyptian peace treaty has held firm ever since.

★ QUOTE OF THE DAY

We are privileged to witness tonight a significant achievement in the cause of peace, an achievement none thought possible a year ago, or even a month ago, an achievement that reflects the courage and wisdom of these two leaders.

Jimmy Carter

September 18

1793: George Washington laid the cornerstone of the U.S. Capitol: In an event full of pomp and pageantry, the president was given an engraved silver plate which he put on the ground. It read:

This South East corner stone, of the Capitol of the United States of America in the City of Washington, was laid on the 18th day of September, in the thirteenth year of American Independence, in the first year of the second term of the Presidency of George Washington, whose virtues in the civil administration of his country have been as conspicuous and beneficial, as his Military valor and prudence have been useful in establishing her liberties, and in the year of Masonry 5793, by the Grand Lodge of Maryland, several lodges under its jurisdiction, and Lodge 22, from Alexandria, Virginia.

Thomas Johnson, David Stuart and Daniel Carroll, Commissioners

Joseph Clark, R. W. G. M.—P. T.

James Hoban and Stephan Hallate, Architects

Collen Williamson, M. Mason

With the president's assistance, the cornerstone was carefully lowered on top of the plate.

The Capitol took nearly a century to complete, with a major setback coming from the massive damage caused by British invaders setting it on fire during the War of 1812. Today, the U.S. Capitol complex includes six congressional office buildings and three Library of Congress buildings.

1850: Millard Fillmore signed the Fugitive Slave Act, which stated that runaway slaves had to be returned to their masters. Part of the Compromise of 1850 (see September 9), it was meant to ease North-South tensions. It did not; the rift deepened. The president himself opposed slavery—he was the first nonslaveholding president aside from John Adams and son John Quincy Adams—yet signed the act anyway, fearing that if he didn't, southern states would secede from the Union. The Fugitive Slave Act was fiercely criticized in the North.

1873: A financial panic set off a six-year economic depression—marring Ulysses S. Grant's second term. It began with the failure of the prominent brokerage firm Jay Cooke & Company, which overextended itself during the rapid expansion of the transcontinental railroad and the land boom that surrounded it.

★ QUOTE OF THE DAY

God knows I detest slavery but it is an existing evil, and we must endure it and give it such protection as is guaranteed by the Constitution.

Millard Fillmore

September 19

1794: George Washington became the only U.S. president to lead troops into battle. The commander-in-chief led 12,950 men of the Constitutional Army into western Pennsylvania to crush the so-called Whiskey Rebellion. The rebellion was a tax protest that began in 1791 against a federal tax upon distilled spirits. Western farmers felt the tax was unfair because it was an "abuse of federal authority wrongly targeting a demographic that relied on crops such as corn, rye, and grain to earn a profit." By 1794, the president believed that the rebellion threatened the stability of the United States itself. But the fact that the militia itself had been called up was enough to end the Whiskey Rebellion. By the time Washington and his men reached Pittsburgh—then considered frontier territory—the rebellion had largely dissolved.

This Day in Presidential History

1796: George Washington's farewell address. After nearly eight years in office, the president—who had been reluctant to take the job in the first place—decided that he would not accept a third term and would, once and for all, retire to his beloved Mount Vernon. In one of the most memorable speeches in American history—never actually delivered as a spoken address but printed in the Philadelphia *Daily American Advertiser* and reprinted soon after in other newspapers—Washington bid the young republic farewell. The president summarized his tenure, cautioned Americans to avoid political infighting, and advised future leaders to avoid permanent alliances with other nations. The comments reflected, in part, what the president felt was partisan criticism of his leadership: Some opponents had actually labeled Washington's policies a betrayal of the Constitution—criticism which offended the president.

The unity of government which constitutes you one people is also now dear to you. It is justly so; for it is a main pillar in the edifice of your real independence, the support of your tranquility at home, your peace abroad, of your safety, of your prosperity, of that very liberty which you so highly prize.

From Washington's farewell address

1881: James Garfield died—victim of an assassin's bullet. More than eleven weeks after being shot as he tried to board a train in Washington (see July 2), the president succumbed to his wound. He was the twentieth president and the second to be assassinated in sixteen years. Historians think the president could have lived had his medical care not been so sloppy and unsanitary. The president's assassin, Charles Guiteau, was swiftly convicted and hanged (see June 30).

★ QUOTE OF THE DAY

Next to freedom and justice is popular education, without which neither freedom nor justice can be permanently maintained.

James Garfield

September 20

1881: Chester Arthur was sworn in following the death of James Garfield. Garfield, president for just six months, had been shot on July 2 and lingered for another two months. Arthur, the twenty-first president, would serve out Garfield's term but would not run himself in 1884. Arthur was a widower; his sister, Mary Arthur McElroy, served as White House hostess for him.

1941: As defense spending soared ahead of World War II, Franklin D. Roosevelt signed the largest tax hike in American history. The Revenue Act of 1941 generated more than $3 billion—the 2016 equivalent of $51 billion—as the Army and Navy rapidly expanded. Within three months, the United States would be attacked, thrusting it into the conflict (see December 7–8).

2001: George W. Bush warned Americans to prepare for a long war against terrorism. Speaking to a joint session of Congress nine days after terrorists attacked New York and Washington, the president outlined his administration's plans to combat global terror. He also named Pennsylvania governor Tom Ridge as the first director of a new cabinet department: Homeland Security. Of Islamic terrorists, Bush said, "We're not deceived by their pretenses to piety," but added that America was not at war with Islam itself.

2007: Citing "unsettling times," George W. Bush assured Americans that the U.S. economy was in good shape. The president's comment came one year after the U.S. housing market began collapsing—erasing an estimated $7 trillion in wealth—and weeks before the stock market, then trading at all-time high, began what would be a 57% collapse (the S&P 500), and a year before a series of government bailouts of the mortgage, banking, and auto industries.

★ QUOTE OF THE DAY

Every nation, in every region, now has a decision to make: Either you are with us, or you are with the terrorists. From this day forward, any nation that continues to harbor or support terrorism will be regarded by the United States as a hostile regime.

George W. Bush

September 21

1931: Another wave of bank closings alarmed Herbert Hoover. Fearing that the United States would go off the gold standard—as Great Britain did—in an attempt to solve its economic crisis, Americans withdrew money from banks and hoarded gold. Over the next month, 827 more banks, depleted of cash, would close.

1939: With World War II under way, Franklin D. Roosevelt asked Congress to amend the Neutrality Acts—so the United States could aid Britain and France. Those countries had declared war on Nazi Germany two weeks before, after German forces invaded Poland. The following spring, the Nazis would turn their attention westward, conquering France, Belgium, the Netherlands, Denmark, and Norway. In September 1940, it would begin bombing Britain itself, ahead of a planned invasion.

★ QUOTE OF THE DAY

We have always held to the hope, the belief, the conviction, that there is a better life, a better world, beyond the horizon.

Franklin D. Roosevelt

September 22

1862: Abraham Lincoln issued the Emancipation Proclamation. Following the Confederate defeat at Antietam—which the president hoped was a turning point in the war (see September 17), the president made the proclamation public. It freed slaves in Confederate or contested areas of the South. But slaves in non-Confederate border states and in parts of the Confederacy under Union control were not included. The president knew that his proclamation was merely a temporary military measure, and that only Congress could end slavery permanently. The proclamation would take effect on New Year's Day (see January 1). The Thirteenth Amendment to the Constitution abolishing slavery would become effective in December 1865—eight months after the president's assassination.

★ QUOTE OF THE DAY

I think slavery is wrong, morally and politically. I desire that it should be no further spread in these United States, and I should not object if it should gradually terminate in the whole Union.

Abraham Lincoln, September 17, 1859

September 23

1944: Republicans attacked Franklin D. Roosevelt's dog. They said that the president had accidentally left behind Fala, a Scottish terrier, during a trip to Alaska—and dispatched a navy destroyer to retrieve the dog, at a cost of $20 million. The story was false. FDR's rival in that presidential election year, New York governor Thomas Dewey, had been criticizing the Roosevelt administration as corrupt and incompetent. The false story about Fala gave the president a chance to hit back. FDR went on to win election to a historic fourth term that November.

1949: The end of America's nuclear monopoly—Harry Truman announced that the Soviet Union had detonated (on August 29) its first atomic bomb. The Soviets, of course, had stolen U.S. atomic secrets during the Manhattan Project—the secret American crash effort to build the bomb during World War II. The news that the U.S.S.R. now had atomic weapons—years ahead of when American officials predicted—sparked alarm. The president soon called for the rapid development in the next stage of nuclear arms—the hydrogen bomb.

★ QUOTE OF THE DAY

I am accustomed to hearing malicious falsehoods about myself—such as that old, worm-eaten chestnut that I have represented myself as indispensable. But I think I have a right to resent [and] object to libelous statements about my dog.

Franklin D. Roosevelt

September 24

1789: George Washington signed the Judiciary Act—creating the Federal Court system. Article III of the Constitution established a Supreme Court, but the authority to create lower federal courts was left to Congress. This new act not only established the structure and jurisdiction of the federal court system, but also created the position of attorney general.

1869: Ulysses S. Grant's presidency was stained by "Black Friday"—a financial panic that was traced to his brother-in-law. The panic began when two railroad entrepreneurs, Jay Gould and James Fisk, Jr., tried to corner the gold market. Teaming up with the president's brother-in-law—Abel Rathbone Corbin—they tried to corner the gold market and force prices up. Learning of the scheme, Grant ordered the Treasury to sell a large chunk of the government's gold—causing prices to crash. It was one of several scandals to occur during Grant's eight years in office.

1955: Dwight Eisenhower had a heart attack, raising doubts about his reelection prospects. The president was in Denver and would spend the next several weeks in a suite at the Fitzsimons Army Hospital (now part of the University of Colorado Anschutz Medical Campus). Many White House staffers and reporters moved to Denver to be near him. He was released on Armistice Day, November 11. In February 1956, doctors said that the president had recovered; Eisenhower went on to win the reelection that November in a landslide.

1957: Dwight Eisenhower ordered troops to Little Rock, Arkansas, to enforce school desegregation. Arkansas officials—including Governor Orval Faubus—had resisted desegregation, as ordered in the Supreme Court's landmark *Brown v. Board of Education* ruling (see May 17). In addition to sending in U.S. troops, the president also federalized the entire 10,000-man Arkansas National Guard, taking control away from Faubus. The forced enrollment of the so-called "Little Rock Nine" in that city's Central High School was a major turning point in the civil rights movement.

★ QUOTE OF THE DAY

Under the leadership of demagogic extremists, disorderly mobs have deliberately prevented the carrying out of proper orders from a Federal court. Local authorities have not eliminated that violent opposition ... proper and sensible observance of the law, then demanded the respectful obedience which the nation has a right to expect from all the people. This, unfortunately, has not been the case at Little Rock.

Dwight Eisenhower

September 25

1894: Grover Cleveland pardoned bigamists, adulterers, and polygamists. The president's proclamation was directed at Mormons who had previously engaged in such activity—considered illegal by the U.S.

government. Then—and now—it is against the law for anyone to be married, at the same time, to multiple partners.

1959: Dwight Eisenhower welcomed the first Soviet leader to visit the United States. The president and Nikita Khrushchev met for two days at Camp David, the presidential retreat in Maryland. The status of Germany, including a divided Berlin, and levels of armaments were discussed. But hopes for warmer ties between Washington and Moscow would soon collapse, after the downing of an American spy plane in Soviet airspace (see May 5 and May 16).

☆ QUOTE OF THE DAY

The best results in the operation of a government wherein every citizen has a share largely depend upon a proper limitation of purely partisan zeal and effort and a correct appreciation of the time when the heat of the partisan should be merged in the patriotism of the citizen.

Grover Cleveland, from his first inaugural address

September 26

1914: Woodrow Wilson signed a bill creating the Federal Trade Commission. It was designed to protect consumers from unscrupulous businesses and help thwart business monopolies.

1960: Richard M. Nixon and John F. Kennedy met in a television debate; presidential campaigns would never be the same. People hearing the Chicago debate on the radio thought Nixon, the sitting vice president, won. But on TV it was a different story. Nixon, who was recovering from the flu and suffering from a knee injury, looked pale, and fast-growing stubble on his face didn't help his appearance. Yet he refused to wear makeup. He also wore a gray suit, which provided little contrast with the background set. Kennedy, on the other hand, had flown in from California with a healthy tan. He also refused makeup, though some historians say he might have gotten a quick touchup just before going onto the set. He wore a dark suit, which stood out against the gray background. In short, Kennedy looked healthy and attractive while Nixon, who quickly began to sweat, didn't. The image that both men projected helped establish television as the most important political medium.

★ QUOTE OF THE DAY

If I were two-faced, would I be wearing this one?

Abraham Lincoln

September 27

1938: With war looming in Europe, Franklin D. Roosevelt wrote to Nazi leader Adolf Hitler appealing for peace. The president was worried about German threats to invade a part of Czechoslovakia called the Sudentenland. Hitler scoffed publicly at FDR's letter—but soon did take over the Sudentenland, and, in March 1939, all of Czechoslovakia itself.

1964: The Warren Commission report on the assassination of President John F. Kennedy was made public. It said that a lone gunman, twenty-four-year-old Lee Harvey Oswald, was solely responsible for the president's murder. The report also blamed the Secret Service for poor preparations for Kennedy's Dallas visit, and for failing (obviously) to sufficiently guard him.

1991: With the Cold War essentially over, George H.W. Bush ordered defense cuts. The president's order resulted in the Pentagon taking B-52 bombers off their full-time alert. The president also ordered some 2,400 short-range land- and sea-based nuclear weapons eliminated, a move he said could save $2 billion a year.

★ QUOTE OF THE DAY

The question before the world today, Mr. Chancellor, is not the question of errors of judgment or of injustices committed in the past. It is the question of the fate of the world today and tomorrow. The world asks of us who at this moment are heads of nations the supreme capacity to achieve the destinies of nations without forcing upon them, as a price, the mutilation and death of millions of citizens. …

Allow me to state my unqualified conviction that history, and the souls of every man, woman, and child whose lives will be lost in the threatened war, will hold us and all of us accountable should we omit any appeal for its prevention. … The conscience and the impelling desire of the people of my country demand that the voice of their government be raised again and yet again to avert and to avoid war.

From Franklin D. Roosevelt's letter to Hitler

September 28

1967: Criticized for escalating the Vietnam War, President Lyndon B. Johnson used a Congressional Medal of Honor ceremony (for Army sergeant David Dolby) to defend his policy. The president told his critics, "The hard reality (is) that only military power can bar aggression and can make a political solution possible." Johnson noted that the United States had offered, several times, to negotiate with North Vietnam but that those offers had been rejected. Johnson felt that in the absence of peace talks, he had no choice but to maintain a sizable U.S. military presence in South Vietnam. But growing public opposition to the war gradually weakened the president politically, and in 1968 he stunned the nation by announcing that he would not run for reelection (see March 31).

★ QUOTE OF THE DAY

No one hates war and killing more than I do.

Lyndon B. Johnson

September 29

1789: George Washington appointed Thomas Jefferson to be the first secretary of state—a move the president would eventually regret. Secretary of State Jefferson argued with Treasury Secretary Alexander Hamilton about fiscal policy, particularly funding debts left over from the Revolutionary War. The powerful James Madison sided with Jefferson, and the two formed a party to oppose the Washington administration. The party was called "the Republican," and became known as the Democrat-Republican. Jefferson's actions and his efforts to undermine Hamilton angered President Washington, and Jefferson left the government. George Washington never forgave Jefferson for his actions, and the two sons of Virginia—who played such crucial roles in the founding of their country—never spoke again.

1907: With Theodore Roosevelt watching, the foundation stone for Washington National Cathedral was laid. The last finial was placed eighty-three years later in the presence of President George H.W. Bush.

★ QUOTE OF THE DAY

Far and away the best prize that life has to offer is the chance to work hard at work worth doing.

Theodore Roosevelt

September 30

1918: In a shift, Woodrow Wilson said he supported the Nineteenth Amendment to the Constitution, giving women the right to vote. The president had been slow to come around on the issue of women's voting rights—until they began protesting in large numbers outside the White House. Some even went on hunger strikes and were force-fed, which appalled the president.

1962: John F. Kennedy ordered Mississippi officials to enroll a black student, James Meredith, in the University of Mississippi. But the desegregation order was resisted by Mississippi governor Ross Barnett. "I shall do everything in my power to prevent integration in our schools," he vowed. The governor was held in contempt by the Department of Justice. The president ordered Mississippi officials to "cease and desist" obstructing justice, federalized the state's National Guard and sent in U.S. marshals to enforce his order. Two people were killed when riots broke out; 3,000 federal troops put an end to the violence. James Meredith, a U.S. Air Force veteran, was often harassed at Ole Miss; he defied this bigotry and graduated in 1963. In 1966, Meredith was shot during a solo 220-mile march aimed at spurring black voter registration. He survived and later finished the march.

Suffragettes picketing at the White House, January 1917. Library of Congress.

★ QUOTE OF THE DAY

Do not pray for easy lives. Pray to be stronger men.

John F. Kennedy

October

October 1

1924: Jimmy Carter was born in Plains, Georgia. He was the thirty-ninth president, serving from 1977 to 1981. A U.S. Naval Academy graduate who served as an engineering officer on a nuclear submarine for several years and as a peanut farmer (he put his farm into a blind trust during his presidency), Carter entered Georgia politics in 1962 and was elected governor eight years later. He was elected to the presidency in 1976, defeating incumbent president Gerald Ford.

The war in Vietnam and the Watergate scandal had eroded faith in government, and Carter came to office promising to restore the public's trust. He indeed was perceived as honest and forthright, yet was also seen—fairly or not—as unable to cope with mounting issues, both at home and abroad. He lost his reelection bid to Ronald Reagan in 1980 by a landslide. Carter's postpresidency—longer than any other ex-president's—

Jimmy Carter. Official White House portrait.

was marked by a focus on resolving conflicts, advancing democracy and human rights and economic and social development. For his efforts he won the Nobel Peace Prize in 2002.

★ QUOTE OF THE DAY

The best way to enhance freedom in other lands is to demonstrate here that our democratic system is worthy of emulation.

Jimmy Carter

October 2

1919: Woodrow Wilson suffered a crippling—and near-fatal stroke. The president had been on a cross-country tour to build support for the Versailles Treaty and League of Nations, but developed blinding headaches and was rushed back to Washington. On October 2, First Lady Edith Wilson found him sprawled on a bathroom floor, and when the president's physician, Cary Grayson, first saw him, he cried out, "My God, the president is dead!" Wilson was alive, but paralyzed and unable to speak.

For the remainder of his presidency, his condition was hidden from the American public and from much of official Washington. It was one of the greatest cover-ups in American history. Edith Wilson often reviewed papers and made decisions on her husband's behalf—becoming, some historians contend, an acting president.

1981: Ronald Reagan's military buildup. The fortieth president, who came to office after an election campaign promising to expand and strengthen America's defense, said on this day that the United States would produce the B-1 bomber—reversing a decision made during the previous administration. The B-1, designed to penetrate Soviet air space by flying at supersonic speeds while jamming enemy radar, had been killed by Jimmy Carter in 1977.

Also on this day, Reagan said that the United States would accelerate the MX missile ("Peacekeeper") program, and embark on development of a "stealth" bomber that would be produced in the 1990s.

★ QUOTE OF THE DAY

One cool judgment is worth a thousand hasty counsels. The thing to do is to supply light and not heat.

Woodrow Wilson

October 3

1789: The first presidential proclamation. George Washington, at the request of Congress, designated November 26 as a day of national thanksgiving.

1993: Two U.S. Army helicopters were shot down by in Mogadishu, Somalia, killing eighteen American soldiers. The United States had been in Somalia since December 1992 on a peacekeeping and humanitarian mission. After the deaths of the American servicemen, Bill Clinton, who became president in January 1993, ordered a withdrawal.

2008: George W. Bush signed a $700 billion bill to bailout banks. The so-called "Troubled Asset Relief Program" (TARP) was designed to use taxpayer dollars to buy mortgage-backed securities and other distressed assets. The purchases, the president and Treasury Secretary Hank Paulson hoped, would bolster confidence in the U.S. economy. The U.S. economy, rocked by a collapse in the housing industry, a plunging stock market, and surging unemployment, was described by some economists and historians as being in the most perilous condition since the Great Depression of the 1930s.

★ QUOTE OF THE DAY

Now therefore I do recommend and assign Thursday the 26th day of November next to be devoted by the People of these States to the service of that great and glorious Being, who is the beneficent Author of all the good that was, that is, or that will be—That we may then all unite in rendering unto him our sincere and humble thanks—for his kind care and protection of the People of this Country previous to their becoming a Nation.

George Washington

October 4

1822: Rutherford B. Hayes was born in Delaware, Ohio. He was the nine-teenth president, serving from 1877 to 1881. Elected president in one of the most controversial elections in American history (see March 3), Hayes served just one term. But following the administrations of Andrew Johnson, who was impeached and nearly thrown out of office, and Ulysses S. Grant, whose administration was tainted by corruption, Hayes was generally seen as a welcome change. He presided over the end of post–Civil War Reconstruction, and through friendships with Alexander Graham Bell and Thomas Edison, focused attention on inventions that gradually transformed the U.S. economy. The White House, in fact, got its first telephone during the Hayes' presidency. The phone number? 1.

President Hayes and First Lady Lucy Hayes were also rather straightlaced, refusing to serve alcohol in the White House. The first lady would go down in history with the nickname "Lemonade Lucy."

1957: Americans were frightened but Dwight Eisenhower took it in stride—after the Soviets beat the United States into space with the first satellite, *Sputnik*. The success of *Sputnik* convinced many Americans that

Rutherford B. Hayes. Library of Congress.

This Day in Presidential History

the United States was falling behind the Soviet Union in science and technology.

Senate Majority Leader Lyndon B. Johnson warned that the Soviets could bomb America from space, and the stock market fell 10% in two weeks. But the president—a former five-star general—thought *Sputnik*'s military threat overstated. The real threat, he thought, was its potential to scare Americans. Eisenhower placed *Sputnik* within the broader context of the Cold War, predicting a long struggle that U.S. economic prowess would win. But the president did order a crash program to develop new defense technologies, and beef up teaching of science, math, engineering, and foreign languages in American schools.

★ QUOTE OF THE DAY

Nothing brings out the lower traits of human nature like office seeking.

Rutherford Hayes

October 5

1829: Chester Arthur was born in Fairfield, Vermont. He was the twenty-first president, serving from 1881 to 1885. He was vice president for just six months before succeeding the assassinated James Garfield.

Because of his love of fine clothing, the president was nicknamed "Elegant Arthur." The presidential dandy, known for his long mutton chop sideburns, had an immense clothes collection, reportedly owning eighty pairs of pants and shoes. Arthur hired the first White House valet and traveled around in a lavish carriage with gold-laced curtains and a family coat of arms. He also thought the White House was run down (it was). He decided to hold a (literally) yard sale—and sold some of Abraham Lincoln's clothes that were still in the executive mansion.

Personal foibles aside, he was seen as a decent president. Of Arthur, one critic said "No man ever entered the presidency so profoundly and widely distrusted—and no one ever retired more generally respected." Even Mark Twain, deeply cynical about politicians, said: "It would be hard indeed to better President Arthur's administration."

1937: In remarks clearly aimed at Nazi Germany and Japan, Franklin D. Roosevelt called for a "quarantine" of aggressor nations. Without

Chester Arthur. Library of Congress.

mentioning them by name, the president said aggressor nations were spending up to 50% of their budget on the military—compared to about 11–12% for the United States.

1947: Harry Truman gave the first presidential speech on TV, asking Americans to cut back on their use of grain in order to help starving Europeans. Few Americans saw the speech: only a few thousand households had TV in 1947; by the early 1950s, millions would.

⭐ QUOTE OF THE DAY

There are many characteristics which go to make a model civil servant. Prominent among them are probity, industry, good sense, good habits, good temper, patience, order, courtesy, tact, self-reliance, manly deference to superior officers, and manly consideration for inferiors.

Chester Arthur, First Annual Message, 1881

October 6

1976: A debate blunder by Gerald Ford gave an opening to his presidential challenger, Jimmy Carter. At the second debate of the presidential campaign, in San Francisco, the president declared that "there is no

This Day in Presidential History

Soviet domination of Eastern Europe and never will be under a Ford administration." Given a chance to clarify his remarks, Ford did not, and Carter pounced.

1979: The first Pope to visit the White House—John Paul II—was feted by Jimmy Carter.

Carter greeted the Polish pontiff in his native tongue: "Niech bedzie bog Pochwalony" ("May God be praised"). The Pope responded, "It gives me great joy to be the first Pope in history to come to the capital of this nation, and I thank almighty God for this blessing."

★ QUOTE OF THE DAY

I am a Ford, not a Lincoln.

> Gerald Ford, modestly describing his lack of oratorial prowess

October 7

1942: In a public statement directed at Nazi Germany, Franklin D. Roosevelt vowed to try "the ringleaders responsible for the organized murder of thousands of innocent persons" for their war crimes. Despite his use of the word "thousands," Roosevelt was certainly referring to the Holocaust, which he had learned of earlier in the year (see July 28). The president died before World War II ended, but the Nuremberg Trials—a series of military tribunals—prosecuted twenty-two top Nazi officials.

Roosevelt was later criticized by some for not doing more to stop the direct extermination of Jews; some said he could have bombed railroad tracks that led to death camps, for instance. But FDR believed that the fastest way to stop the killing of innocent civilians was to win the war as quickly as possible—by taking the fight to the enemy itself.

1963: John F. Kennedy signed the Limited Nuclear Test Ban Treaty. The pact with Great Britain and the Soviet Union—the only other nuclear powers at that time—capped eight years of negotiations, which resulted in all three countries agreeing to ban the testing of nuclear weapons in the atmosphere, space, and underwater. Underground tests would be allowed, as no radioactive debris fell beyond the boundaries of the nation conducting the test. The United States, Britain, and Soviet Union also pledged to work towards complete nuclear disarmament, a goal that has proven to be elusive.

2001: The War on Terror: Bush announced a U.S. attack on Afghanistan. Three weeks after terrorists attacked New York and Washington with hijacked commercial airliners, George W. Bush announced the beginning of "Operation Enduring Freedom," a U.S. military offensive in Afghanistan. Its goal, the president said, was to crush the Taliban and al Qaeda, the Islamic terror group behind the 9/11 attacks. Bush warned that the United States would take the war on terrorism to any country that sponsored or harbored terrorists.

In 2001, the United States considered seven nations terrorist states: Cuba, Iran, Iraq, Libya, North Korea, Sudan, and Syria. In 2006, Libya was removed from the list. In 2008, the Bush administration also removed North Korea from its terror list, even though that communist nation had successfully tested its first nuclear weapon two years before.

October 8

1888: Grover Cleveland signed the Chinese Exclusion Act, which restricted Chinese immigration to the United States. Cleveland wanted immigrants who would assimilate to American culture and the English language; he had no interest in those who he believed would not.

1953: Dwight Eisenhower announced that the Soviet Union had successfully tested a hydrogen bomb. In a news conference, he warned Americans that the U.S.S.R. had the "capability of atomic attack on us, and such capability will increase with the passage of time."

1998: The House of Representatives voted to move ahead with impeachment proceedings against Bill Clinton. The president was subsequently charged with perjury and obstruction of justice. He was impeached by the House, but acquitted by the Senate.

★ QUOTE OF THE DAY

In opening our vast domain to alien elements the purpose of our lawgivers was to invite assimilation, and not to provide an arena for endless antagonism. The paramount duty of maintaining public order and defending the interests of our own people may require the adoption of

This Day in Presidential History

measures of restriction, but they should not tolerate the oppression of individuals of a special race.

Grover Cleveland, 1886

October 9

1869: The death of Franklin Pierce was announced by Ulysses S Grant. Pierce was the fourteenth president, serving from 1853 to 1857. "Baby" Pierce, as he was called because he was forty-nine when he became president, is the only chief executive from New Hampshire. Pierce, regarded as one of the worst presidents for his failure to stop the United States from sliding into civil war, suffered politically after he backed repeal of the Missouri Compromise on slavery. The Missouri Compromise was an 1820 agreement between pro- and antislavery factions in Congress. It banned slavery in the former Louisiana Territory north of the thirty-sixth parallel, except within the boundaries of the proposed state of Missouri.

★ QUOTE OF THE DAY

Frequently the more trifling the subject, the more animated and protracted the discussion.

Franklin Pierce

October 10

1890: Hoping to protect U.S. manufacturers from foreign competition, Benjamin Harrison signed the McKinley Tariff, boosting protective tariffs of U.S. goods by nearly 50%. The tariff—named for the person who introduced the bill in Congress, future president William McKinley—gave Harrison and future presidents expanded powers in foreign trade. It did not sit well with American consumers, however, who saw the price of many products soar. Republicans lost their majority in the House of Representatives, and in the 1892 presidential election, Harrison, also a Republican, was swept out of the White House. Higher tariffs also angered America's trade partners, who argued for retaliatory tariffs on American goods.

1951: Harry Truman's Mutual Security Act. A week after the Soviet Union conducted its second nuclear weapons test, President Truman said that the United States would provide military and economic aid to "free peoples." It was a clear message to both the Soviets and China that America would do whatever it could to help democratic nations resist the spread of communism. In practical terms, this meant that the United States would provide everything from guns, tanks, and airplanes to books, farming equipment, irrigation pumps, and medical supplies. Signing the Mutual Security Act, Truman called it a "great collective effort of the free nations to build a better world." Truman's successor, Dwight D. Eisenhower, abolished the Mutual Security Act in 1953.

1957: Dwight Eisenhower apologized for a racial insult. After the finance minister of Ghana—Komla Agbeli Gbedemah—had been refused service at a restaurant in Dover, Delaware, an appalled and embarrassed president offered his apologies. African diplomats were often the target of racism in the United States. Eisenhower knew it tarnished America's image abroad—which didn't help his broader goal of winning the hearts and minds of people during the Cold War. Such problems would continue for years, however, with diplomats from new countries in Africa and Asia facing housing discrimination and being turned away from places like restaurants and barber shops.

1973: Richard M. Nixon's vice president—Spiro Agnew—resigned. Agnew, snared in a tax-evasion scandal, quit—becoming just the second vice president in American history to step down (John Calhoun in 1832 was the other). He was also fined $10,000 and sentenced to three years' probation. Agnew's resignation triggered the Twenty-fifth Amendment to the Constitution, requiring President Richard M. Nixon to select a new vice president (see October 12).

★ QUOTE OF THE DAY

I believe that the United States as a government, if it is going to be true to its own founding documents, does have the job of working toward that time when there is no discrimination made on such inconsequential reason as race, color, or religion.

Dwight Eisenhower

October 11

1910: Ex-president Theodore Roosevelt became the first president to fly in an airplane. He flew for four minutes in a Wright Brothers plane over St. Louis. But sitting presidents wouldn't begin flying until Franklin D. Roosevelt, in secret, flew on a dangerous World War II mission to Casablanca, Morocco, for talks with British prime minister Winston Churchill.

1986: The climactic summit of the Cold War: Reagan and Gorbachev met in Iceland. A year after their first meeting in Geneva, Switzerland, Ronald Reagan and Soviet leader Mikhail Gorbachev met in Reykjavik, the capital of Iceland, to continue talks about curbing their intermediate range nuclear missiles in Europe. But the talks collapsed when Gorbachev proposed limiting America's Strategic Defense Initiative (SDI).

One of Reagan's key objectives, SDI ("Star Wars" to its opponents) was a proposed space-based defense shield that would, in theory, knock down Soviet nuclear missiles. Reagan had promised the American people that he would never give up SDI, which was then in its research stage. As talks continued, the stakes rose dramatically. At one point, Reagan offered to eliminate all ballistic missiles within a decade—while reserving the right to deploy strategic defenses. Gorbachev proposed eliminating *all* nuclear weapons within a decade—if Reagan dropped SDI. The president, briefly tantalized, said no, and the summit ended, apparently in failure. "Reagan wanted so badly to build it (SDI) and Gorbachev wanted so badly to stop it," wrote Ken Adelmenm, an arms control advisor to the president.

But the Reykjavik talks reflected the degree to which both the United States and Soviet Union—the world's two leading military powers— were willing to make concessions; a year later Reagan and Gorbachev signed the INF treaty—an agreement to limit intermediate range nuclear missiles.

Some historians think Soviet leader Gorbachev was anxious for the United States to drop SDI because of his belief that the U.S.S.R. could not keep up with the United States in military technology or military spending. The Soviet economy was buckling during the 1980s; in 1989, Gorbachev would look on passively as the Berlin Wall fell and Moscow's East European allies broke away. Gorbachev would be briefly overthrown in 1991; the Soviet Union itself collapsed and dissolved later that year.

2002: Former president Jimmy Carter won the Nobel Peace Prize for his "decades of untiring effort" on human rights and economic and social development. The committee had wanted to give Carter the prize years earlier, for his stewardship of the Camp David Accords—the peace deal between Israel and Egypt—but was prevented from doing so by a technicality: Carter had not been nominated by the official deadline.

But after he left office, Carter and his wife Rosalynn created the Atlanta-based Carter Center to advance human rights and alleviate human suffering. Since 1984, they have worked with Habitat for Humanity to build homes and raise awareness of homelessness. Among his many accomplishments, Carter has helped to fight disease and improve economic growth in developing nations and has served as an observer at numerous political elections around the world. For these efforts, the Nobel committee called Carter the best ex-president the United States has ever had. Three other U.S. presidents have won the Nobel Peace Prize: Theodore Roosevelt, Woodrow Wilson, and Barack Obama.

★ QUOTE OF THE DAY

America did not invent human rights. In a very real sense human rights invented America.

Jimmy Carter

October 12

1901: Theodore Roosevelt renamed 1600 Pennsylvania Avenue "the White House." Since John Adams became the first president to live in the grand mansion at 1600 Pennsylvania Avenue NW, the building was often called "The "President's House" or "The Executive Mansion." Roosevelt did away with this, changing the official name to one that most Americans used: "The White House."

1970: Richard M. Nixon pulled 40,000 troops out of Vietnam. Continuing with his "Vietnamization" policy aimed at turning responsibility for fighting North Vietnam over to the South Vietnamese, the president said the 40,000 American troops would be home by Christmas. Nixon's withdrawal from Vietnam was steady: when he became president in January 1969, there were 540,000 Americans there; by the end of 1970 there were 335,000. A year later there were 160,000. By early 1973, after a peace deal

This Day in Presidential History

had been signed with communist North Vietnam, the remaining Americans—including prisoners of war—came home.

1973: Richard M. Nixon chose a new vice president: House Minority Leader Gerald Ford of Michigan. Ford replaced Spiro Agnew, who resigned two days earlier (see October 10). Following Senate confirmation, Ford was sworn in on December 6. Ten months later Ford succeeded Nixon himself, when the president resigned during the Watergate scandal. Gerald Ford thus became the only man in American history to serve as both vice president and president without being elected by the American people to either office.

2000: Bill Clinton condemned a terrorist attack. In Aden, Yemen, an American destroyer, the U.S.S. *Cole*, was badly damaged when a motorized rubber dinghy loaded with explosives pulled up alongside and blew up. The explosion ripped a 40-by-40-foot hole in the port (left) side of the ship. Seventeen sailors were killed and thirty-nine wounded in the attack, which was carried out by two suicide bombers thought to be members of Saudi exile Osama bin Laden's al Qaeda terrorist network. An outraged Clinton called the terror attack "a despicable and cowardly act. We will find out who was responsible and hold them accountable." In 2002, a CIA-operated drone fired a missile at a vehicle in Yemen carrying Abu al-Harithi, a suspected planner of the bombing plot. He was killed.

☆ QUOTE OF THE DAY

To announce that there must be no criticism of the president, or that we are to stand by the president, right or wrong, is not only unpatriotic and servile, but is morally treasonable to the American public.

Theodore Roosevelt

October 13

1792: Construction began on the White House, with the laying of its cornerstone. Commissioners presided over the ceremony, in which a polished brass plate was pressed into a layer of wet mortar, which had been spread across a foundation stone. A stone was placed on top of this, and master mason Collen Williamson nudged it into place. President Washington, tending to the nation's business in Philadelphia, was not present, but was the recipient of at least one toast given in his honor that evening.

The White House was the first public building to be erected in Washington, D.C. In 1790, the commissioners of the District of Columbia offered a prize of $500 to the architect who submitted the best design for the mansion. Hundreds of proposals were submitted, including one from Thomas Jefferson, who submitted his design anonymously. But the commissioners chose instead the blueprint of a young Irish immigrant, James Hoban. Hoban modeled it after one of the grandest buildings in Dublin, the Leinster House.

Construction—mostly by slave labor—took eight years and cost $232,000, about $75 million in 2017 terms. George Washington selected the site, but he never lived there (the only president who never lived in the executive mansion). Since John Adams moved in on November 1, 1800, every president of the United States has called the White House home.

The White House was first known as the "Presidential Palace," and later the "Executive Mansion," until Theodore Roosevelt changed its permanent name to the "White House" in 1901. Even before this, Washingtonians often called it the White House, because its white-gray color stood out amid nearby buildings, which were almost always red brick.

1970: A gloomy report on Vietnam was given to Richard M. Nixon, which said the massive American war in that southeast Asian country could not be won as long as the Viet Cong, a communist fighting force in South Vietnam, remained intact. The U.S. war in Vietnam, which had begun in earnest in 1964, had peaked in 1968 and 1969, when Nixon became president—and the commander in chief was looking for a way out.

★ QUOTE OF THE DAY

Let us raise a standard to which the wise and honest can repair; the rest is in the hands of God.

George Washington

October 14

1890: Dwight D. ("Ike") Eisenhower was born in Denison, Texas. He was the thirty-four president, serving from 1953 to 1961. Eisenhower was really christened David Dwight; he reversed his name when he enrolled at the U.S. Military Academy at West Point in 1911. As an army general in World

This Day in Presidential History   **275**

War II, he led the allied invasion of Nazi-occupied North Africa in 1943, and Operation Overlord—invasion of Nazi-occupied France (D-Day)—on June 6, 1944. He was later promoted to the rank of general in the army and given a fifth star, one of just nine men in American history to be accorded that honor.

With the exception of a sharp recession in 1958–1959, Eisenhower's two terms as president were marked by a rapidly growing U.S. economy and significant social change. The Supreme Court's *Brown vs. Board of Education* ruling in 1954—arguably the most important ruling of the twentieth century—said that school segregation was unconstitutional; in 1957 the president dispatched troops to Little Rock, Arkansas, to make sure that the law was enforced.

On the world stage, Cold War tensions with the Soviet Union and China flared. Eisenhower condemned the 1956 Soviet invasion of Hungary but took no action. He also condemned an Israeli, British, and French invasion of Egypt, and pressured them to withdraw. Eisenhower ordered CIA coups in Iran and Guatemala, and, as the space age dawned, started the National Aeronautics and Space Administration (NASA).

An aggregation of rankings by presidential historians and political scientists, released by C-SPAN in 2017, rated Dwight Eisenhower as the ninth-greatest U.S. president.

1912: Former president Theodore Roosevelt was shot in the chest while giving a speech in Milwaukee, Wisconsin, by a mentally ill former tavern

Dwight D. Eisenhower. Official White House portrait.

keeper, John Flammang Schrank. Roosevelt, the former Republican president (1901–1909) who was now seeking that office as a member of the Progressive Party, was hit in the chest by a .32 caliber bullet. But thanks to a Roosevelt's heavy coat, a glasses case, and a thick, folded copy of his speech, the bullet only inflicted a flesh wound. Announcing that he had been shot, he pulled the torn and bloodstained speech from his breast pocket and boasted, "It takes more than one bullet to kill a Bull Moose." He spoke for nearly an hour and then went to the hospital. He finished second in that year's four-man presidential race, with Democrat Woodrow Wilson also defeating Republican William Howard Taft (the presidential incumbent) and socialist Eugene Debs.

★ QUOTE OF THE DAY

Though force can protect in emergency, only justice, fairness, consideration and cooperation can finally lead men to the dawn of eternal peace.

Dwight D. Eisenhower

October 15

1860: Why did Abraham Lincoln have a beard? He received a letter from an eleven-year-old girl, Grace Bedell, saying he would look better with one. Lincoln agreed. In Bedell's letter, written on October 15, 1860—just a few weeks before the 1860 election—she told Lincoln, "I have got 4 brothers, and part of them will vote for you any way and if you let your whiskers grow I will try and get the rest of them to vote for you. You would look a great deal better for your face is so thin. All the ladies like whiskers and they would tease their husbands to vote for you and then you would be President." On October 19, Lincoln replied to the "dear little miss": "Do you not think people would call it a piece of silly affect[at]ion if I were to begin it now?" But days after his election, the president-elect changed his mind. "Billy," he reportedly told his barber, "let's give them a chance to grow."

On February 16, 1861, as president-elect Lincoln was traveling to Washington to be sworn in, his train passed through Grace's hometown of Westfield, New York. He asked to meet her and young Grace met Lincoln—who by then had grown his now-famous beard.

1974: Gerald Ford signed a bill aimed at overhauling campaign finance reform. The Federal Elections Campaign Act placed legal limits on campaign contributions; it also created the Federal Election Commission (FEC), an independent agency responsible disclosing campaign finance information and oversee the public funding of presidential elections.

☆ QUOTE OF THE DAY

No man will ever carry out of the Presidency the reputation which carried him into it.

Thomas Jefferson

Lincoln may have grown a beard for another reason. He knew he wasn't a particularly attractive man, and often cracked jokes about his homeliness. During one of his famous debates with Stephen Douglas, Douglas called him two-faced. Lincoln turned and appealed to the crowd. "If I had another face," he asked, "do you think I'd wear this one?"

October 16

1854: Abraham Lincoln condemned slavery. Lincoln, a lawyer and former one-term congressman from Illinois, delivered a speech on the Kansas-Nebraska Act, which Congress had passed five months earlier. The future president attacked it, saying slavery was "immoral."

The Kansas-Nebraska Act allowed two new territories—Kansas and Nebraska—to join the United States, with the citizens of each given the power to determine whether slavery would be allowed or disallowed. Abolitionists like Lincoln hoped to convince lawmakers in the new territories to reject slavery. He believed the law went against the founding American principle that "all men are created equal." Lincoln was determined to outlaw the spread of slavery to new states, but worried that outlawing it in states where it already existed might lead to civil war. He hoped that by confining slavery to the South, "it would surely die a slow death."

Lincoln's eloquent opposition to slavery raised his political profile across the nation; although he lost an Illinois senate race to Stephen Douglas in 1858, he would win the presidency in 1860.

1901: Theodore Roosevelt shocked the nation by dining with a black man—Booker T. Washington—at the White House. The president caused a national sensation by having dinner with Washington, the African American educator who had become a close friend. Other presidents had invited African–Americans to meetings at the White House, but never for a meal. And segregation was law in 1901. The president was later praised by some but fiercely criticized by others; Washington received death threats.

1962: The Cuban Missile Crisis began. John F. Kennedy was informed that the Soviet Union was placing nuclear missiles in Cuba that were capable of destroying most of the United States. It was the beginning of the Cuban Missile Crisis—a tense thirteen-day standoff—that nearly led to nuclear war between the United States and the Soviet Union. The standoff gave birth to the term Mutual Assured Destruction (MAD), in which both sides understood that they would each be destroyed in a nuclear conflict.

★ QUOTE OF THE DAY

In the long history of the world, only a few generations have been granted the role of defending freedom in its hour of maximum danger. I do not shrink from this responsibility—I welcome it.

John F. Kennedy, from his inaugural address

October 17

1859: James Buchanan ordered U.S. Marines—led by Robert E. Lee—to retake Harper's Ferry, Virginia (now West Virginia), after the town had been seized by abolitionist John Brown. Brown had hoped that his raid would spark a nationwide revolt of slaves and had asked two leading abolitionists—Frederick Douglass and Harriet Tubman—to join him. Tubman was ill and declined, while Douglass thought Brown's plan faulty and declined to participate. Lee of course, would soon resign his U.S. military commission (he was in the Army) to lead the Confederate Army of Northern Virginia during the Civil War.

1973: Richard M. Nixon coped with an oil embargo. After the president ordered U.S. military assistance to Israel, which had been attacked by its Arab neighbors, OPEC—the Organization of Petroleum Exporting Countries—began an oil embargo against America. The embargo sparked

This Day in Presidential History   **279**

widespread energy shortages in the United States. Gasoline prices soared, and the country fell into a deep recession. By the time the embargo ended in March 1974, the average retail price of gas had climbed to 84 cents per gallon from 38 cents per gallon. Americans responded by ditching big, gas-guzzling cars for smaller, fuel-efficient ones. At one point, worries over energy supplies were so great that the Nixon administration contemplated seizing Middle East oil fields.

1974: Gerald Ford testified to Congress on Nixon's pardon. In a rarity for an American president, Ford traveled to Capitol Hill to testify to Congress as to why he had pardoned his predecessor, Richard M. Nixon, for his involvement in the Watergate scandal. Rather than be impeached and removed from office, Nixon chose to resign in August; a month later Ford pardoned him for crimes "he committed or may have committed." Ford told lawmakers that legal proceedings or further punishment against Nixon would only further polarize the public; he wanted America to move on. Ford's popularity fell. The Nixon pardon probably cost him votes in his failed effort to win the presidency in 1976. Had he won just 3,687 more votes in Hawaii and 5,559 in Ohio, he would have won.

1975: A car slammed into Gerald Ford's limo. A month after two assassination attempts (see September 5 and September 22), the president's car was hit as it drove through an intersection in Hartford, Connecticut. The president was not hurt. The intersection had not been secured by police and the Secret Service and the other driver, nineteen-year-old James Salamites, had a green light. After questioning Salamites and his teenage passengers, police cleared him of any wrongdoing. The incident caused a major review of security procedures for presidential motorcades. The president later phoned Salamites to see how he was doing.

☆ QUOTE OF THE DAY

We would needlessly be diverted from meeting those challenges if we as a people were to remain sharply divided over whether to indict, bring to trial, and punish a former president, who already is condemned to suffer long and deeply in the shame and disgrace brought upon the office he held. Surely, we are not a revengeful people. We have often demonstrated a readiness to feel compassion and to act out of mercy. As a people, we have a long record of forgiving even those who have been our country's most destructive foes.

Yet, to forgive is not to forget the lessons of evil in whatever ways evil has operated against us. And certainly the pardon granted the former president will not cause us to forget the evils of Watergate-type offenses or to forget the lessons we have learned that a government which deceives its supporters and treats its opponents as enemies must never, never be tolerated.

Gerald Ford

Gerald Ford's testimony to Congress on his pardon of former President Richard M. Nixon was only the third time in American history that a sitting president has testified before Congress. On February 13, 1862, Abraham Lincoln testified to the House Judiciary Committee about the leak of his state of the union message to a New York newspaper; and on August 19, 1919, Woodrow Wilson encouraged the Senate Foreign Relations committee to pass the Versailles Treaty (it didn't).

October 18

1867: The United States formally took possession of Alaska after purchasing the territory from Russia for $7.2 million, or less than two cents an acre. Alaska was huge: 586,412 square miles, about twice the size of Texas. Its purchase, authorized by President Andrew Johnson, was championed by Secretary of State William Seward. At the time, the purchase of Alaska was regarded as a joke by the American people—"Seward's Folly," it was called.

1962: John F. Kennedy played coy with the Soviets on Cuba. With photos of Soviet nuclear missiles in Cuba within arms' reach, the president was told by Soviet foreign minister Gromyko that the U.S.S.R. had no offensive weapons there. Kennedy knew that Gromyko was lying. He went on TV four days later to announce a naval quarantine of Cuba and demanded that Moscow remove its missiles from Cuba.

★ QUOTE OF THE DAY

If the rabble were lopped off at one end and the aristocrat at the other, all would be well with the country.

Andrew Johnson

October 19

1960: Dwight Eisenhower ordered a U.S. trade embargo against Cuba; everything was banned but medicine and food.

1973: Watergate continued closing in on Richard M. Nixon; he rejected an Appeals Court decision ordering him to turn over audio tapes related to Watergate scandal. The next day, all hell would break loose—with what came to be known as the "Saturday Night Massacre" (see October 20).

1987: Ronald Reagan blamed soaring federal deficits for the biggest one-day crash of stocks—22%—in American history. In response to the stock market crash, Reagan said he would consider raising taxes as part of a deficit-reduction package. Earlier in his administration Reagan had signed off on higher taxes on gasoline and personal income—and the 1986 Tax Reform Act also raised $420 billion (approximately $770 billion in 2016 dollars) by raising corporate taxes and closing loopholes.

☆ QUOTE OF THE DAY

If a nation expects to be ignorant and free, in a state of civilization, it expects what never was and never will be.

Thomas Jefferson

October 20

1964: Herbert Hoover died at New York City. He was the thirty-first president, serving from 1929 to1933. Hoover—one of just three men to be elected president without being elected to any previous office or having a high military rank (William Taft and Donald Trump were the others)—took office during a time of great prosperity and progress, but seven months after being sworn in, the stock market collapsed, ushering in the Great Depression. Hoover and Congress fought the Depression with tactics that appeared to make things even worse. The Smoot-Hawley Tariff act repressed trade. The top personal income tax bracket jumped from 25% to 63%. Corporate taxes increased as well. Historians generally regard Hoover's presidency—which ended with the landslide election of Franklin Roosevelt in 1932—as a failure.

This Day in Presidential History

1973: Richard M. Nixon's Saturday Night Massacre blew Watergate wide open. The president, trying to contain Watergate, fired his own attorney general, Elliot Richardson, Deputy Attorney General William Ruckelshaus, and the Watergate special prosecutor Archibald Cox. It caused a national uproar; and talk of impeachment—from both parties—grew.

★ QUOTE OF THE DAY

About the time we can make the ends meet, somebody moves the ends.

Herbert Hoover

October 21

1902: Theodore Roosevelt helped settle a crippling strike by coal miners. Miners in Pennsylvania had walked off the job that spring, and with winter approaching, the prospect of a winter coal shortage weighed heavily on the president's mind. Roosevelt asked both union leaders and mine operators to the White House, where an end to the strike was negotiated. The gesture helped underscore what the president called his "Square Deal" for the American people.

1921: In the first public remarks by a sitting president on the subject, Warren Harding—in Alabama—condemned the lynching of African Americans. Although the number of lynchings had been declining since the late nineteenth century, data shows that they were still occurring in 1921 at the rate of more than one per week. Harding—a progressive Republican who supported full civil rights for blacks—voiced support for anti-lynching bills, which were soon passed by the House—but defeated in the Senate.

1972: Richard M. Nixon gave the Environmental Protection Agency greater powers to regulate the sale and use of pesticides. The EPA was first proposed by Nixon and began operations in 1970 after the president signed an executive order (see December 2).

1984: Acknowledging his own age, President Reagan said he would not make an issue of presidential opponent Walter Mondale's youth and inexperience. Reagan's line during his second debate with former vice president Mondale was a response to a poor performance in their first debate, when Reagan said he was "confused," didn't know what city he was in, and said soldiers wore "wardrobes."

This Day in Presidential History

★ QUOTE OF THE DAY

Congress ought to wipe the stain of barbaric lynching from the banners of a free and orderly, representative democracy.

Warren Harding

October 22

1962: Going public with his knowledge of Soviet nuclear missiles in Cuba, John F. Kennedy demanded their removal and threatened war. Speaking on TV, the president announced a naval "quarantine" of Cuba and warned that any Soviet missiles fired anywhere in the Western hemisphere would be regarded as an attack on the United States, "requiring a full retaliatory response."

1965: Lyndon B. Johnson signed the Highway Beautification Act. The president said its goals were to limit advertising billboards, junkyards, and general ugliness along America's interstate highways. The act was the pet project of First Lady Lady Bird Johnson, who believed that removing ugliness from the nation's roadways would make America a better place to live.

★ QUOTE OF THE DAY

Ask not what your country can do for you—but what you can do for your country.

John F. Kennedy, from his inaugural address

October 23

1983: An outraged Ronald Reagan condemned a terror bombing that killed 241 U.S. servicemen. The bombing of a Marine Corps base in Beirut, Lebanon, was the worst day for the Marines since World War II. The president had sent troops to Lebanon earlier in 1983, hoping to stabilize that civil-war ravaged country. Hezbollah, a terrorist group linked to Iran, took credit for the bombing. The president chose not to retaliate and

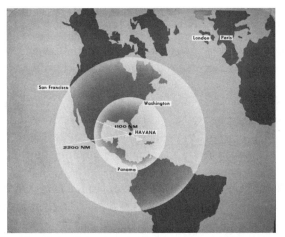

Nuclear missiles placed in Cuba by the Soviet Union sparked the most danger-ous chapter of the Cold War: the Cuban Missile Crisis. John F. Kennedy's calm and determined management of the standoff prevented nuclear war. United States. Department of Defense. Department of Defense Cuban Missile Crisis Briefing Materials. John F. Kennedy Presidential Library and Museum, Boston.

later ordered a withdrawal of American forces from Lebanon. Reagan would never again send ground troops there—or anywhere in the Middle East. Osama bin Laden, the leader of the terrorist group al Qaeda—which would attack New York and Washington in 2001 (see September 11) later said that Reagan's failure to respond to a series of terror attacks convinced him that America was weak—and could be attacked.

1973: Richard M. Nixon agreed to turn over nine secret Watergate record-ings to Federal Judge John Sirica. Citing executive privilege, the president at first had refused to comply with the judge's order, which was issued on August 29, 1973. But as pressure from the media and public grew, Nixon relented.

☆ QUOTE OF THE DAY

We should all recognize that these deeds make so evident the bestial nature of those who would assume power if they could have their way and drive us out of that area that we must be more determined than ever that they cannot take over that vital and strategic area of the earth or, for that matter, any other part of the earth.

Ronald Reagan

This Day in Presidential History

October 24

1861: Abraham Lincoln received the first transcontinental telegram. It was sent to him from San Francisco by California's chief justice, Stephen J. Field. Like radio in the 1920s, television in the 1950s, or the Internet today, the telegraph ushered in dramatic changes in the way Americans communicated with each other. Just two days after Lincoln received the telegraph from California, the federal government halted its use of the famous Pony Express and turned to what Western Union called "lightening lines" to spread communications nationwide. The telegraph would have vital military applications as well; the president spent long hours in the telegraph room (located in the War Department next door to the White House) during the Civil War.

1929: The Great Depression began with "Black Thursday"—a massive Wall Street crash. Followed five days later with yet another plunge ("Black Tuesday"), it began a decade-long collapse that affected much of the western world. At first, President Herbert Hoover downplayed the crash, declaring on October 25 that "the fundamental business of the country, that is, the production and distribution of commodities, is on a very sound and prosperous basis." But as the downturn worsened, efforts by Hoover to combat it proved ineffective; his re-election bid in 1932 would be crushed by Franklin D. Roosevelt.

1951: Truman ended the official state of war with Germany, six years after World War II ended. Germany had surrendered in 1945, but a formal treaty had never been signed. A formal end to the war was delayed by sparring between the United States, Britain, and France with the Soviet Union over the status of German territory, including the divided city of Berlin.

1973: Richard M. Nixon vetoed the War Powers Resolution, aimed at limiting a president's ability to wage war. The president objected to the bill, introduced by Senator Jacob K. Javits of New York, which stipulated that a commander-in-chief had to report to Congress 48 hours after sending troops into combat. The law also said that presidents could also keep troops in combat for just 60 days (and a 30-day withdrawal period) unless they had Congressional approval for longer deployments. Congress later overrode Nixon's veto.

★ QUOTE OF THE DAY

The Founding Fathers understood the impossibility of foreseeing every contingency that might arise in this complex area. They acknowledged

This Day in Presidential History

the need for flexibility in responding to changing circumstances. They recognized that foreign policy decisions must be made through close cooperation between the two branches and not through rigidly codified procedures.

Richard M. Nixon, on his veto of the War Powers Resolution

October 25

1892: First Lady Caroline Harrison died from tuberculosis, sending President Benjamin Harrison into mourning. Mrs. Harrison was one of three First Ladies to die while their husband was in office. Letitia Tyler (1842) and Ellen Wilson (1914) were the others.

1926: The Supreme Court ruled that presidents could fire members of the cabinet at their own discretion. The ruling nullified the 1868 Tenure of Office Act, which required consent of the Senate before a president could remove a member of the cabinet.

1983: Ronald Reagan ordered U.S. Marines to invade the Caribbean island of Grenada and rescue 1,000 Americans from its Marxist regime. About 6,000 U.S. troops landed on the tiny island, located off the coast of Venezuela, and the Marxist government fell within a week. Sixteen U.S. troops were killed during the operation.

★ QUOTE OF THE DAY

Freedom is never more than one generation away from extinction. We didn't pass it to our children in the bloodstream. It must be fought for, protected, and handed on for them to do the same.

Ronald Reagan

October 26

1826: John Quincy Adams hailed the opening of the first part of the Erie Canal. The president, a staunch supporter of infrastructure programs, thought the Canal would boost the U.S. economy by linking population

This Day in Presidential History

centers on the East coast with agricultural areas further inland. The Erie Canal would eventually span 363 miles from Lake Erie to New York City.

1994: With Bill Clinton looking on, Israeli Prime Minister Rabin and Jordan's King Hussein signed a peace treaty. The treaty normalized relations between the two countries and resolved longstanding territorial disputes. The treaty, which was closely linked with ongoing efforts to create peace between Israel and the Palestinian Authority, made Jordan just the second Arab country after Egypt to normalize relations with Israel.

2001: In the wake of the September 11, 2001, terror attacks on the United States, George W. Bush signed the Patriot Act, a series of security measures aimed at preventing future attacks. The Patriot Act, which stood for "Providing Appropriate Tools Required to Intercept and Obstruct Terrorism," gave the federal government broad new powers to gather intelligence, improved information sharing among intelligence agencies and eased restrictions on communications surveillance:

- The Treasury Department could now better regulate financial transactions involving foreigners and U.S. companies
- Law enforcement and immigration officials were given broader discretion to detain (indefinitely) and deport immigrants
- Intelligence agencies had greater ability to use "roving wiretaps" on telephone, e-mail, and financial records
- Searches of homes and businesses ("the records provision") without the owner's or occupant's permission or knowledge
- Better surveillance of the so-called "lone wolves" who might be operating on their own

There have been several legal challenges since 2001 to the Patriot Act; federal courts have ruled that some are unconstitutional. Civil rights supporters have said the provisions trample upon the individual liberties of American citizens.

2006: George W. Bush signed a bill to construct a fence on the United States-Mexican border. The goal was to build a 700-mile-long barrier along key points of America's southern border, to curb illegal immigration, drug trafficking, and potential terrorists. By April 2009 the Department of Homeland Security had erected about 613 miles of the barrier along portions of the border, ranging from California to Texas. The rest of the 700-mile fence was never built. The entire U.S.-Mexican border is approximately 2,200 miles long.

★ QUOTE OF THE DAY

We will bankrupt ourselves in the vain search for absolute security.

Dwight Eisenhower

October 27

1810: James Madison issued a proclamation authorizing the annexation of Western Florida, which was thought to be—but wasn't—part of the 1803 Louisiana Purchase.

1858: Theodore Roosevelt was born in New York City. He was the 26th president, serving from 1901 to 1909. After the 1901 assassination of William McKinley, Roosevelt, at 42, became the youngest-ever president—though the youngest person *elected* was John F. Kennedy.

If ever there was a man born for his era, it was "TR." As the curtain rose on the twentieth century, the United States had quietly, and rather quickly, become a great world power. Straddling a continent, protected by the buffer of two vast oceans, rich in natural resources, industrializing rapidly, and not the least bit hesitant about embracing the future, America and its bespectacled new leader could be defined in exactly the same way: forward-thinking, brash, and supremely confident. Historians generally rank him as the fifth-greatest president, and for his efforts to preserve the environment, Theodore Roosevelt's bust is one of four carved onto Mount Rushmore.

1941: Ten days after a German U-boat torpedoed a U.S. destroyer (the *Kearney*), Franklin D. Roosevelt told Americans: "America has been attacked, the shooting has started." The president stopped short of declaring war on Germany, though, given that many Americans remained reluctant to get into another European conflict. Another U.S. destroyer, the *Reuben James,* would be sunk three days later, killing 115 Americans. The United States and Germany would declare war on each other in December (see December 11).

Theodore Roosevelt in 1907. Library of Congress.

★ QUOTE OF THE DAY

Nobody cares how much you know, until they know how much you care.

Theodore Roosevelt

October 28

1886: In New York harbor, Grover Cleveland dedicated the "The Statue of Liberty Enlightening the World"—more commonly known as the Statue of Liberty. Lady Liberty, a gift from the people of France, has served as a symbol of freedom ever since. "We will not forget that liberty here made her home; nor shall her chosen altar be neglected," the president said.

1962: The Cuban Missile Crisis ended when the Soviet Union agreed to remove nuclear missiles from Cuba. President John F. Kennedy, hours from ordering a U.S. attack on Cuba, accepted the Soviet offer and ended a U.S. naval quarantine. The Cuban Missile Crisis—easily the most dangerous chapter of the Cold War—nearly led to nuclear war between the United States and Soviet Union. Analysts believe that a nuclear exchange between the two superpowers would have killed 100 million Americans (then 55% of the U.S. population) and 100 million Soviets.

1998: Bill Clinton signed the Digital Millennium Copyright Act, aimed at strengthening copyright protections posed by the internet.

★ QUOTE OF THE DAY

The cost of freedom is always high, but Americans have always paid it.

John F. Kennedy

October 29

1901: William McKinley's assassin was executed. Leon Czolgosz was electrocuted just 45 days after the president's death; McKinley lingered for eight days after being shot in Buffalo, New York.

1940: As Franklin D. Roosevelt looked on, the first peacetime draft in American history was held. Five weeks earlier, the president had signed the Selective Service and Training Act, requiring men aged 21-35 to register. Nazi Germany's defeat that spring of Denmark, Norway, the Netherlands, Belgium, and France—leaving Britain all alone to fight Adolf Hitler—made a draft a real possibility. U.S. military spending also began to rise sharply.

1975: Gerald Ford refused to bail out New York City from a fiscal crisis. Instead of a bailout, the president advised the nation's biggest city to adopt fiscal restraint and make cutbacks. A famous headline in the *New York Daily News* the next day blared: "Ford to City—Drop Dead," a phrase that the president certainly did not utter.

1994: A man fired at least 29 shots at the White House with a semi-automatic rifle. President Bill Clinton was inside at the time. The gunman, Francisco Martin Duran, was tackled by three tourists. Found with a suicide note in his pocket, Duran was sentenced to 40 years in prison.

★ QUOTE OF THE DAY

We are mustering all our resources, manhood, and industry and wealth to make our nation strong in defense. For recent history proves all too clearly, I am sorry to say, that only the strong may continue to live in freedom and in peace.

Franklin D. Roosevelt

October 30

1735: John Adams was born in Braintree, in the Province of Massachusetts Bay. He was the second U.S. president, serving from 1797 to 1801. Known as "the Atlas of Independence," Adams was, of course, one of the Founding Fathers. He was also the first vice-president, serving under George Washington.

Adams is regarded by some historians as a better political philosopher than politician, yet his career was marked by numerous accomplishments that highlighted his political skills. His eloquent arguments for independence inspired others, including his widely published papers attacking the Stamp Act of 1765 and the legality of British taxation of the colonies without political representation.

Adams was the first president to live in the White House, moving in on November 1, 1800. First Lady Abigail was famous for hanging laundry

John Adams. Library of Congress.

This Day in Presidential History

in the East Room. As president, he nominated John Marshall to be chief justice of the Supreme Court. It was one of the most momentous appointments in the high court's history: Marshall would serve for 34 years. President Adams also handled the "Quasi-War" with France in 1798. A dispute over trade routes sparked naval battles, but the president's diplomatic efforts prevented a broader war. Historians credit the president for securing the peace while standing up to a major European power.

He would die, as would Thomas Jefferson, on July 4, 1826—the 50th birthday of the United States.

1953: Dwight Eisenhower signed a National Security Council document saying the U.S. nuclear arsenal must be expanded to meet the growing Soviet threat. The president saw atomic weapons as the best deterrent to Soviet power, but feared the U.S. economy couldn't support both military and domestic spending.

★ QUOTE OF THE DAY

Liberty cannot be preserved without general knowledge among the people.

John Adams

October 31

1941: Mount Rushmore—featuring 60-foot busts of Presidents Washington, Jefferson, Lincoln, and Theodore Roosevelt—was completed. Four hundred laborers led by sculptor Gutzon Borglum worked on the herculean task that was begun in October 1927. The presidents chosen for Mount Rushmore symbolized America's founding (Washington) political philosophy (Jefferson), preservation (Lincoln), and conservation (Roosevelt).

1956: Breaking with key allies, Dwight Eisenhower condemned a British, French, and Israeli attack on Egypt (the Suez Crisis)—and said the United States would not help them. As the world focused on the Suez Crisis, Soviet tanks rolled into Hungary to crush an uprising there. Eisenhower refused to get involved in that crisis either, saying he would not aid the Hungarian freedom fighters. The Hungarian rebellion was crushed by

Moscow. Eisenhower's refusal to help either the Israelis or the anti-Soviet freedom fighters didn't mar his successful re-election just days later.

1968: Five days before the presidential election Lyndon B. Johnson announced a halt to the bombing of North Vietnam. It didn't last.

☆ QUOTE OF THE DAY

The peace we seek and need means much more than mere absence of war. It means the acceptance of law, and the fostering of justice, in all the world.

Dwight Eisenhower

November

November 1

1800: John Adams became the first president to move into the President's House—known today, of course, as the White House. Construction on the mansion wasn't even finished when Adams' carriage arrived at 1600 Pennsylvania Avenue (First Lady Abigail would arrive a month later). But their furniture, which had been brought from Philadelphia, was in place and the famous Gilbert Stuart portrait of George Washington—the only president who never lived in the White House—had been proudly hung.

In a note the next day to his wife, Adams expressed his wish that "may none but honest and wise men (shall) ever rule under this roof." Adams himself would only live in the house for five months. His reelection bid was defeated by Thomas Jefferson, and President and Mrs. Adams returned to their native Massachusetts in February 1801.

1828: Andrew Jackson was elected as the seventh president of the United States, defeating the incumbent president John Quincy Adams. Jackson, a Democrat, won with 56% of the popular vote and 178 electoral votes to Adams's 83 (the election took place over several days).

1950: Harry Truman survived an assassination attempt. The attack on Truman by Puerto Rican nationalists took place at Blair House, across from the White House, where the president was living while the White House was being renovated. Secret Service officer Leslie Coffelt was killed during the attack. The president watched the gunfight from his open window, just a few feet away, until a passerby shouted at him to take cover.

★ QUOTE OF THE DAY

A Constitution of Government once changed from Freedom, can never be restored. Liberty, once lost, is lost forever.

John Adams

James K. Polk. Library of Congress.   **Warren G. Harding.** Library of Congress.

November 2

1795: James Knox Polk was born in Pineville, North Carolina. He was the eleventh president, serving from 1845 to 1849. Polk is best known for leading the nation into the Mexican-American War, a conflict that resulted in the United States expanding all the way to the Pacific Coast, making it a true continental power. The United States also added the Oregon territory during Polk's tenure. Altogether, the United States grew more during Polk's presidency than at any other time.

1852: Franklin Pierce was elected the fourteenth president of the United States. Pierce, the New Hampshire Democrat, received 50.8% of the popular vote and 254 electoral votes to Winfield Scott's (the New Jersey Whig) 43.9% and 42, respectively.

1865: Warren G. Harding was born in Blooming Grove, Ohio. He was the twenty-ninth president, serving from 1921 to 1923. To this day, Harding's winning margin in the election of 1920—26.17 points over James Cox—remains the largest in American history.

1880: In the tightest race in U.S. history, James A. Garfield was elected the twentieth president of the United States. Garfield, the Ohio Republican, won the popular vote over Pennsylvania Democrat Winfield Scott Hancock by just 1,898 votes. The electoral vote margin was 214 to 155.

1948: Harry S. Truman, president since the 1945 death of Franklin D. Roosevelt, was elected in his own right. The thirty-third president, who was considered an underdog, defeated New York Governor Thomas Dewey, with 303 electoral votes and 49.6% of the popular vote to Dewey's 189 and 45.1%, respectively. A third-party candidate, Strom Thurmond of the Dixiecrat party, won 39 electoral votes and 2.9% of the popular vote.

1976: Jimmy Carter was elected the thirty-ninth president of the United States. The Georgia Democrat got 50.1% of the popular vote and 297 electoral votes to incumbent president Gerald Ford's 48.0% of the popular vote and 240 electoral votes. Ford won twenty-seven states, the most ever by a losing candidate.

2004: George W. Bush was reelected. The forty-third president won 50.7% of the popular vote and 286 electoral votes; Democratic challenger John Kerry got 48.3% of the popular vote and 251 electoral votes.

November 3

1896: William McKinley was elected the twenty-fifth president of the United States. The Ohio Republican won 51.0% of the popular vote and 271 electoral votes to Democratic challenger William Jennings Bryan's 46.7% and 176, respectively.

1908: William Howard Taft was elected the twenty-seventh president of the United States. The Ohio Republican won 51.6% of the popular vote and 321 electoral votes to Democratic challenger William Jennings Bryan's 43.0% and 162, respectively. It was Bryan's third and final attempt to win the presidency.

1936: Franklin D. Roosevelt was reelected. The thirty-second president won in a crushing landslide, beating Republican challenger Alf Landon by 60.8% to 36.5% in the popular vote and 523-8 in the electoral college.

★ QUOTE OF THE DAY

Without the assistance of that Divine Being who ever attended him, I cannot succeed. With that assistance I cannot fail.

Lyndon B. Johnson, quoting Abraham Lincoln

This Day in Presidential History

1964: Lyndon B. Johnson was elected. The president—who assumed office a year before following the assassination of John F. Kennedy (see November 22), won in a huge landslide, getting 61.1% of the popular vote to Republican challenger Barry Goldwater's 38.5% and 486 electoral votes to Goldwater's 52.

1992: Bill Clinton was elected the forty-second president of the United States. In a three-man race, Clinton, the Arkansas Democrat received 43.0% of the popular vote and 370 electoral votes. The incumbent president George H.W. Bush got 37.4% and 168 electoral votes. Ross Perot, an independent candidate from Texas got 18.9% of the vote—but no electoral votes.

November 4

1796: The Washington administration agreed to pay protection money to safeguard American shipping in the Mediterranean. The yearly U.S. "tribute" to the Pasha of Tripoli helped guarantee the peaceful transit of American cargo ships.

1856: James Buchanan was elected the fifteenth president of the United States. In a three-man race, the Pennsylvania Democrat won 45.3% of the popular vote and 174 electoral votes. Republican John Fremont of California received 33.1% and 114 electoral votes, and former President Millard Fillmore, running as the American Party's candidate, won 21.5% of the popular vote and 8 electoral votes.

1884: Grover Cleveland was elected the twenty-second president of the United States. In one of the closest races in U.S. history, Cleveland, the New York Democrat, got 48.9% of the popular vote to Maine Republican James Blaine's 48.3%. The electoral vote margin was 219-182. It was the first Democratic win since 1856.

1924: Calvin Coolidge was elected. The Republican Coolidge, who had become the thirtieth president after the sudden death of Warren Harding in 1923 (see August 2), won 54.0% of the popular vote and 382 electoral votes. Democrat Charles Bryan of West Virginia won 28.8% of the popular vote and 136 electoral votes, while Wisconsin's Burton Wheeler, the Progressive candidate, 16.6% of the popular vote and 13 electoral votes.

1939: With World War II under way, Congress agreed to Franklin D. Roosevelt's proposal to let Allied nations buy American weapons. FDR's changes to the Neutrality Act were clearly aimed at benefiting Britain and France, which had just declared war on Nazi Germany. Roosevelt successfully argued that U.S. neutrality laws prior to the war may have given passive "aid to an aggressor" because it denied aid to victimized nations.

1952: Dwight Eisenhower was elected the thirty-fourth president of the United States. The former general, a Republican, won easily over Democrat Adlai Stevenson, getting 55.2% of the popular vote and 442 electoral votes to Stevenson's 44.3% and 89, respectively.

1979: Iranian students took sixty-six Americans hostage. The seizure of the U.S. embassy in Tehran sparked a 444-day crisis; the failure of President Jimmy Carter to end it would play a large role in his losing reelection bid the next year.

1980: Ronald Reagan was elected the fortieth president of the United States. The Republican, a former two-term governor of California, beat the incumbent president Jimmy Carter with just 50.7% of the popular vote—but a crushing 489 electoral votes. Carter got 41.0% of the popular vote and 49 electoral votes. An independent candidate, John Anderson, got 6.6% of the popular vote but no electoral votes.

2008: Barack Obama was elected the forty-fourth president of the United States. The Illinois Democrat—the first African–American president—got 52.9% of the popular vote to Arizona Republican John McCain's 45.7%. Obama won 352 electoral votes; McCain 173.

★ QUOTE OF THE DAY

If there is anyone out there who still doubts that America is a place where all things are possible, who still wonders if the dream of our Founders is alive in our time, who still questions the power of our democracy, tonight is your answer.

Barack Obama

November 5

1862: Abraham Lincoln fired, for the second time, General George McClellan as commander of the Union Army. Lincoln was frustrated that McClellan seemed unable to engage Confederate General Robert E. Lee's

Army of Northern Virginia. Lincoln gave McClellan two chances, and the General capitalized on neither of them. It was the second instance that particularly infuriated Lincoln. At Antietam, Maryland, on September 17, 1862—still the single bloodiest day in American history—McClellan, despite knowing Lee's plan and having a superior force at his disposal, fought Lee to a standstill but failed to defeat him. He also failed to pursue Lee's forces as they withdrew across the Potomac River to Virginia. McClellan, Lincoln famously said, has a "case of the slows."

1872: Ulysses S. Grant was reelected. The eighteenth president, a Republican, won 55.6% of the popular vote and 286 electoral votes to Democrat Horace Greeley's 43.8% of the popular vote and 66 electoral votes.

1912: Woodrow Wilson was elected the twenty-eighth president of the United States. In a crowded four-man field, Democrat Wilson beat sitting Republican president William Howard Taft, former Republican president Theodore Roosevelt (the Progressive Party nominee), and Socialist Eugene Debs. Wilson got just 41.8% of the popular vote but 435 electoral votes. Roosevelt got 26.4% of the popular vote and 88 electoral votes, while Taft got 23.2% of the popular vote and 8 electoral votes. Debs got 6.0% of the popular vote and no electoral votes.

1940: Franklin D. Roosevelt was reelected. The thirty-second president, a Democrat, beat Wendell Willkie with 54.7% of the popular vote and 449 electoral votes. It was a record third term for FDR, who broke the unwritten rule established by George Washington that limited presidents to two terms in office.

1968: Capping one of the most turbulent years in American history, Richard M. Nixon was elected the thirty-seventh president of the United States, defeating Vice President Hubert Humphrey. Nixon won 43.4% of the popular vote and 301 electoral votes to Humphrey's 42.7% and 191, respectively. Alabama governor George Wallace, the American Independent Party's candidate, got 13.5% of the popular vote and 46 electoral votes.

1996: Bill Clinton was reelected. With 49% of the vote, the president easily defeated Republican Kansas Senator Bob Dole, who got 41%. Clinton, the forty-second president, became the first Democrat since Franklin D. Roosevelt to win a second term in the White House.

2003: George W. Bush signed a bill banning late-term abortion. It was the first law to ban an abortion procedure since the Supreme Court's landmark 1973 *Roe v. Wade* decision.

☆ QUOTE OF THE DAY

Our (political) process works in this country when we have devoted, dedicated people giving their all in battle for a cause that they believe in.

Richard M. Nixon

November 6

1860: With the Civil War about to begin, Abraham Lincoln was elected as the sixteenth president of the United States. The Illinois Republican won 39.8% of the popular vote and 180 electoral votes in a four-man race. The Illinois Republican beat Stephen Douglas, the Northern Democratic candidate (29.5% of the popular vote and 12 electoral votes), Southern Democratic candidate John Breckenridge (18.1% of the popular vote and 72 electoral votes), and Constitutional Union candidate John Bell (12.6% of the popular vote and 39 electoral votes).

1900: William McKinley was reelected. In a rematch with his 1896 rival William Jennings Bryan, McKinley—the twenty-fifth president—won 51.6% of the popular vote and 292 electoral votes. Bryan received 45.5% and 155, respectively.

1956: Dwight Eisenhower was reelected. In a rematch with his 1952 rival Adlai Stevenson, Eisenhower, the thirty-fourth president, won with 57.4% of the popular vote and 457 electoral votes. Stevenson got 42.0% of the popular vote and 73 electoral votes.

1984: Ronald Reagan was reelected in a landslide. The fortieth president—at seventy-three the oldest ever elected to a second term—routed his Democratic rival Walter Mondale, winning 58.8% of the popular vote and 525 electoral votes. Mondale, the former vice president, won 40.6% of the popular vote and the electoral votes of just one state—his home state of Minnesota—and the District of Columbia.

☆ QUOTE OF THE DAY

I fully appreciate the present peril the country is in, and the weight of responsibility on me.

Abraham Lincoln, in a December 22, 1860, letter

This Day in Presidential History

November 7

1848: Zachary Taylor, running as the Whig candidate, was elected the twelfth president of the United States. "Old Rough and Ready," as the general was known, got 47.3% of the popular vote and 163 electoral votes, while Democratic rival William Butler got 42.5% of the popular vote and 127 electoral votes. A third candidate was former president Martin Van Buren, who ran as the Free Soil candidate; he got 10% of the vote but failed to win any electoral votes.

1916: Woodrow Wilson was reelected. Running on a "He kept us out of War" slogan, the twenty-eighth president won 49.2% of the popular vote and 277 electoral votes, to Republican Charles Evans Hughes's 46.1% of the popular vote and 254 electoral votes. A swing of just 3,800 votes in California would have given the election to Hughes.

1944: Franklin D. Roosevelt won an unprecedented fourth term as president. Seeing the United States through World War II, FDR got 53.4% of the popular vote to New York Republican Thomas Dewey's 45.9%. The electoral college was nowhere near as close: the president crushed Dewey 432 to 99.

1972: Richard M. Nixon was emphatically reelected. Riding a wave of popularity, the thirty-seventh president swamped Democrat George McGovern, winning 60.7% of the popular vote and 520 electoral votes, to McGovern's 37.5% and 17, respectively. Nixon carried forty-nine states—losing only Massachusetts and the District of Columbia.

1973: "Project Independence" was Richard M. Nixon's name for a crash effort to wean the United States off of imported oil. The president announced the effort after oil exporting nations began an embargo to cut off supplies. He said that through conservation and scientific and technologically driven development of alternative sources of energy, the United States could be energy self-sufficient by 1980.

★ QUOTE OF THE DAY

It is time to get on with the great tasks that lie before us. I have tried to conduct myself in this campaign in a way that would not divide our country, not divide it regionally or by parties or in any other way, because

I very firmly believe that what unites America today is infinitely more important than those things which divide us.

Richard M. Nixon

November 8

1864: Abraham Lincoln was re-elected, swamping George McClellan—the Civil War general Lincoln fired—with 55% of the popular vote and 212 of 233 electoral votes.

1892: Getting revenge on President Benjamin Harrison, Grover Cleveland was elected the twenty-fourth president of the United States. Cleveland, first elected to the presidency in 1884, lost the reelection to Harrison in 1888. But facing off again, Cleveland turned the tables, winning 46% of the popular vote and 277 electoral votes to Harrison's 43% of the popular vote and 145 electoral votes. Cleveland became the only president elected to two nonconsecutive terms.

1904: Theodore Roosevelt was elected. TR, who became the twenty-sixth president after the assassination of William McKinley in 1901 (see September 6 and 14), trounced Democrat Alton B. Parker by 56% to 37% in the popular vote and 226-140 in the electoral vote.

1932: Franklin D. Roosevelt was elected the thirty-second president of the United States. FDR, the Democratic governor of New York, crushed President Herbert Hoover, winning the popular vote 57.4% to 39.7% and the electoral college 472-59. It was the first of an unprecedented—and never to be repeated—four straight wins by FDR.

1988: George H.W. Bush was elected the forty-first president of the United States. Bush—the first sitting vice president to be elected to the presidency in 152 years—beat Massachusetts governor Michael Dukakis with 53.4% of the popular vote and 426 electoral votes, to Dukakis's 45.6% and 111, respectively.

2016: Billionaire Donald Trump was elected forty-fifth president of the United States. A New York real estate and construction magnate who moved into brand licensing and reality television, Trump won 306 electoral votes to Democratic challenger Hillary Clinton's 232. But he became the fifth president to have lost the popular vote, winning 46.1% to Clinton's 48.2%. Trump, seventy, was the oldest person ever elected to a first term as president.

★ QUOTE OF THE DAY

To those who supported me, I will try to be worthy of your trust, and to those who did not, I will try to earn it, and my hand is out to you and I want to be your president, too.

George H.W. Bush

November 9

1863: Abraham Lincoln and his future assassin John Wilkes Booth met face-to-face at Ford's Theatre. The president, taking a break from his Civil War responsibilities, attended a play at Ford's called *The Marble Heart*, in which Booth was the star. During the play, Booth, in character as the play's villain, Raphael, twice wagged his finger in the president's face and threatened him, noted Mary Clay, who was with the president and Mrs. Lincoln that night. "When he came a third time I was impressed by it, and said, 'Mr. Lincoln, he looks as if he meant that for you.' 'Well,' he said, 'he does look pretty sharp at me, doesn't he?'"

1901: Worried about Japan's growing power, Theodore Roosevelt established a U.S. naval base in the Philippines. The base at Subic Bay was

The Panama Canal represented America's—and Theodore Roosevelt's—willingness to do big things. Here TR, on the first trip abroad by a sitting president, examines a steam shovel that helped link the Pacific and Atlantic oceans. Library of Congress.

This Day in Presidential History

on territory the United States had won from Spain during the Spanish-American war of 1898. Roosevelt wanted to move the Navy's entire base of Pacific operations to Subic Bay, but encountered intense political opposition. The headquarters of the U.S. Pacific fleet was soon established in Pearl Harbor, on the Hawaiian island of Oahu.

1906: Theodore Roosevelt became the first sitting president to leave the country. The president and First Lady Edith Roosevelt went to Panama to inspect the building of the Panama Canal. The trip lasted seventeen days.

1989: George H.W. Bush hailed the fall of the Berlin Wall. In a year of sweeping change, communist governments across Eastern Europe fell one by one. The dramatic highlight was the announcement by the East German government that the Berlin Wall—since 1961 (see August 13) a hated symbol of both the Cold War and communist oppression—would be opened. The fall of the wall was a huge victory for the United States and its western allies, but the diplomatically sensitive Bush said he wouldn't provoke the Soviet Union by dancing on it. Bush, in fact, saw it as a sign that the Soviet Union and its young leader Mikhail Gorbachev were serious about reform and better relations with the western world.

★ QUOTE OF THE DAY

He does look pretty sharp at me, doesn't he?

> Abraham Lincoln on John Wilkes Booth—at Ford's Theatre,
> seventeen months before Booth murdered him

November 10

1954: Dwight Eisenhower dedicated the Marine Corps War Memorial in Arlington, Virginia. The U.S. Marine Corps was created on this day in 1775.

2001: George W. Bush said the United States would, if needed, attack any nation that presented a threat to American security. As proof, Bush cited Operation Enduring Freedom, the American-led invasion of Afghanistan, which he had launched the previous month (see October 7). The president's speech at the United Nations came two months after terrorists attacked New York and Washington (see September 11).

This Day in Presidential History

★ QUOTE OF THE DAY

We act to defend ourselves and deliver our children from a future of fear. We choose the dignity of life over a culture of death. We choose lawful change and civil disagreement over coercion, subversion, and chaos. These commitments—hope and order, law and life—unite people across cultures and continents. Upon these commitments depend all peace and progress. For these commitments, we are determined to fight.

George W. Bush

November 11

1919: Woodrow Wilson proclaimed the first Armistice Day, to honor the nation's veterans. Coming one year to the day after the end of World War I—"the war to end all wars"—Wilson said "Armistice Day will be filled with lots of pride in the heroism of those who died in the country's service and with gratitude for the victory, both because of the thing from which it has freed us and because of the opportunity it has given America to show her sympathy with peace and justice in the councils of the nations." Armistice Day is now known, of course, as Veterans Day.

1921: Warren Harding dedicated the Tomb of the Unknowns at Arlington National Cemetery. Holding unidentified remains of U.S. soldiers, the tomb is inscribed: "Here Rests in Honored Glory an American Soldier Known but to God." Guarded solemnly around the clock, the Tomb of the Unknowns is a must see for any visitor to Washington. Of Arlington National Cemetery, it is said to be "Where valor proudly sleeps."

1963: Two weeks to the day before he was buried there, John F. Kennedy visited Arlington National Cemetery. Earlier that year, in a previous visit, the president, admiring the view had remarked "I could stay here forever."

★ QUOTE OF THE DAY

Great is the guilt of an unnecessary war.

John Adams

This Day in Presidential History

November 12

1921: With military tensions rising in Asia, Warren Harding convened the Washington Naval Armament Conference. World War I had only ended three years before, but rising Japanese militarism in Asia and an international arms race sparked fears of a new war. The world's top naval powers—Britain, France, Italy, Japan and the United States signed a treaty limiting the size of their navies.

1979: With the Iranian hostage crisis under way, Jimmy Carter cut off oil imports from Iran. Carter was advised that the Iranians might be planning attacks against American oil tankers, and ended shipments immediately. The Iranian hostage crisis, which began on November 4, 1979, involved the storming of the American Embassy in Tehran and the seizure of sixty-six Americans. Thirteen women and African-Americans were released on November 19 and 20. The remaining fifty-three Americans were held hostage for 444 days, to the very end of Carter's presidency on January 20, 1981. The crisis itself hurt the president's popularity and contributed to his defeat.

★ QUOTE OF THE DAY

America does face a difficult task and a test. Our response will measure our character and our courage. I know that we Americans shall not fail.

Jimmy Carter

November 13

1789: George Washington completed the first presidential road trip, a four-week stagecoach trip through northern states.

1945: Harry Truman established a panel to look into the settlement of Jews in Palestine. In the wake of World War II and the Holocaust, the president realized that Jewish refugees needed a safe place to live; Israel was founded on his watch.

1986: In an Oval Office address to the nation, Ronald Reagan denied that there had been an arms-for-hostages deal with Iran. There was. Reagan later admitted that money from Iranian arms sales had been used to buy weapons for U.S.-backed rebels in Nicaragua.

This Day in Presidential History

★ QUOTE OF THE DAY

There is a price tag on human liberty. That price is the willingness to assume the responsibilities of being free men. Payment of this price is a personal matter with each of us.

James Monroe

November 14

1862: Abraham Lincoln approved a plan by General Ambrose Burnside to capture the Confederate capital of Richmond, Virginia. It would be a mistake. It led to the disastrous Battle of Fredericksburg on December 13, in which the Army of the Potomac was dealt one of its worst defeats at the hands of General Robert E. Lee's Army of Northern Virginia.

1972: Richard M. Nixon threatened North Vietnam with "swift and severe" action if it violated a pending ceasefire agreement. The agreement was indeed violated and the president ordered the "Christmas bombing" of North Vietnam. A peace treaty was signed a month after that.

1979: As the Iranian hostage crisis deepened, Jimmy Carter ordered all Iranian assets in the United States frozen. The hostage crisis dragged on until the final day of the president's administration (see January 20); the assets themselves remained frozen for decades after that.

1998: Bill Clinton agreed to pay $850,000 to settle a sexual harassment lawsuit. The out-of-court settlement with Paula Jones contributed to the president's impeachment by the House of Representatives—only the second presidential impeachment in history. Under the agreement, the president made no apology and admitted no wrongdoing. Jones charged that when Clinton was governor of Arkansas in 1991 and she was a state employee, he dropped his pants in front of her and propositioned her. Clinton denied the charge.

★ QUOTE OF THE DAY

He mocks the people who proposes that the government shall protect the rich and that they in turn will care for the laboring poor.

Grover Cleveland

November 15

1939: Franklin D. Roosevelt laid the cornerstone of the Jefferson Memorial. Arguably the most beautiful of all the monuments and memorials in Washington, it sits in West Potomac Park and features a 19-foot statue of Mr. Jefferson looking across the Tidal Basin at the White House. It is composed of circular marble steps, a portico and circular colonnade with ionic columns, which support a graceful dome. Its principal architect, John Russell Pope, designed it with Rome's Pantheon and the Jefferson's own design for the Rotunda at the University of Virginia in mind. The walls around Jefferson's statue are inscribed with his writings, including, of course, his Declaration of Independence, written in 1776.

1990: George H.W. Bush signed the Clean Air Act, aimed at reducing acid rain and smog, as well as banning the use of leaded gas in cars by the end of 1995. Both the House and Senate overwhelmingly passed bills that contained the bulk of Bush's proposals.

★ QUOTE OF THE DAY

We hold these truths to be self-evident: that all men are created equal, that they are endowed by their Creator with certain inalienable rights, among these are life, liberty, and the pursuit of happiness, that to secure these rights governments are instituted among men.

Thomas Jefferson, from the Declaration of Independence

November 16

1933: Franklin D. Roosevelt established diplomatic ties with the Soviet Union. After the Bolshevik revolution in 1917, the new government said it would not honor its foreign debts; relations were severed by President Woodrow Wilson. The United States remained hostile toward Russia and the Soviet Union (which was formally founded in 1922) until FDR took office in 1933 and sought to reestablish ties.

1961: John F. Kennedy ordered an increase in military aid to South Vietnam, but did not commit U.S. combat troops. The president was concerned at the advances being made by the communist Viet Cong, but did not want to become involved in a land war in Vietnam.

1973: Richard M. Nixon urged Congress to authorize construction of the Alaskan oil pipeline. Part of the president's "Project Independence" (see November 7) to wean itself off of dependence on oil imports, Nixon said the pipeline would help the United States become more energy self-sufficient. Congress did approve the pipeline.

★ QUOTE OF THE DAY

I trust that the relations now established between our peoples may forever remain normal and friendly, and that our Nations henceforth may cooperate for their mutual benefit and for the preservation of the peace of the world.

> Franklin D. Roosevelt, in a letter to the Soviet foreign minister

November 17

1973: As the Watergate scandal deepened, Richard M. Nixon, in a news conference, said he wasn't a crook. The president, under growing scrutiny about his possible involvement in the scandal, denied profiting in any way from his years in public service. "I made my mistakes, but in all of my years of public life, I have never profited, never profited from public service—I earned every cent," he said. "And in all of my years of public life, I have never obstructed justice. And I think, too, that I could say that in my years of public life, that I welcome this kind of examination, because people have got to know whether or not their president is a crook. Well, I am not a crook. I have earned everything I have got."

If anything, the news conference only raised more questions about Watergate. The president's insistence that "I'm not a crook" was used against him—and to this day is associated with him and the scandal he tried to suppress. In April 1974, the Internal Revenue Service ordered Nixon to pay more than $400,000 in back taxes for making improper deductions.

★ QUOTE OF THE DAY

People have got to know whether or not their president is a crook. Well, I am not a crook. I have earned everything I have got.

> Richard M. Nixon

November 18

1886: Chester Arthur died in New York City. He was the twenty-first president, serving from 1881 to 1885. He died from complications of Bright's disease, a kidney ailment. Arthur had been vice president for just six months when he became president after the assassination of President James Garfield.

1963: During a Florida motorcade, John F. Kennedy ordered Secret Service agents off the back of his open limousine—so people could get a better view of him. The president, who liked to be seen by the voters, grew weary of having agents so close to him all the time. "Keep those Ivy League charlatans off the back of the car," he said, in jest. Kennedy liked the agents—he was close to many of them—but sometimes thought his own security was a bit much. Kennedy also had the roof of his limousine (which wasn't bulletproof) taken off that day—and four days later in Dallas.

★ QUOTE OF THE DAY

If it were not for the reporters, I would tell you the truth.

Chester Arthur

November 19

1794: The Jay Treaty was signed with Britain, fulfilling George Washington's goal of avoiding another war with that country. The Jay Treaty was named for Supreme Court Chief Justice John Jay, who was sent to London by the president to negotiate with the British.

1831: James Garfield was born in Moreland Hills, Ohio. He was the twentieth president, serving six months before his assassination in 1881. Garfield became the second of four presidents to be assassinated.

1863: Abraham Lincoln gave what is arguably the greatest of all presidential speeches: the 272-word Gettysburg Address. The speech, delivered at the dedication of the Soldiers' National Cemetery in Gettysburg—site of the pivotal Civil War battle four months earlier—took just over two minutes to deliver, but summed up, in Lincoln's characteristic eloquence and brevity, why the war was being waged. Lincoln emphasized the principles

James Garfield. Library of Congress.

of human equality and said the Union would be preserved with "a new birth of freedom."

Four score and seven years ago, our fathers brought forth on this continent a new nation, conceived in liberty, and dedicated to the proposition that all men are created equal. . . .

Now we are engaged in a great civil war, testing whether that nation, or any nation, so conceived and dedicated, can long endure. We are met on the great battlefield of that war. We have come to dedicate a portion of that field, as a final resting place for those who here gave their lives that the nation might live. It is altogether fitting and proper that we should do this.

But in a larger sense, we can not dedicate, we can not consecrate, we can not hallow this ground. The brave men, living and dead, who struggled here, have consecrated it, far above our poor power to add or detract. The world will little note, nor long remember what we say here, but it can never forget what they did here. It is for us the living, rather, to be dedicated here to the unfinished work which they who fought here have thus far so nobly advanced. It is rather for us to be here dedicated to the great task remaining before us—that from these honored dead we take increased devotion to that cause for which they gave the last full measure of devotion—that we here highly resolve that these dead shall not have died in vain—that this nation, under God, shall have a new birth of freedom—and that government of the people, by the people, for the people, shall not perish from the earth.

1919: A crushing blow to Woodrow Wilson. The Senate rejected the Versailles Treaty. The key element of the treaty—negotiated in Europe by the president after the end of World War I—was the creation of the League of Nations (a precursor to today's United Nations). The League was designed to be an organization that would work to defuse geopolitical tensions and make the world "safe for democracy." But Republicans, led by Majority Leader and Foreign Relations Committee Chairman Henry Cabot Lodge, voted not to ratify the pact. The president by this time was gravely ill, having suffered a devastating stroke after making a grueling cross-country trip to sell the Treaty to the American people (see October 2).

1985: Ronald Reagan and Soviet premier Mikhail Gorbachev held their first summit meeting. The Geneva gathering was the first meeting between U.S and Soviet heads of state since 1979.

★ QUOTE OF THE DAY

This government of the people, by the people, for the people, shall not perish from the earth.

Abraham Lincoln

November 20

1920: Woodrow Wilson won the Nobel Peace Prize for his peacemaking efforts in Europe after World War I. Paralyzed by a crippling stroke, the president was unable to attend the Nobel ceremony.

1962: John F. Kennedy signed an executive order ordering an end to housing discrimination. The president's order prohibited federally funded housing agencies from denying housing or funding for housing to anyone based on race, color, creed, or national origin.

★ QUOTE OF THE DAY

Mankind has not yet been rid of the unspeakable horror of war. I am convinced that our generation has, despite its wounds, made notable progress. But it is the better part of wisdom to consider our work as one begun.

Woodrow Wilson

November 21

1864: Did Abraham Lincoln write this famous letter? The president allegedly wrote a letter of condolence to a Lydia Bixby, who reportedly lost five sons in the Civil War. Ironically, Mrs. Bixby herself was said to have supported the Confederacy, and records show that two, not five, of her sons died. Scholars have never been able to prove conclusively that Lincoln wrote the letter, which was portrayed in the 1998 film *Saving Private Ryan*. Many Lincoln experts believe he did, though others say his secretary John Hay was the author. It reads:

Executive Mansion,

Washington, November 21, 1864.

Dear Madam,

I have been shown in the files of the War Department a statement of the Adjutant General of Massachusetts that you are the mother of five sons who have died gloriously on the field of battle. I feel how weak and fruitless must be any word of mine which should attempt to beguile you from the grief of a loss so overwhelming. But I cannot refrain from tendering you the consolation that may be found in the thanks of the Republic they died to save. I pray that our Heavenly Father may assuage the anguish of your bereavement, and leave you only the cherished memory of the loved and lost, and the solemn pride that must be yours to have laid so costly a sacrifice upon the altar of freedom.

Yours, very sincerely and respectfully,

A. Lincoln

1973: Richard M. Nixon's attorney, J. Fred Buzhardt, revealed the presence of an eighteen-minute gap in a White House tape recording related to

Watergate. It was a "smoking gun" that only deepened the mystery of the president's involvement in the scandal.

1974: The Freedom of Information Act was passed over Gerald Ford's veto. It today provides expanded access to government files and allows secrecy classifications to be challenged in court and justified by the appropriate federal authorities.

1989: A bill banning smoking on most domestic flights was signed into law by George H.W. Bush.

★ QUOTE OF THE DAY

The most practical kind of politics is the politics of decency.

Theodore Roosevelt

November 22

1943: Franklin D. Roosevelt demanded the unconditional surrender of Japan during a meeting in Cairo with British prime minister Winston Churchill and Chinese Generalissimo Chiang Kai-shek. At the Sextant Conference in the Egyptian capital, the leaders said that in addition to surrendering unconditionally, Japan must also relinquish conquered Chinese territory, grant Korea its independence, and give up all Pacific territory seized after 1914.

1963: Riding in an open car in Dallas, Texas, John F. Kennedy was assassinated. The thirty-fifth president, Kennedy was the youngest person ever elected, the fourth to be murdered, and, at just forty-six years of age, the youngest president to die. As his casket lay in the back of Air Force One, Vice President Lyndon B. Johnson was sworn in as the thirty-sixth president.

Twenty-four-year-old Lee Harvey Oswald was quickly arrested and charged with the president's murder—and that of a policeman—but within two days was himself gunned down by a Dallas nightclub owner, Jack Ruby. The killing of Oswald sparked talk of a conspiracy that has never abated, though no conclusive evidence has ever surfaced that one existed. Two of the most definitive books on the assassination—William Manchester's massive *The Death of a President* and Gerald Posner's *Case*

Closed—make the case that Oswald, and Oswald alone, planned and carried out the president's assassination.

Kennedy, who had come close to death on prior occasions in his life, often made odd remarks about dying. His favorite poem, for example, was Alan Seeger's "I Have a Rendezvous with Death." In Fort Worth, Texas, on the morning of his assassination, Kennedy remarked on the crowds he encountered in Houston, which he visited the night before: "Last night would have been a hell of a night to assassinate a president."

★ QUOTE OF THE DAY

Last night would have been a hell of a night to assassinate a president.

President Kennedy, joking on the morning of his assassination

When John F. Kennedy was killed, there were no federal laws on the books for killing a president, so justice for prior assassinations was meted out in different ways. Because Abraham Lincoln was commander in chief, the coconspirators of his assassin, John Wilkes Booth, were tried in military court. But Charles Guiteau, who killed James Garfield sixteen years later, was tried in federal court by the district attorney for the District of Columbia. William McKinley's assassin, Leon Czolgosz, was tried in a New York state court. In 1963, accused assassin Lee Harvey Oswald was charged—and would have been tried—under Texas law for murdering Kennedy and Dallas police officer J.D. Tippit.

November 23

1804: Franklin Pierce was born in Hillsborough, New Hampshire. He was the fourteenth president, serving between 1853 and 57. "Baby" Pierce, as he was called because has 49 when he became president, is the only president from New Hampshire. Regarded as an ineffectual president, Pierce suffered politically after he backed repeal of the Missouri Compromise on slavery. The Missouri Compromise was an 1820 agreement between pro- and antislavery factions in Congress. It banned slavery in the former Louisiana Territory north of the parallel 36°30' north except within the boundaries of the proposed state of Missouri. Pierce's personal life was tragic: all three of his sons died young, including one son who died in

Franklin Pierce. Library of Congress.

a train accident that nearly killed president-elect Pierce and soon-to-be first lady Jane.

1921: In a move that strengthened prenatal care in the United States, Warren Harding signed the Promotion of the Welfare and Hygiene of Maternity and Infancy Act (also known for its sponsors as the Sheppard-Towner Act). Congress and the president acted after learning that about 80% of American women were not receiving proper care when pregnant. The act gave matching federal funds to states for maternal and child care.

1963: President for just twelve hours, Lyndon B. Johnson was nearly shot by a Secret Service agent guarding LBJ at his Washington home. The agent, Gerald Blaine, said that he heard rustling in the trees. Fearing an attack on the new president, Blaine picked up his machine gun and aimed it at the person—Johnson himself, who had stepped outside for some fresh air.

★ QUOTE OF THE DAY

The storm of frenzy and faction must inevitably dash itself in vain against the unshaken rock of the Constitution.

Franklin Pierce

This Day in Presidential History

November 24

1784: Zachary Taylor was born in Barboursville, Virginia. He was the twelfth president, serving from 1849 to 1850. Known as "Old Rough and Ready" for his distinguished forty-year Army career, Taylor had no interest in politics, until he was urged to run as a Whig in the 1848 presidential election. Although a slave owner himself—and the last president to own slaves while in office—Taylor angered many Southerners for his moderate stance on the issue. The president died on July 9, 1850, just sixteen months after taking office, probably of gastroenteritis. Taylor was the second of three Whig presidents, the last being Millard Fillmore. Taylor was also the second president to die in office.

1963: The accused assassin of President John Kennedy—Lee Harvey Oswald—was gunned down in Dallas, fueling speculation of a conspiracy. Shortly before Oswald was to have been transferred from Dallas police headquarters to the Dallas county jail, Jack Ruby, a longtime friend—or gadfly—of the Dallas police, had been in a nearby Western Union shop wiring money to an employee. He went into the garage just as Oswald emerged and shot him. Often untold is the fact that Oswald's departure was delayed by Oswald himself—after he requested to put on a sweater. Had he not done this, he would have left minutes before Ruby arrived.

Zachary Taylor. Library of Congress.

This Day in Presidential History

★ QUOTE OF THE DAY

It would be judicious to act with magnanimity towards a prostrate foe.

Zachary Taylor

November 25

1957: Dwight Eisenhower suffered a stroke in the Oval Office, impairing his speech. In 1958, the president wrote a letter giving Vice President Nixon the authority to take over if he became incapacitated. This—and the assassination of President John F. Kennedy—led to the ratification of the Twenty-fifth Amendment in 1967 (see February 10).

1963: Three days after his assassination, John F. Kennedy was buried with full military honors at Arlington National Cemetery. Jacqueline Kennedy, his thirty-four-year-old widow, won the world's admiration for her dignified bearing as she marched behind her husband's horse-drawn coffin. A photo of John F. Kennedy Jr. saluting was arguably the most memorable and heartbreaking moment—it was also the boy's third birthday.

1973: Because of gasoline shortages, Richard M. Nixon asked Americans to drive less and for gas stations to close for twenty-seven hours on weekends. To save energy, the president also called for a 50-mph speed limit and limits on air travel. Nixon urged citizens to not hang Christmas lights.

1986: Ronald Reagan now admitted that money from Iranian arms sales had been used to buy weapons for U.S.-backed rebels in Nicaragua. Many Americans were angry that Reagan appeared to be doing business with Iran—while publicly labeling it a terrorist state. The Iran-Contra affair quickly became a constitutional scandal; there was talk of impeaching the president. Eleven White House officials were convicted (some convictions were overturned on appeal).

★ QUOTE OF THE DAY

Our independence will depend on maintaining and achieving self-sufficiency in energy.

Richard M. Nixon

This Day in Presidential History

November 26

1789: George Washington marked America's first official Thanksgiving by attending services at St. Paul's Chapel in New York City, and by donating beer and food to imprisoned debtors in the city. He had issued the first-ever presidential proclamation (see October 3) ordering that the holiday be observed.

1941: Franklin D. Roosevelt signed a bill officially establishing the fourth Thursday in November as Thanksgiving Day. The bill updated a proclamation by Abraham Lincoln that Thanksgiving would fall on the last Thursday of the month.

2002: George W. Bush signed a bill creating the Department of Homeland Security. Citing "the dangers of a new era," the president said the cabinet-level department would integrate and oversee twenty-two existing federal security agencies, such as the Immigration and Naturalization Service, Coast Guard, and Border Patrol.

★ QUOTE OF THE DAY

America, of course has countless things for which to be thankful on this November 26. But I think the most important is this: for the first Thanksgiving in the last four, we sit down to our traditional Thanksgiving feast without the fear of the casualty list hanging over us. We don't, longer, have to worry about the killing in Korea.

Dwight Eisenhower

November 27

1963: Lyndon B. Johnson asked Congress to honor John F. Kennedy's legacy by passing civil rights legislation. The president, speaking just five days after President Kennedy's assassination, told lawmakers to "resolve that John Fitzgerald Kennedy did not live—or die—in vain."

1965: With 120,000 troops in Vietnam, the Pentagon asked Lyndon B. Johnson for 280,000 more. The president agreed. At the height of the Vietnam War (1968), U.S. troop strength peaked at 538,000. A total of 58,000 Americans were killed during the war.

1973: Richard M. Nixon signed the Emergency Petroleum Allocation Act. The goal: free the United States of all oil imports by 1980. The president acted in the wake of an Arab oil embargo against the United States; it caused gas prices to soar, rationing, and a deep recession. When Nixon signed the act (also known as "Project Independence") in 1973, the United States imported 36% of the petroleum it used. In 2016: 24%.

★ QUOTE OF THE DAY

The time has come for Americans of all races and creeds and political beliefs to understand and to respect one another. So let us put an end to the teaching and the preaching of hate and evil and violence. Let us turn away from the fanatics of the far left and the far right, from the apostles of bitterness and bigotry, from those defiant of law, and those who pour venom into our Nation's bloodstream.

Lyndon B. Johnson

November 28

1943: In Iran, Franklin D. Roosevelt attended the Tehran Conference to plot World War II strategy with British prime minister Winston Churchill and Soviet premier Josef Stalin—the first meeting of the "Big Three." The 7,000-mile journey was a strain on Roosevelt, whose health was deteriorating, but the conference was of such importance that he made the trip. One of the main goals of the conference, which was held at the Soviet embassy in the Iranian capital, was to agree on a timetable for a second front in Europe against Nazi Germany. It was decided that "Operation Overlord," as the invasion of France would be called, would begin in May 1944 and coincide with a Soviet attack on Germany's eastern border. Stalin also agreed to enter the Pacific war against Japan.

★ QUOTE OF THE DAY

No power on earth can prevent our destroying the German armies by land, their U-boats by sea, and their war plants from the air. Our attack will be relentless and increasing.

Franklin D. Roosevelt, December 1, 1943

This Day in Presidential History

November 29

1963: Lyndon B. Johnson formed the Warren Commission to investigate the assassination of President Kennedy, which had occurred the week before. The commission—chaired by Supreme Court Chief Justice Earl Warren—would conclude that Lee Harvey Oswald, acting alone, and not as part of a conspiracy, murdered Kennedy. Future president Gerald Ford served on the commission.

1990: George H.W. Bush signed the Immigration Act of 1990. It was the most extensive revision to U.S. immigration laws in more than a half century—and allowed for the admission of 700,000 aliens each year.

☆ QUOTE OF THE DAY

The administration of justice is the firmest pillar of government.

George Washington

November 30

1950: Harry Truman said if necessary, he would use atomic weapons to end the Korean War. The president's threat came days after China entered the war, joining North Korea in attacks on American and United Nations troops. The top Allied commander in Korea, General Douglas MacArthur, also advocated bombing China, but his disagreements with the president led to his firing in 1951 (see April 11). Sandwiched between World War II and Vietnam, the Korean War—"the forgotten war"—killed 36,516 Americans in three years.

1993: Bill Clinton signed the Brady Bill requiring handgun buyers to wait five days while a background check was conducted. It was named for James Brady, the press secretary to former president Ronald Reagan, who was shot in the head during an attempted assassination in 1981 (see March 30). Reagan himself endorsed the bill vigorously.

☆ QUOTE OF THE DAY

This bill—on a nationwide scale—can't help but stop thousands of illegal handgun purchases.

Ronald Reagan, endorsing the Brady Bill

This Day in Presidential History

December

December 1

1824: The disputed presidential election was given to the House of Representatives to resolve. Four men ran for president that year—Andrew Jackson, John Quincy Adams, William Crawford, and Henry Clay—but none won a majority of electoral votes, as required by the Twelfth Amendment to the Constitution. During the election, Jackson, who won the popular vote, won the most electoral votes as well: ninety-nine. That gave him a plurality, but a majority—131 of 261—was needed. Lawmakers would eventually give the presidency to Adams (see February 9).

1834: Andrew Jackson said the federal government was once again debt free. In his State of the Union address—delivered by mail to Congress—the president said the Treasury had a surplus on $6.7 million. Jackson, who hated debt—calling it a curse and "a moral failing"—was ruthless in making sure that the federal government avoided red ink. He blocked spending bills and sold off federal assets—mostly land—to raise revenue.

1955: A black boycott of the Montgomery, Alabama, bus system began, eliciting Dwight Eisenhower's moral—but not political—support. The president told his cabinet he was "much impressed with the moderation of the negroes in Alabama." But the president also considered the boycott a state's right issue, and saw no reason for the federal government to get involved.

★ QUOTE OF THE DAY

Free from public debt, at peace with all the world, and with no complicated interests to consult in our intercourse with foreign powers, the present may be hailed as the epoch in our history the most favorable for the settlement of those principles in our domestic policy which shall be best calculated to give stability to our Republic and secure the blessings of freedom to our citizens.

Andrew Jackson

This Day in Presidential History

December 2

1812: The election of 1812 concluded, with James Madison re-elected. He defeated DeWitt Clinton with 51% of the popular vote and 128 of 217 electoral votes.

1823: In what came to be known as the Monroe Doctrine, James Monroe said the Western Hemisphere would be off limits for colonization by, or interference from, foreign powers. The president's comments, made in his State of the Union address, were aimed at Britain, Spain, France, and Russia, the latter of which had settlements in what is today central California. Numerous presidents, including James Polk, Theodore Roosevelt, John F. Kennedy, and Ronald Reagan, have used the Monroe Doctrine to justify policies over the past two centuries.

1954: Dwight Eisenhower signed a defense pact with Taiwan after Communist China bombed the Taiwanese islands of Quemoy and Matsu.

1970: Richard M. Nixon signed an executive order creating the Environmental Protection Agency. As concern over air and water quality and other environmental issues grew, Nixon proposed the agency after he became president in 1969. Its mission is "to protect human health and the environment."

★ QUOTE OF THE DAY

The American continents, by the free and independent condition which they have assumed and maintain, are henceforth not to be considered as subjects for future colonization by any European powers.

James Monroe

December 3

1901: In a 20,000-word State of the Union speech, Theodore Roosevelt asked Congress to curb the power of trusts. He stated: "Great corporations exist only because they are created and safeguarded by our institutions; and it is therefore our right and our duty to see that they work in harmony with these institutions." The president's administration sued dozens of what it considered monopolies, such as John D. Rockefeller's Standard Oil and J.P. Morgan's Northern Securities Co. (railroads).

This Day in Presidential History

1929: Herbert Hoover reassured Americans that the worst of the recent stock market crash was over and that the economy was fine. The president was wrong; the Great Depression was just beginning. The worst year: 1932, when unemployment reached 23.6%; the economy shrank 13.4%.

★ QUOTE OF THE DAY

Wisdom oft times consists of knowing what to do next.

Herbert Hoover

December 4

1816: Voting—which began November 1—was concluded in the presidential election between James Monroe, the Democratic-Republican candidate, and Federalist candidate Rufus King. Monroe, of Virginia, was the easy victor, becoming the fifth president of the United States with 183 electoral votes and 68.2% of the popular vote, to King's 34 electoral votes and 30.9% of the popular vote.

1844: James K. Polk was elected the eleventh president of the United States. The only president who also served as Speaker of the House, Polk pledged to serve just one term and kept his word. He had four key goals for his presidency and achieved all of them: acquisition of California (won via war with Mexico), settlement of a boundary dispute with Britain over the Oregon territory, lowering of trade tariffs, and reestablishment of the independent treasury system. Under Polk, the United States became a true continental power.

1981: Ronald Reagan signed an executive order allowing the CIA to engage in domestic counterintelligence. It permitted the collection and retention of "information obtained in the course of a lawful foreign intelligence, counterintelligence, international narcotics, or international terrorism investigation" and "information that may indicate involvement in activities that may violate federal, state, local, or foreign laws."

1992: George H.W. Bush ordered 28,000 Marines to Somalia. The East African country was being torn apart by civil war; the outgoing president wanted to help with the distribution of humanitarian aid. He called the military mission "God's work." But the Americans soon found themselves drawn into the civil war—with disastrous results (see October 3).

Martin Van Buren. Library of Congress.

★ QUOTE OF THE DAY

Peace, plenty, and contentment reign throughout our borders, and our beloved country presents a sublime moral spectacle to the world.

James Polk

December 5

1782: Martin Van Buren was born in Kinderhook, New York. He was the eighth president, serving from 1837 to 1841. Born to parents of Dutch descent, Van Buren was the first president to be born an American citizen, and the only president not to have spoken English as a first language. Van Buren is one of only two people who served as secretary of state, vice president, and president. The other: Thomas Jefferson. There is some debate as to whether Van Buren's nickname—"Old Kinderhook"—spurred use of the phrase "OK" in the United States.

1804: Thomas Jefferson was officially reelected. Fellow Democratic-Republican and the first governor of New York, George Clinton, would be vice president.

1832: The election of 1832 concluded, with Andrew Jackson winning a second term with 54% of the popular vote and 219 of 286 electoral votes.

1898: William McKinley vowed to build a canal in Latin America. In his State of the Union address, which was read to both Houses of Congress, McKinley said a canal connecting the Pacific and Atlantic oceans was of strategic importance to the United States. After his assassination in 1901, his successor, Theodore Roosevelt, would oversee the construction of such a canal—through Panama.

1994: Bill Clinton and four former Soviet Republics agreed to slash nuclear weapons. The Strategic Arms Reduction Treaty (START I) pact signed in Budapest, Hungary, aimed to eliminate more than 9,000 warheads.

1996: Bill Clinton named Madeline Albright as secretary of state. Albright was the first woman ever appointed to the nation's top diplomatic post. There have now been three female secretaries of state: Albright; Condoleezza Rice, who served in the administration of George W. Bush, and Hillary Clinton, who served in the administration of Barack Obama.

★ QUOTE OF THE DAY

As to the presidency, the two happiest days of my life were those of my entrance upon the office and my surrender of it.

Martin Van Buren

December 6

1820: James Monroe was reelected. The president easily won a second term, winning 231 electoral votes to John Quincy Adams's 1.

1865: The Thirteenth Amendment to the Constitution—which abolished slavery—was ratified. Abraham Lincoln, assassinated eight months earlier, would have been gratified. He had come to the conclusion early in his presidency that a constitutional amendment was necessary to end slavery—though his priority in fighting the Civil War itself had been to preserve the Union, and not necessarily to end slavery. The amendment stated, "Neither slavery nor involuntary servitude, except as a punishment for crime whereof the party shall have been duly convicted, shall exist within the United States, or any place subject to their jurisdiction."

1904: Theodore Roosevelt made the case for U.S. military intervention abroad. In his State of the Union, the president, building upon the Monroe

Doctrine, said America was obliged to be an "international police power" in the Western hemisphere as needed in "flagrant cases of wrongdoing or impotence."

1923: The first presidential address was broadcast on the radio by Calvin Coolidge. *The New York Times*, noting the significance of using this new technology, said the president's voice "will be heard by more people than the voice of any man in history." The speech, Coolidge's first State of the Union, paid tribute to the late president Warren Harding and outlined his goals in domestic and foreign policy. Radio's true power would not become apparent for another decade, though—when Franklin D. Roosevelt gave the first of his Fireside Chats (see March 12).

1973: Gerald Ford was sworn in as vice president. Ford, the longtime House Minority Leader, was selected as vice president by Richard M. Nixon after the resignation of Spiro Agnew (see October 10).

★ QUOTE OF THE DAY

It is only when the people become ignorant and corrupt, when they degenerate into a populace, that they are incapable of exercising their sovereignty.

James Monroe

December 7

1808: James Madison was elected the fourth president of the United States. Madison—the Democratic-Republican candidate—won 64.7% of the popular vote and 122 electoral votes to Federalist candidate Charles Pinckney's 32.4% and 47, respectively. It was one of only two times in American history that a sitting vice president—George Clinton, who had served Thomas Jefferson's second term—would continue to serve in that role under a new president. The other? John C. Calhoun, who served as vice president under President John Quincy Adams but stayed on, for a time, under President Andrew Jackson.

1836: The election 1836 concluded with Martin Van Buren, the incumbent vice president, winning the presidency with 51% of the popular vote and 170 of 294 electoral votes.

1931: Herbert Hoover turned away "hunger marchers" at the White House. Protestors demanding jobs descended on Washington, D.C. They tried to give the president a petition but were denied entry at the White House gates. There were more than eight million Americans unemployed at the time—about 15.8% of the labor force.

1941: A sneak attack by Japan on the U.S. naval base at Pearl Harbor, Hawaii, thrust the United States into World War II. The attack killed 2,459 Americans—the third-single bloodiest day in American history. Franklin D. Roosevelt would ask Congress the next day to declare war, calling December 7 "a date which will live in infamy." America would soon declare war on two of Japan's allies—Germany and Italy—after those countries declared war on the United States first (see December 11).

★ QUOTE OF THE DAY

Let every nation know, whether it wishes us well or ill, that we shall pay any price, bear any burden, meet any hardship, support any friend, oppose any foe to assure the survival and the success of liberty.

John F. Kennedy

December 8

1801: Thomas Jefferson mailed in his first State of the Union—setting the standard for more than a century. Since Jefferson thought that traveling to Congress and speaking before lawmakers in person was imperious and would make him seem like a king, his address was read to Congress by a clerk in the House of Representatives. The move reflected Jefferson's love for simplicity and dislike of ceremony. The next president to deliver a State of the Union in person would be Woodrow Wilson on December 2, 1913.

1993: Bill Clinton signed NAFTA—the North American Free Trade Act. The pact, negotiated during the administration of George H.W. Bush, eliminated numerous trade barriers between the United States, Canada, and Mexico—creating the world's largest free trade zone.

2003: George W. Bush signed a bill to expand Medicare. The bill added prescription drug benefits to the health program, and provided billions of dollars in incentives for private insurance companies to cover Medicare subscribers. Critics warned the Medicare expansion would mean trillions of dollars in spending for future taxpayers, particularly as the so-called "baby boomers" born between 1946 and 1964 began to retire.

★ QUOTE OF THE DAY

Medicare is a great achievement of a compassionate government, and it is a basic trust we honor. Medicare has spared millions of seniors from needless hardship. Each generation benefits from Medicare. Each generation has a duty to strengthen Medicare, and this generation is fulfilling our duty.

George W. Bush

December 9

1941: With the United States now officially at war with Japan, Franklin D. Roosevelt warned Americans to brace for a long conflict. The war—the second deadliest in American history—would last for three years and eight months, until Japan's surrender in 1945 (see August 14).

1950: With the Korean War under way, Harry Truman banned U.S. exports to Communist China. The Chinese had just intervened in the war, launching a deadly surprise attack that took American forces by surprise; the situation was so grave that the president contemplated using nuclear weapons (see November 30).

1967: Lyndon B. Johnson's daughter married in the White House. In an East Room ceremony, Lynda Bird Johnson, twenty-three, married Captain Chuck Robb (U.S. Marines), twenty-eight.

1980: After former Beatle John Lennon was shot to death on December 8, 1980, president-elect Ronald Reagan said he opposed stronger handgun laws. Three months later, Reagan—by then president—was shot and nearly assassinated by John Hinckley. The handgun used by Hinckley to shoot the president was easily bought at a Tennessee pawn shop. Reagan later backed the Brady Bill (see November 30) and an assault weapons ban.

1992: George H.W. Bush ordered 1,800 Marines to Mogadishu, Somalia. The Marines were part of a multinational peacekeeping force that was trying to restore order in that war-torn country. But attacks against the peacekeeping force soon began. In 1993, two U.S. Army helicopters would

This Day in Presidential History

be shot down by rebels, killing eighteen American troops (see October 3). Bill Clinton, by then president, would order a withdrawal.

★ QUOTE OF THE DAY

We are now in this war. We are all in it—all the way. Every single man, woman, and child is a partner in the most tremendous undertaking of our American history.

Franklin D. Roosevelt

December 10

1796: John Adams was declared the winner of the presidential election, with Thomas Jefferson becoming vice president. The election, held from November 4 to December 7, was the first contested U.S. presidential election and the only one in which a president and vice president were elected from opposing tickets. Adams, the Federalist candidate, won 71 electoral votes and 53.4% of the popular vote. Jefferson the Democratic-Republican candidate, won 68 electoral votes and 46.6% of the popular vote. Jefferson would turn the tables on Adams four years later.

1832: The road to the Civil War: Andrew Jackson issued the Nullification Proclamation.

South Carolina had said that federal tariffs (passed in 1828 and 1832) on certain imported goods were harmful and unconstitutional. But the president's proclamation said that it was illegal for any state to determine which federal laws to abide by and which to ignore, and that states had no authority to nullify those laws. Jackson believed in states' rights. But he also believed that power granted to the federal government by the Constitution was supreme—and that he would use force if necessary, to uphold it. The nullification crisis and battle over states' rights would contribute to the outbreak of the Civil War in 1861.

1906: Theodore Roosevelt was awarded the Nobel Peace Prize. The Nobel committee praised the president for his role in ending the Russo-Japanese War in 1905. Three sitting presidents (Roosevelt, Woodrow Wilson, and Barack Obama) and one ex-president (Jimmy Carter) have been awarded the Nobel Peace Prize.

★ QUOTE OF THE DAY

The ordinance is founded, not on the indefeasible right of resisting acts which are plainly unconstitutional and too oppressive to be endured; but on the strange position that any one State may not only declare an act of Congress void, but prohibit its execution.

Andrew Jackson

December 11

1930: The Great Depression deepened with the closing of the Bank of the United States in New York City. The bank—with more than 400,000 depositors—was the largest to date of the more than 1,300 bank closings across the country. Days before, President Herbert Hoover asked Congress to fund a massive public works program for the growing ranks of unemployed. Lawmakers would soon allocate $116 million for a jobs program.

1941: Germany and Italy declared war on the United States—and the United States responded in kind. Germany and Italy were allies of Japan, and after Japan's attack on Pearl Harbor, drawing America into the war, Germany and Italy joined in the fight against the United States.

★ QUOTE OF THE DAY

The long known and the long expected has thus taken place. The forces endeavoring to enslave the entire world now are moving toward this hemisphere.

Never before has there been a greater challenge to life, liberty, and civilization.

Delay invites greater danger. Rapid and united effort by all of the peoples of the world who are determined to remain free will insure a world victory of the forces of justice and of righteousness over the forces of savagery and of barbarism.

Franklin D. Roosevelt

December 12

1806: Thomas Jefferson sought to ban the slave trade. In his State of the Union message to Congress (read on this day by a congressional clerk), the president—himself a slave owner—asked Congress to pass a law making international slave trading a crime. Such a law was needed, Jefferson said, to "withdraw the citizens of the United States from all further participation in those violations of human rights... which the morality, the reputation, and the best of our country have long been eager to proscribe." Congress soon passed such a law (see March 2).

1998: The House Judiciary Committee approved a fourth and final article of impeachment against Bill Clinton. The full House went on to impeach the president on charges of perjury and obstruction of justice. But in a Senate trial, Mr. Clinton was acquitted and allowed to remain in office.

2000: In a landmark Supreme Court decision, George W. Bush was declared the winner of the 2000 presidential election. Ending a five-week standoff, the Court's 5-4 ruling blocked further recounts in Florida, thus awarding the state's 25 electoral votes—and the presidency—to Bush, the Texas governor, over Vice President Al Gore. Bush's margin of victory in the deadlocked state was just 537 votes.

★ QUOTE OF THE DAY

This young century will be liberty's century.

George W. Bush

December 13

1918: Woodrow Wilson landed in France and became the first sitting U.S. president to visit Europe. He was traveling to the Versailles peace conference, which concerned World War I peace negotiations and planning for the League of Nations (see January 8). The president would spend six months in Europe, the longest time any president would spend abroad.

2000: President-elect George W. Bush and Vice President Al Gore paid tributes to one another—and America's democratic process—as the divisive 2000 election finally came to an end. A five-week electoral standoff had been resolved the day before, and Gore, the loser, said of Bush: "Neither he nor I anticipated this long and difficult road; certainly neither of us wanted it to happen. Yet it came, and now it has ended—resolved, as it must be resolved, through the honored institutions of our democracy." Bush was also gracious: "Americans share hopes and goals and values far more important than any political disagreements. Republicans want the best for our nation, and so do Democrats. Our votes may differ, but not our hopes."

2001: George W. Bush told Russia that the United States would pull out of a key arms control pact. The president said the United States would withdraw from the 1972 Anti-Ballistic Missile Treaty, allowing it to conduct antimissile defense tests.

★ QUOTE OF THE DAY

A truly American sentiment recognizes the dignity of labor and the fact that honor lies in honest toil.

Grover Cleveland

December 14

1799: With what are believed to be his final words —"'Tis well"—George Washington died. He was the first president of the United States, serving from 1789 to 1797. Washington was also the commander of the Continental Army during the Revolutionary War from 1775 to 1783. Because of his role in the American Revolution and in the formation of the United States, Washington is called "Father of His Country." Historians today generally regard Washington as the second or third greatest president.

1916: Woodrow Wilson vetoed an immigration bill. The president objected to the bill's tough restrictions, which banned "alcoholics, contract laborers, epileptics, feeble-minded persons, idiots, illiterates, imbeciles, insane persons, paupers, persons afflicted with contagious disease, persons being mentally or physically defective, persons with constitutional psychopathic inferiority, political radicals, polygamists, prostitutes, and vagrants" from entering the United States. Wilson's veto would be overridden by Congress in 1917.

2012: A shooting at Sandy Hook Elementary School in Newton, Connecticut, took twenty-six lives—twenty of them children. Barack Obama would call it the worst day of his presidency.

★ QUOTE OF THE DAY

Perseverance and Spirit have done Wonders in all ages.

George Washington

George Washington would be quite familiar with today's nasty political atmosphere: His enemies accused him of everything from treason to bribery. "I am accused of being the enemy of America," he wrote, "and subject to the influence of a foreign country."

December 15

1791: Virginia became the tenth state to ratify the Bill of Rights, making the ten amendments part of the U.S. Constitution. George Washington had called for their ratification in his first inaugural address in 1789.

1978: Jimmy Carter said the United States would grant full diplomatic recognition to Communist China and cut off ties with Taiwan. The president also ended a treaty obligating the United States to defend Taiwan if it were attacked by China. The move outraged Republicans, who challenged a president's right to cancel a treaty without Senate approval. Their case went to the Supreme Court, which threw the challenge out, thus supporting Carter's position.

★ QUOTE OF THE DAY

Big jobs usually go to the men who prove their ability to outgrow small ones.

Theodore Roosevelt

December 16

1907: Theodore Roosevelt's Great White Fleet. As the twentieth century dawned, the United States found itself a world power. The president, eager to display America's might—and its desire for peace—dispatched a U.S. Navy fleet consisting of sixteen battleships and various escorts on a goodwill trip around the world. The ships, painted white, were welcomed at many ports; their journey, which ended two weeks before Roosevelt left office in 1909, was one of the president's proudest accomplishments.

1950: Harry Truman declared a national emergency, following the entry of Communist China into the Korean War. The president was so worried that he considered using atomic weapons. Nine were sent to the region. He also ordered price and wage controls to be imposed on the U.S. economy.

★ QUOTE OF THE DAY

I do not think much of a man who is not wiser today than he was yesterday.

Abraham Lincoln

December 17

1942: The United States and ten other Allied governments issued a joint statement condemning Nazi Germany's "bestial policy of cold-blooded extermination" of the Jews. Franklin D. Roosevelt received intelligence of the Holocaust throughout 1942 (see July 26), and on December 13, the American public learned of it from a radio broadcast by CBS journalist Edward R. Murrow, who spoke of "a horror beyond what imagination can grasp ... there are no longer 'concentration camps'— we must speak now only of 'extermination camps.'" Rather than bomb train tracks that led to concentration camps like Auschwitz, Franklin Roosevelt thought that the best way to stop the mass murder of Jews was to defeat Germany itself, a decision later second-guessed by critics.

1975: A woman who tried to kill Gerald Ford was sentenced to life in prison. In Sacramento, California, just three months earlier (see September 5), Lynette Alice "Squeaky" Fromme pulled a .45-caliber pistol as the president came within two feet of her. Fromme—a disciple of Charles Manson—was quickly subdued by Secret Service agents. Ford testified in her trial, the first criminal trial in U.S. history that had oral testimony from a sitting president.

☆ QUOTE OF THE DAY

It was simply the hand with the weapon in it, at a height between my knee and my waist, approximately.

Gerald Ford, describing the moment he saw Fromme's gun pointed at him

December 18

1915: Woodrow Wilson married Edith Bolling Galt. Wilson's first wife, Ellen, had died the year before, devastating the president. His personal physician introduced Wilson, fifty-nine, to Edith, who was forty-three and claimed to be a descendant of Pocahontas. Wilson enjoyed having Edith sit with him in the Oval Office while he conducted business, leading to accusations that she had undue influence over the president. This became evident in 1919 when Wilson suffered a stroke (see October 2) after a national tour to win support for the League of Nations. The stroke left the president partially paralyzed, and, for two months, essentially unable to speak. In one of the greatest cover-ups in U.S. history, Wilson's illness was hidden from the American people by Edith, the president's personal physician, and a few White House staffers. Edith essentially became acting president, making decisions on her husband's behalf.

1972: Richard M. Nixon announced the "Christmas bombing" of North Vietnam, a massive campaign designed to bring the North Vietnamese to the negotiating table. Talks had collapsed on December 13, with each side blaming the other. A furious Nixon unleashed "Operation Linebacker II," in which B-52 bombers and fighter-bombers dropped over 20,000 tons of bombs on Hanoi and Haiphong. The bombings would continue until December 29, when the North Vietnamese agreed to resume peace talks. The United States lost fifteen of its B-52s and eleven other aircraft during the two week onslaught. North Vietnam said that over 1,600 civilians were killed.

★ QUOTE OF THE DAY

All great change in America begins at the dinner table.

Ronald Reagan

December 19

1998: The House of Representatives impeached Bill Clinton, charging him with lying under oath to a federal grand jury and obstructing justice. Clinton, the second president to be impeached (see February 24), was later acquitted in a Senate trial. The House decision to impeach came after a four-year investigation into the president and First Lady Hillary Clinton's alleged involvement in an assortment of real estate, fund-raising, and sexual harassment scandals. An independent prosecutor, Kenneth Starr, learned of an affair between Clinton and a White House intern, Monica Lewinsky. The president had denied the affair, but when questioned by Starr, tried to invoke executive privilege to avoid responding. Starr then charged the president with obstruction of justice, forcing Clinton testify before a grand jury in August 1998. In that testimony, the president acknowledged that he had an "inappropriate" relationship with Lewinsky. But he insisted that his testimony was "legally accurate."

2008: With the U.S. auto industry facing collapse, George W. Bush announced a $17 billion bailout of General Motors and Chrysler. The bailout—which followed prior bailouts of mortgage giants Fannie Mae and Freddie Mac (see September 7) and banks (see October 3) was designed to protect a vital industry afloat. The president required that the automakers radically restructure their businesses so they could return to profitability. The U.S. economy had shed 1.9 million jobs in the last four months of 2008; the president hoped the bailout would help stem further losses.

★ QUOTE OF THE DAY

If we were to allow the free market to take its course now, it would almost certainly lead to disorderly bankruptcy. In the midst of a financial crisis and a recession, allowing the U.S. auto industry to collapse is not a responsible course of action. The question is how we can best give it a chance to succeed.

George W. Bush

December 20

1860: South Carolina seceded from the Union. James Buchanan was still president, but the secession was seen as a response to the election of Abraham Lincoln as president. In his State of the Union message to Congress, Buchanan rejected the right of any state to leave the Union—but blamed northern states for what he called their "long-continued and intemperate interference...with the question of slavery." Six other Southern states—Mississippi, Florida, Alabama, Georgia, Louisiana, and Texas—would soon secede as well. When President Buchanan left office on March 4, 1861, the Union was down to twenty-five states—from thirty-two.

1989: George H.W. Bush ordered "Operation Just Cause"—an invasion of Panama. The president ordered the arrest of that country's military dictator Manuel Noriega, who had been indicted in the United States on drug trafficking charges. Noriega surrendered on January 3, 1990, was convicted, and sent to prison. The invasion took the lives of twenty-three American soldiers.

★ QUOTE OF THE DAY

What is right and what is practicable are two different things.

James Buchanan

December 21

1970: The Odd Couple: Elvis Presley visited Richard M. Nixon. "The King" asked the president if he could help in the U.S. war on drugs. Elvis even brought a gun into the White House—a .45 Colt—and gave it to Nixon as a gift. The photo of Nixon and Elvis remains, to this day, one of the most popular items for visitors to the National Archives.

This Day in Presidential History

The president meets the king: Richard M. Nixon welcomes Elvis Presley to the Oval Office in December 1970. Presley, a known drug user, asked to be a federal agent in the war in drugs. Nixon arranged for him to get a federal agent's badge. And—unthinkable today—Presley brought a handgun into the mansion, a gift for the president. Official White House photography by Ollie Atkins.

1987: Ronald Reagan urged Congress to support an international cap and trade treaty designed to protect the Earth's fragile ozone layer. It was called the Montreal Protocol and was necessary, the president said, "to protect public health and the environment from potential adverse effects of depletion of stratospheric ozone."

1987: Richard M. Nixon encouraged Donald Trump to run for office. In a letter to the real estate mogul, the former president said, "You will be a winner!"

1988: A U.S.-bound jumbo jet, Pan Am Flight 103, en route from London to New York, exploded over Lockerbie, Scotland, killing all 259 passengers and crew members (including 189 Americans) and 11 people on the ground. Residents of the town described a flash in the sky followed by a huge, deafening roar—before debris and bodies rained down upon them. The terror attack on Flight 103—the latest in string of attacks on American targets in the 1980s (most of which went unanswered)—was traced to Libya.

★ QUOTE OF THE DAY

My concern today is not with the length of a person's hair but with his conduct.

Richard M. Nixon

December 22

1807: Thomas Jefferson signed the Embargo Act—aimed at ending British and French harassment of American merchant ships. Britain and France were at war, and the United States was neutral—but that didn't stop either British or French forces from seizing American ships and plundering their goods for wartime use. The Embargo Act was meant to hurt both Britain and France by cutting off trade, but historians say it wound up hurting the U.S. economy itself.

1864: An unusual Christmas gift: Abraham Lincoln was offered the city of Savannah, Georgia, by conquering Union General William T. Sherman. Sherman's army captured the port city after his famous March to the Sea from Atlanta.

1999: Bill Clinton urged Americans to keep calm, despite fears of terrorism. Those fears were justified: eight days before, an alert border patrol agent became suspicious of a man attempting to cross into Washington State from Canada. The man, Ahmed Ressam, was an Algerian member of al Qaeda who lived in Montreal; a search of his car turned up bomb-making equipment—he was planning to bomb Los Angeles International airport on New Year's Eve.

★ QUOTE OF THE DAY

The only legitimate right to govern is an express grant of power from the governed.

William Henry Harrison

December 23

1913: Woodrow Wilson signed the Federal Reserve Act, which created the Federal Reserve. The Federal Reserve enabled the government to better control U.S. monetary supply, and established a framework for regulating banks and credit.

1988: Ronald Reagan, speaking two days after the terror bombing of Pan Am 103, called it "a tragedy that steals the hopes and dreams from our society."

This Day in Presidential History

★ QUOTE OF THE DAY

Politics is such a torment that I advise everyone I love not to mix with it.

Thomas Jefferson

December 24

1923: Calvin Coolidge pushed a button to light the first national Christmas tree ever displayed on the White House grounds. The first president to have an indoor Christmas tree in the White House was Benjamin Harrison in 1889.

1929: A fire roared through the West Wing, destroying the Oval Office—capping a bad first year in office for Herbert Hoover. After the blaze, the president had it restored to its former self. His successor, Franklin D. Roosevelt, chose to renovate and further expand the West Wing to accommodate his larger staff—and the office would be moved to its current location in the southeast corner of the West Wing.

1943: In his end-of-the-year radio address, Franklin D. Roosevelt announced that General Dwight Eisenhower would be Supreme Commander of the allied force that would invade Nazi-held western Europe. The date for the invasion, a closely held secret, had been set for May 1944. Weather delayed the actual invasion until June (see June 6).

1992: George H.W. Bush pardoned former Defense Secretary Caspar Weinberger and five others for their involvement in the Reagan-era Iran-Contra scandal. The scandal led to talk of impeaching President Reagan and resulted in the convictions of eleven Reagan administration staffers (some were overturned on appeal). Bush's pardons were the last chapter in the six-year arms-for-hostages deal.

★ QUOTE OF THE DAY

Don't interfere with anything in the Constitution. That must be maintained, for it is the only safeguard of our liberties.

Abraham Lincoln

December 25

1868: Andrew Johnson granted an unconditional pardon to all Confederate soldiers from the Civil War. In his Christmas Day proclamation, the president said he hoped his pardon would that it would "renew and fully restore confidence and fraternal feeling among the whole people, and their respect for and attachment to the National Government, designed by its patriotic founders for the general good."

★ QUOTE OF THE DAY

Let your heart feel for the afflictions and distress of everyone, and let your hand give in proportion to your purse.

George Washington

December 26

1972: Harry Truman died in Kansas City, Missouri. The thirty-third president, he served from 1945 to 1953. Vice president for just three months when Franklin D. Roosevelt died, Truman became president just as World War II was ending in Europe. He made the grave decision to drop two atomic bombs on Japan, which brought the Pacific war to an end. He oversaw the Marshall Plan (see April 3), Berlin Airlift (see May 1), Korean War (see June 25), and creation of NATO—the North Atlantic Treaty Organization (see April 4). The last president without a college degree, Truman was known for his honesty and accountability: a famous sign on his Oval Office desk said "The Buck Stops Here." Truman was unpopular when he retired in 1953, but historians today consider him one of the ten greatest presidents in American history.

★ QUOTE OF THE DAY

A politician is a man who understands government. A statesman is a politician who's been dead for 15 years.

Harry Truman

Harry Truman was a stickler for punctuality; he kept six clocks in the Oval Office. He was also the sharpest dressed president; the former Kansas City haberdasher owned a reported 486 ties!

2006: Gerald Ford died in Rancho Mirage, California. The thirty-eighth president, he served from 1974 to 1977. Ford was the only person in American history to become both vice president and president without ever being elected to either office—and is thus called the "Accidental President." A longtime congressman from Michigan, Ford became vice president when President Richard M. Nixon selected him to replace Spiro Agnew, after Agnew resigned in October 1973 (see October 10). Ford became president ten months later when Nixon himself resigned in the Watergate scandal (see August 8–9). In his first address to the nation after being sworn in, Ford told Americans that "Our long national nightmare is over. Our constitution works." A month after being sworn in, Ford pardoned Nixon, causing critics to charge that the two men made a deal. Ford denied it, but it contributed to his loss in the 1976 election.

Gerald Ford played both center and linebacker on the University of Michigan football teams that went undefeated and won back-to-back national championships in 1932 and 1933. Offered NFL contracts by both the Detroit Lions and Green Bay Packers; Ford chose to attend Yale Law School instead.

⭑ QUOTE OF THE DAY

Truth is the glue that holds governments together. Compromise is the oil that makes governments go.

Gerald Ford

December 27

1944: Franklin Roosevelt ordered the military to seize property of the retailer Montgomery Ward, after it refused to comply with World War II labor agreements. As America fought on two fronts, Roosevelt said the United States would not tolerate any labor walkouts that might cripple the war effort.

2001: Three months after terrorists attacked the United States, the Bush administration said it would hold Taliban and al Qaeda prisoners at the U.S. Navy base at Guantanamo Bay, Cuba. The first twenty captives arrived on January 11, 2002. Guantanamo—an American base since 1903—was considered outside U.S. legal jurisdiction, and the Bush administration asserted that detainees were not entitled to any protections of the Geneva Conventions. But the Supreme Court ruled (in *Hamdan v. Rumsfeld* on June 29, 2006) that they were entitled to the minimal protections listed under Common Article 3 of the Geneva Conventions.

★ QUOTE OF THE DAY

Our commanders in the field are demanding weapons in increasing quantities so that they may hit the enemy harder and harder. The supreme effort of all of us here at home is imperative if we are to give them what they need. Nothing less will suffice. The Government of the United States cannot and will not tolerate any interference with war production in this critical hour.

Franklin D. Roosevelt

December 28

1856: Woodrow Wilson was born in Staunton, Virginia. He was the twenty-eighth president, serving from 1913 to 1921. Wilson, the eighth (and, for now, last) president from Virginia, was perhaps America's best-educated chief executive, attending Princeton and the University of Virginia Law School before earning his doctorate in political science from Johns Hopkins. He later became president of Princeton and then governor of New Jersey.

In 1912, in a four-way race between Wilson, President William Howard Taft, former president Theodore Roosevelt, and socialist Eugene Debs, Wilson, a Democrat, was elected with just 42% of the popular vote—but got the required majority of the electoral vote.

In Wilson's first year in office, the Federal Reserve was created; he also signed into law the nation's first income tax since the Civil War. In 1914, he signed a bill banning child labor.

Reelected in 1916 with the slogan "he kept us out of war," Wilson won narrowly. But America would enter World War I in 1917 (see April 2).

Woodrow Wilson at his first Inauguration, March 4, 1913. Library of Congress.

The war was over in a year-and-a-half, and Wilson, making the first trip to Europe by a sitting president, helped negotiate the Versailles Treaty and organize the League of Nations (a precursor to today's United Nations).

But the Senate rejected the Versailles Treaty, a crushing blow to Wilson. In the fall of 1919, he embarked on a national tour to build support for it. He became ill, returned to Washington, and suffered a near-fatal stroke that left him partially paralyzed and unable to speak. His condition was largely hidden from the American people for the remainder of his presidency. He left office in 1921 and died in 1924.

★ QUOTE OF THE DAY

If you want to make enemies, try and change something.

Woodrow Wilson

December 29

1790: George Washington told the Seneca Nation that the United States was dedicated to friendship with Indians. The president told native leaders that "you cannot be defrauded of your lands…you possess the right to

This Day in Presidential History

Andrew Johnson. Matthew Brady. Library of Congress.

sell, and the right of refusing to sell." Later history of U.S. relations with Native Americans showed that this was hardly the case—and a century to the day after Washington's expressions of peace came the Wounded Knee massacre of the Lakota tribe. It occurred during the presidency of Benjamin Harrison.

1808: Andrew Johnson was born in Raleigh, North Carolina. After the assassination of Abraham Lincoln, he became the seventeenth president and served from 1865 to 1869. Johnson was impeached for trying to fire War Secretary Edwin Stanton. The Senate later acquitted Johnson by one vote (see May 16).

1940: Franklin D. Roosevelt's "Arsenal of Democracy" speech. In his end-of-the-year fireside chat, the president, noting that Nazi Germany had conquered most of Europe, warned that the United States must beef up its defenses—quickly—and do all it can to help Great Britain, which was then being bombed and under threat of an invasion by Nazi Germany. "Never before since Jamestown and Plymouth Rock has our American civilization been in such danger as now," FDR warned. Twelve months later, America would be at war with Germany, Japan, and Italy (see December 7 and 11).

This Day in Presidential History

1970: Seeking to improve workplace safety, Richard M. Nixon signed the Occupational Health and Safety Act (OSHA). It gives the government more power to set workplace safety standards for jobs in the United States.

★ QUOTE OF THE DAY

Frankly and definitely there is danger ahead—danger against which we must prepare. But we well know that we cannot escape danger, or the fear of danger, by crawling into bed and pulling the covers over our heads... we have no excuse for defeatism. We have every good reason for hope—hope for peace, hope for the defense of our civilization and for the building of a better civilization in the future.

Franklin D. Roosevelt

December 30

1853: Franklin Pierce's biggest achievement—the Gadsden Purchase Treaty—was signed.

It gave the United States approximately 45,000 square miles of territory that had belonged to Mexico. The president and his secretary of state Jefferson Davis wanted the land—which now comprises New Mexico and a quarter of southern Arizona—for a proposed southern transcontinental railroad. The treaty also resolved outstanding differences between the two nations stemming from the 1848 Treaty of Guadalupe Hidalgo that ended the Mexican-American War. But the treaty also stirred new tensions over the expansion of slavery—an issue that the Pierce administration failed to solve.

1969: Richard M. Nixon signed a sweeping tax reform bill, cutting taxes for most Americans, but raising them on the rich. The president's Tax Reform Act also exempted nine million low-income citizens from paying any taxes at all; it also sharply raised Social Security benefits.

★ QUOTE OF THE DAY

It isn't sufficient just to want—you've got to ask yourself what you are going to do to get the things you want.

Franklin D. Roosevelt

December 31

1970: Richard M. Nixon signed what was arguably the most important environmental bill in U.S. history: The Clean Air Act Amendments. It required the Environmental Protection Agency (created on Nixon's watch) to develop and enforce regulations to protect people from breathing polluted air. It created regulations that helped remove sulfur and nitrogen dioxide, carbon monoxide, ozone, and lead from the air—saving countless lives.

1977: Visiting Iran, Jimmy Carter called it "an island of stability," and praised the Shah. In a New Year's Eve toast, the president noted "the respect and admiration and love" Iranians had for the Shah—who was overthrown a year later by Islamic fundamentalists.

★ QUOTE OF THE DAY

It was by one Union that we achieved our independence and liberties, and by it alone that they can be maintained.

James Monroe

Appendix

How Do Historians Rate the Presidents?

Here is C–SPAN's "Historians Survey of Presidential Leadership," released in February 2017, along with the years they lived and served as president. (This list does not include Donald Trump, who had, at the time of writing, just assumed the presidency on January 20, 2017.)

1. Abraham Lincoln *(1809–1865, president from 1861–1865)*
2. George Washington *(1732–1799, president from 1789–1797)*
3. Franklin D. Roosevelt *(1882–1945, president from 1933–1945)*
4. Theodore Roosevelt *(1858–1919, president from 1901–1909)*
5. Dwight D. Eisenhower *(1890–1969, president from 1953–1961)*
6. Harry S. Truman *(1884–1972, president from 1945–1953)*
7. Thomas Jefferson *(1743–1826, president from 1801–1809)*
8. John F. Kennedy *(1917–1963, president from 1961–1963)*
9. Ronald Reagan *(1911–2004, president from 1981–1989)*
10. Lyndon B. Johnson *(1908–1973, president from 1963–1969)*
11. Woodrow Wilson *(1856–1924, president from 1913–1921)*
12. Barack Obama *(1961– , president from 2009–2017)*
13. James Monroe *(1758–1831, president from 1817–1825)*
14. James K. Polk *(1795–1849, president from 1845–1849)*
15. Bill Clinton *(1946– , president from 1993–2001)*
16. William McKinley *(1843–1901, president from 1897–1901)*
17. James Madison *(1751–1836, president from 1809–1817)*
18. Andrew Jackson *(1767–1845, president from 1829–1837)*
19. John Adams *(1735–1826, president from 1791–1801)*
20. George H.W. Bush *(1924– , president from 1989–1993)*

21. John Quincy Adams *(1767–1848, president from 1825–1829)*

22. Ulysses S. Grant *(1822–1885, president from 1869–1877)*

23. Grover Cleveland *(1837–1908, president from 1885–1889 and 1893–1897)*

24. William H. Taft (*1857–1930, president from 1909–1913)*

25. Gerald Ford *(1913–2006, president from 1974–1977)*

26. Jimmy Carter *(1924– , president from 1977–1981)*

27. Calvin Coolidge *(1872–1933, president from 1923–1929)*

28. Richard M. Nixon *(1913–1994, president from 1969–1974)*

29. James Garfield *(1837–1881, president from March–September 1881)*

30. Benjamin Harrison *(1833–1901, president from 1889–1893)*

31. Zachary Taylor *(1784–1850, president from 1849–1850)*

32. Rutherford B. Hayes *(1822–1893, president from 1877–1881)*

33. George W. Bush *(1946– , president from 2001–2009)*

34. Martin Van Buren *(1782–1862, president from 1837–1841)*

35. Chester Arthur *(1829–1886, president from 1881–1885)*

36. Herbert Hoover *(1874–1964, president from 1929–1933)*

37. Millard Fillmore *(1800–1874, president from 1850–1853)*

38. William Henry Harrison *(1773–1841, president from March to April 1841)*

39. John Tyler *(1790–1862, president from 1841–1845)*

40. Warren Harding *(1865–1923, president from 1921–1923)*

41. Franklin Pierce *(1804–1869, president from 1853–1857)*

42. Andrew Johnson *(1808–1875, president from 1865–1869)*

43. James Buchanan *(1791–1868, president from 1857–1861)*

Index

immigrants quarantined, 197;
Pendleton Act, 18–9;
sells Lincoln's belongings, 266;
sworn in 252–3
assault weapons ban:
explained, 130, 245;
Reagan supports, 130, 245
assassination attempts:
Bush, George H. W., 176;
Bush, George W., 136;
Ford, 172, 238, 249, 336–7;
Jackson, 34;
Nixon, 58;
Reagan, 98–9, 171, 232;
Roosevelt, Franklin, 52;
Roosevelt, Theodore, 276–7;
Truman, 295
assassinations:
Garfield, 179, 181, 252;
Kennedy, 258, 315–6, 319;
Lincoln, 112, 113, 185;
McKinley, 239–40, 245, 291;
Robert Todd Lincoln's presence at,
181
Atlee, Clement, 195–6
atomic bomb:
Hiroshima, 213;
Nagasaki, 213, 215;
Soviet Union's first, 255;
Truman informed of test, 196.
See also Manhattan Project
Auschwitz-Birkenau, 205

Babcock, Orville, 136
Bank War, 189, 242
Bao Dai, 198
Barnett, Ross, 260
Bay of Pigs ("Operation Zapata"),
86, 115, 128
Beauregard, P. G. T., 198
Bedell, Grace, 277
Belarus, 145
Bell, Alexander Graham, 19, 115, 265

Bell, John, 301
Begin, Menachem, 77, 94, 249–50
Bergen-Belsen, 132
Berlin Wall:
built, 219;
falls, 305;
Kennedy speech, 176;
Reagan speech, 163–4
bin Laden, Osama:
inspired by Reagan, 285;
Kenya, Tanzania embassies
bombed, 214;
killed, 128;
Sept. 11 Commission, 168;
U.S.S. Cole, 274
Bitburg, 132
Black Friday panic, 124, 255–6
Black Thursday (1929 stock market
crash), 286
Blaine, Gerald, 317
Blaine, James, 298
Boulder (Hoover) Dam, 174
Bradley, Omar, 203
Brady, James, 98, 322
Brady Bill, 99, 322
Brady, Matthew, 51
Booth, Edwin, 181
Booth, John Wilkes:
assassinates Lincoln, 112;
at Lincoln's inauguration, 72
encounters Lincoln at Ford's
Theatre, 304;
killed, 122–3;
vows to kill Lincoln, 109
Brandeis, Louis, 32
Breckenridge, John, 301
Bretton Woods Conference, 180–1
Brooklyn Bridge, 146
Brown, John, 279
Brown vs. Board of Education, 96,
141, 256
Bryan, Charles, 298
Bryan, William Jennings:

This Day in Presidential History

This Day in Presidential History

This Day in Presidential History

Index

This Day in Presidential History

This Day in Presidential History

This Day in Presidential History

This Day in Presidential History

This Day in Presidential History

Index

Johnson, Andrew, 148, 207, 281;
Johnson, Lyndon B., 5, 11, 16, 27,
84, 90, 100, 104, 165, 170, 182,
231, 259, 297, 321;
Kennedy, 25, 57, 68, 115, 137, 144,
147, 151, 156, 161–2, 162, 176,
219, 261, 279, 284, 291, 316, 329;
Lincoln, 2, 23, 36, 50, 66, 74, 77,
93, 101, 113, 114, 119, 131, 147,
155, 168, 181, 191, 199, 205, 212,
226, 227, 254, 258, 301, 305, 313,
336, 342;
Madison, 48, 85, 117, 154–5, 178, 229;
McKinley, 118, 219, 239, 246;
Monroe, 13, 126, 308, 324, 328,
349;
Nixon, 3, 12, 29, 30, 51, 58, 120,
135, 169, 173, 198, 215, 221,
286–7, 301, 302–3, 310, 319, 340;
Obama, 92, 129, 211, 299;
Pierce, 152, 270, 317;
Polk, 38, 76, 139, 167, 326;
Reagan, 32, 43, 52, 78, 87, 99, 116,
123, 130, 132, 141, 153, 157, 171,
218, 230, 285, 287, 322, 338;
Roosevelt, Franklin D., 4, 28, 35,
41, 56, 80, 81, 109, 111, 133, 142,
149, 158, 172, 182, 185, 220, 228,
234, 254, 255, 258–9, 291–2,
310, 321, 331, 332, 345, 348;
Roosevelt, Theodore, 8, 14, 50, 238,
260, 274, 290, 315, 335;
Taft, 179, 248;
Taylor, 319;
Truman, 98, 103, 107, 109, 122,
135, 138, 140, 157, 177, 178, 196,
208, 213, 230, 343;
Trump, 165;
Tyler, 65, 106;
Van Buren, 202, 327;
Washington, 18, 40, 55, 59, 62, 105,
108, 114, 133, 187, 194, 195, 223,
264, 275, 322, 335, 343;

Wilson, 39, 63, 102, 188, 264, 314, 346
Rabin, Yitzhak, 77, 245
Radio Act of 1927, 60
Randolph, Edmund, 61
Reagan, Ronald:
air traffic controllers, 212;
arms talks with Soviet Union, 27;
"Ash Heap of History" speech, 160;
assassination attempt, 98–9, 171,
232;
assault weapons ban, 130, 245;
Beirut Embassy bombing, 116;
Bergen-Belsen, 132;
Bitburg, 132;
Brady Bill, 99, 322;
bio, 42–3, 157;
cap and trade treaty, 105, 340;
Challenger disaster, 32;
China visit, 123;
CIA, 325;
Clean Water Act, 41;
debates Mondale, 283;
election of 1980, 299;
election of 1984, 301;
"Evil Empire," 78;
farewell address, 14;
Gorbachev summits, 272, 313;
Grenada invasion, 287;
hot mic scare, 218;
inaugural, 24–5;
Iran-Contra, 63, 74, 307, 319;
Japanese relocation and internment
reparation, 56;
Libya, 79–80–113;
Marine barracks bombing, 284–5;
Martin Luther King Jr., 17;
military buildup, 263;
Monroe Doctrine and, 324;
"9-1-1 Emergency Day," 230;
O'Connor nominated for Supreme
Court, 187;
Pan Am 103 bombing, 340, 341;
Polish sanctions, 56;

This Day in Presidential History

This Day in Presidential History

This Day in Presidential History

This Day in Presidential History

This Day in Presidential History

About the Author

Paul Brandus, a frequent speaker at presidential libraries and the author of the acclaimed *Under This Roof: A History of the White House and Presidency* (Lyons Press, 2015), is an award-winning independent member of the White House press corps. He founded *West Wing Reports* in 2009 (Twitter @WestWingReport) and reports for television and radio clients across the United States and overseas. He is also a contributing columnist for *USA Today* and a financial columnist for *MarketWatch* and *Dow Jones*. He previously spent five years as a journalist in Moscow and several years as a New York-based network television producer and writer. He also worked for several years in the investment industry.